Important: Do not remove this
date due reminder.

DATE DUE

THE LIBRARY STORE   #47-0205

Charlie Chaplin's
Red Letter Days

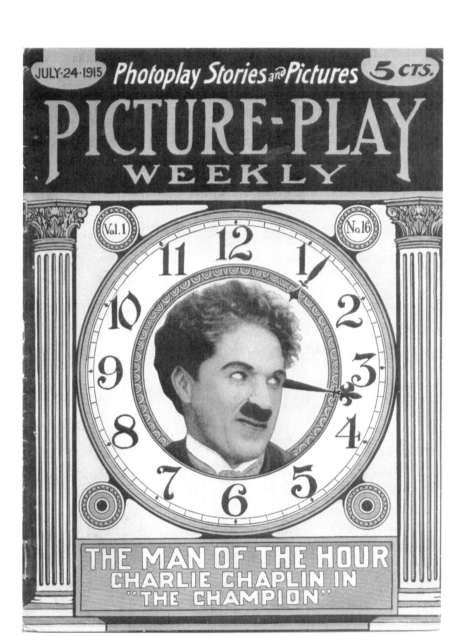

Picture-Play Weekly was one of many magazines that both profited from and promoted Chaplin's growing fame.

Charlie Chaplin's
Red Letter Days

At Work with
the Comic Genius

FRED GOODWINS

Edited by DAVID JAMES

Annoted by DAN KAMIN

ROWMAN & LITTLEFIELD
Lanham • Boulder • New York • London

Published by Rowman & Littlefield
A wholly owned subsidiary of The Rowman & Littlefield Publishing Group, Inc.
4501 Forbes Boulevard, Suite 200, Lanham, Maryland 20706
www.rowman.com

Unit A, Whitacre Mews, 26-34 Stannary Street, London SE11 4AB

Thanks to Grey Smith of Heritage Auctions for providing images of the original release posters of *The Champion, The Floorwalker, One A.M.,* and *The Rink.*

British Library Cataloguing in Publication Information Available

Library of Congress Cataloging-in-Publication Data

Names: Goodwins, Fred, 1891–1923 author. | James, David, 1964– editor. |
   Kamin, Dan, 1946- editor.
Title: Charlie Chaplin's Red letter days : at work with the comic genius /
   Fred Goodwins ; edited by David James and Dan Kamin.
Description: Lanham : Rowman & Littlefield, [2017] | Includes bibliographical
   references and index.
Identifiers: LCCN 2016043506 (print) | LCCN 2017003916 (ebook) | ISBN
   9781442278080 (hardback : alk. paper) | ISBN 9781442278097 (electronic)
Subjects: LCSH: Chaplin, Charlie, 1889-1977—Criticism and interpretation.
Classification: LCC PN2287.C5 G66 2017 (print) | LCC PN2287.C5 (ebook) | DDC
   791.4302/8092—dc23
LC record available at https://lccn.loc.gov/2016043506

∞™ The paper used in this publication meets the minimum requirements of
American National Standard for Information Sciences—Permanence of Paper
for Printed Library Materials, ANSI/NISO Z39.48-1992.

Printed in the United States of America

Contents

Introduction

Red Letter Days

On February 26, 1916, a British magazine called *Red Letter* began a series of thirty-seven articles about Charlie Chaplin by Fred Goodwins, an actor who became part of Chaplin's stock company in early 1915. By the end of 1914 Chaplin had become the most popular actor in films, and reporters were clamoring for access and interviews. What makes Goodwins's articles stand out is that he was a working member of the company, and therefore a privileged eyewitness to Chaplin's revolutionary transformation of crude slapstick into cinematic art.

Equally remarkable is how unguarded Chaplin is throughout the series. This is largely because Goodwins was not only a member of the company, but also one of the studio's core British members. Chaplin had cut his artistic teeth in the British music hall, and he surrounded himself with fellow music hall veterans. There were deep and unspoken levels of understanding between these countrymen, and their jovial spirit of camaraderie comes across clearly in the articles. The presence of old colleagues also elicits a good deal of spontaneous reminiscing on the comedian's part, as well as some surprisingly frank reflections on his current concerns, including his controversial decision not to return to England and enlist to fight in the Great War.

The series is studded with gems of information and insight about Chaplin's working methods during this critical time of his artistic development. In addition, in the months leading up to Goodwins's series the magazine published a rich array of Chaplin-related material that captures a world in the grip of Chaplin fever, including Chaplin covers on many of the issues, "Red Letter Photocards," which were postcards given away with the magazine that featured stills from Chaplin's 1915 Essanay films, and a series of strikingly well-drawn cartoon strips featuring Charlie causing his characteristic mayhem. It was all fodder for an eager public that couldn't get enough of their comic hero. To illustrate the book we have included a selection of Red Letter Photocards, along with posters, sheet music, and magazines of the era.

The articles constitute a unique and vivid account of the ebb and flow of life at the Chaplin studio. They both deepen our understanding of Chaplin's artistry and shed new light on his personality. They also shed new light on the personalities of Chaplin's unsung collaborators, such as his beloved costar Edna Purviance, his gigantic nemesis Eric Campbell, and the other familiar faces that populate his films.

The text has never been reprinted, nor even referred to in the vast body of literature on Chaplin published since then. This volume contains everything Goodwins wrote (truncating only the longish article titles the magazine supplied to entice readers and most of his references to photos we have not reprinted). In addition, we have included as appendixes three anonymous articles published in *Red Letter* that cover Chaplin's exhilarating trip to New York in February 1916, when he signed the historic Mutual contract that made him the highest-paid star in Hollywood—indeed, the highest-paid employee of any kind in the world—and affirmed his status as the most famous and popular person alive.

The magazines were discovered in the British Library in 2013 by Dr. David James, the editor of this book. James worked with Chaplin expert Dan Kamin, who annotated the articles to highlight their revelations. The two of us hope that the resulting book will be as pleasurable for today's readers as the original articles were for readers in 1916.

1

Charlie's "Last" Film

February 26, 1916

The world is ringing with the name of Chaplin. The little comedian's vogue is today undoubtedly even greater than it has ever been, but nowadays we have "Chaplin everything" thrust under our noses, until we are beginning to lose sight of the great vital import of the name, representing as it does the most phenomenal rise to the most phenomenal fame any man or woman has ever achieved in the history of the world, and, what is greater, the world-wide triumph of a style of comedy and a sense of humour that is distinctively British.

[Goodwins begins his series by appealing to his readers' pride in the way Chaplin's "distinctively British" humor has swept the world. His claim that Chaplin had become not only the most famous person alive, but the most famous person who had ever lived, might be considered a bit premature in 1916, since it wasn't until the late teens that Chaplin's films were widely distributed in China, India, and some of the other non-Western regions,[1] as well as war-torn European countries such as France. By 1920, though, the extent of Chaplin's fame was indisputable. "He is as universal as laughter and as common as tears," was the way another writer eloquently put it in 1926.[2] Chaplin himself was known to boast that people who had never heard of Jesus Christ could imitate his distinctive comic walk.[3]]

But there is something more in the comedian than that great sense of humour and that omnipotent personality. There is the soul of a great human being. I have written certain articles for the press of both Continents upon

1

Chaplin as a personality and as a worker, but the little Britisher's utter humanity is so essentially a part of all that the name of Chaplin conveys that I feel bound to write about a wonderful week I have just spent with him during the taking of his last Essanay picture.

[*Goodwins is refreshingly frank in admitting that the purpose of his articles is to idolize Chaplin as a person as much as the public was currently idolizing his screen character. During 1915 Chaplin had been alternately startled, bemused, flattered, irritated, and alarmed by the avid public interest in his private life. He resented the intrusiveness of this attention but recognized its publicity value. He also understood that he needed to control the content as much as possible, and hence Goodwins's transition from actor to actor/publicist. Had Goodwins kept his focus on beatifying his boss, the series would almost certainly have been little but fan magazine drivel. But while there's a fair amount of fawning in the articles, luckily for us Goodwins realized that depicting Chaplin in the white heat of artistic creation would be far more interesting to readers. He was also astute enough to sense that even describing the mundane day-to-day operations of Chaplin's comedy studio, as he does in the next installment when production is halted by torrential downpours, would make good copy.*]*

It was quite a while since I had been in the Essanay studio here, and I always remembered it as the scene of furious activity. In those days a host of men of every trade and profession connected with the motion picture industry bustled around the stage or held brief conferences with the comedian upon the production in hand, what time he was wont to stroll up and down the big expanse of flooring, his tiny hands thrust deep into his pockets, preoccupied, thinking, at times almost absent-minded. The atmosphere was one of tense thought, one of striving and struggling after ideas to put into celluloid form for the amusement of the whole civilised globe—all the time looking ahead. By that atmosphere one was apt to judge the comedian in a light other than the real one. Assuredly a man's true self shows best when his mind is at ease.

That is why this last week—pretty positively the last but one under the Essanay banner—has shown my little friend to be something more than even I had believed him, for his immediate mission is all but fulfilled, his mind at ease once more.

When this picture is finished he proposes—and who would not in his position?—to launch out upon his own account together with his brother Sydney,

The Chaplin craze. Ten of his Essanay films were fictionalized in *Picture-Play Weekly* and reprinted in *The Charlie Chaplin Book*, one of the first books devoted to a movie star. Edna Purviance was Chaplin's leading lady from 1915 through 1923.

who at the time of writing is in New York arranging the finance of the new syndicate.

The picture as yet has no title. It was started over seven months ago as a six-reel comedy-dramatic feature entitled *Life*, but took so much time and labour (and therefore deprived the public of several of his regular two-reel releases) that he was impelled to drop it. I saw it run off in the projecting room recently, and all the time Charlie sat beside me, exclaiming "Gee, how I'd set my heart on this! It would have been the greatest thing I have ever attempted." *[There is more about* Life *in chapter 6.]*

It had been Charlie's original intention to leave the abandoned feature behind him when he took his final departure from the Essanay plant, and to make his last picture a brand-new one, entitled *Insurance*. We made up for it several days, but still nothing happened, and we had nothing particular to do.

The picture, however, never materialised, for, as his engagement with the Essanay Company neared its end, the thought of those reels of splendid work lying abandoned upon the cutting-room shelves began to fret Charlie, and finally he conceived the idea of utilising the cream of it, and by adding the necessary extra material, and then cutting down the whole to the requisite two thousand feet, forming a two-reeler worthy of his last release under the old contract. So highly did the Essanay Company think of the proposal that they arranged to put the comedian on a sharing basis for that one last picture, splitting cost and profit evenly with him.

So far so good, and then came the inevitable difficulty. Nearly all the actors concerned in the original story had left the Essanay Company in the seven months that had elapsed since he had first begun his feature, and in order to match up the new scenes with those already taken he must get them together again by hook or crook.

Of all the trouble it incurred I need not tell. For over a week Jesse Robbins, the studio manager, and Chaplin himself whirled around Southern California in automobiles, 'phoning, telegraphing, and calling until they were on the verge of despair.

It was a fine old quandary! Billy Armstrong, the most wonderful supporter Chaplin has ever had, was under contract as a featured comedian with the David Horsley Company, and therefore legally prevented from returning;

Charles Insley, who played the footpad, was lost track of completely; and so on throughout almost the entire cast. All that remained of the original company were Chaplin himself, "Bud" Jamieson (the mountain of flesh who played in *Charlie the Champion [British title of* The Champion, *Chaplin's third Essanay film]* and thereafter), James Kelly (G. P. Huntley's[4] pa-in-law, by the way), and myself.

Things were at a deadlock, then, until suddenly Armstrong got to hear of the predicament. With the characteristic loyalty of the brother Britisher, he immediately offered to jump his contract and come back, for the sole purpose of helping Charlie out. This of course was out of the question, but they finally did achieve their purpose by arranging with the Horsley Company to release Billy without salary until Charlie was through with him. It is needless to add that the Essanay Company saw to it that the boy did not lose by his devotion to the old banner.

Of Insley, however, nothing could be gathered, and it finally fell to Wesley Ruggles, a member of the present stock company, to make up as nearly as possible the same as the missing actor. So cleverly has he accomplished this that only the sharpest of eyes will ever detect the difference when the picture comes to be shown. *[Evidently Chaplin didn't agree, because he cut all the Insley footage out of the film. While Insley didn't make the final cut, Goodwins did; he plays the second street preacher Chaplin encounters and one of the indolent cops summoned to Edna's home.*

In the film, which was eventually released as Police, *Chaplin skillfully recycled some of his* Life *material, but it was Essanay that proved to be the real masters of creative reuse. In 1918 the company, without his permission, took the unused* Life *footage and cobbled it together with footage from several of his other films and newly shot scenes to produce a spurious "new" Chaplin film,* Triple Trouble. *Insley plays the crook in the doss-house sequence of* Triple Trouble, *and, contrary to Goodwins's assertion, it's not hard to tell him from Ruggles, who appears in the film in flipped-around* Police *footage, and, to add to the confusion, in some of the newly shot footage as well. Filmographies invariably list Ruggles and not Insley as the crook in* Triple Trouble.*]*

I am only relating this little incident in order to show how Chaplin, once his mind is set on what he considers the right thing, allows nothing to swerve him from it.

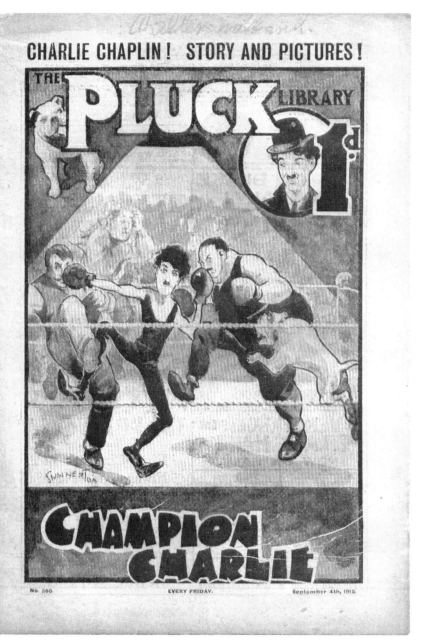

Cartoonists had a field day with Charlie's distinctive costume and antics.

All that remained, then, was to start in on the filming of the additions to the story.

First of all, we needed a lot of burglary scenes, and several locations were suggested as suitable for the work but Chaplin had his own views about the appearance of the house he desired, so nothing would do but that we all go out to his own beautiful home in Hollywood, the sunniest part of the city, right in the heart of the studio district. So a couple of huge touring cars bore us out through the long, palm-fringed Hollywood Boulevard to the picturesque side avenue where Chaplin's home nestles back from the roadside.

How different he seemed with all that mental stress temporarily put behind him! He lay back among the soft upholstery of his car, and, breathing a sigh of relief, murmured—

"Well, boys, this has been a great year for me, but you'll never realise how it feels to know you're going to take a couple of weeks' hard-earned vacation after two years of solid driving life I have had. I've got the finish of this story all mapped out, and there's nothing to bother my head about except getting it filmed. Let's take life a bit easy."

Then he fell into talking about old times in England—of *Sherlock Holmes*, of his *Eight Lancashire Lads* days, of *Casey's Court [Chaplin was actually in* Casey's Circus, *the successor to the popular* Casey's Court *show]*, and, lastly, of his Karno engagements. Often he touched upon his early struggles and privations, his hardships—and, oh, how real those hardships were! It may fall to my lot to chronicle them someday, but the time is not yet ripe.

He loves to talk with us, his British "boys," in the form of slang peculiar to the British professional—an odd mixture of old Romany and the familiar rhyming-slang of the Cockney.

Somehow, whenever we get together, the conversation seems bound to switch from the King's English into that cryptic vocabulary that only the British theatrical man can understand. I don't think it altogether pleases the American boys at times. They are inclined to get the impression that we are commenting upon them with no particular favour, and it would be bad form, I suppose, if it weren't so utterly unconscious.

Presently Charlie stuck his head out of the car, and looked up at the sky, which was becoming overcast.

"How's the light, Harry?" he queried the cameraman. "It looks as if it was going to 'parney' pretty soon. Well, we shouldn't worry. If it starts we'll all

IF YOU WANT TO LOOK LIKE CHARLIE CHAPLIN,

Let your hair grow long and curl it till it looks like this

Pull a bit of wool off the mat and stick under your nose,

Buy a pair of old boots, too big for you, and turn out your toes,

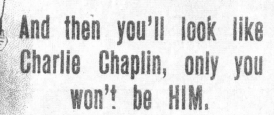

And then you'll look like Charlie Chaplin, only you won't be HIM.

Part of Charlie's appeal was that everyone could imitate him—or try to!

go back down town and get some 'mangari' at the Louvre." *[Parney (rain) is derived from* pani, *the Hindustani word for water, and* mangari *(food) from the Italian word for eating.]*

And 'parney' it certainly did within half-an-hour, so he promptly instructed the chauffeur to turn and go back to Los Angeles for lunch.

"The Louvre" is, ironically enough, a big German restaurant in town, and we created something of a sensation, even in picture-blasé Los Angeles, when the entire company walked into the big dining-room in full war-paint. First came James Kelly and John Rand (the cook in *Charlie Shanghaied [British title of* Shanghaied*]*; then Leo White (a Manchester boy, well known to you by his characterisation of the French Count in many of Chaplin's recent pictures[5]); next, Billy Armstrong (Crouch End,[6] every inch of him!), clad as a wretched miser; then Ruggles, in his footpad makeup; Bud Jaimieson, as a very "lady-like" tramp;[7] myself, as an American police captain, with a monocle and wristwatch; and, lastly, Charles Chaplin, in the garb that needs no description from me or anyone else.

Altogether, including the chauffeurs and property-men, we numbered fifteen, and by the time Charlie was in the whole assembly was looking at us.

As he made his way down the centre aisle the leader of the orchestra gave a quick word of instruction, and the band struck up "The Chaplin Glide." *[During 1915 dozens of songs were published about Chaplin in America and Britain to capitalize on the public's fascination with his characteristic comic gestures, funny walk, and the ever-increasing wealth of his offscreen self. This one goes:*

> *With his little derby hat,*
> *And his breeches and all that,*
> *And the way he swings his bamboo cane around,*
> *And when he takes those corner glides,*
> *With those funny feet he slides,*
> *He's the guy that gets the money,*
> *Ev'rybody says he's funny*
> *In that Charlie Chaplin ragtime glide.]*

The little comedian's eyes shone, and he grinned cheerily as that big assembly of German diners burst into whole-hearted applause in recognition of the genius in their midst. They knew he was British; they knew it was their creed

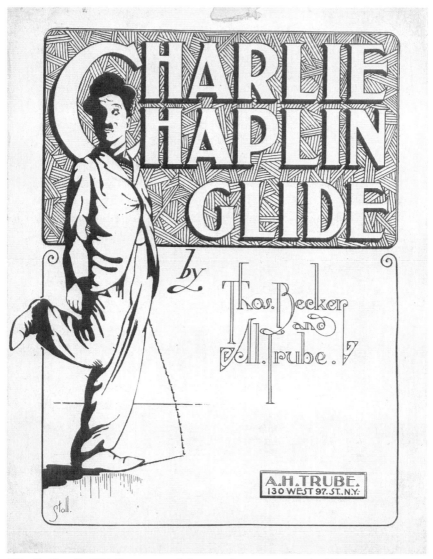

"Charlie Chaplin Glide" was one of dozens of songs written in 1915 to capitalize on the craze.

to hate us because of our nationality, just as we despise them because of theirs and all that it signifies; but genius and human feeling have no nationality or creed, and thus there was for the nonce a truce between us.

Something seemed to rise in my throat as I grew to realise the strength that must lie in that little fellow's appeal when a thing like this could happen literally in the midst of the enemy, and I found myself vaguely wondering if his influence over humanity might not be strong enough to appreciably sway the decision in this titanic war of ours. I spoke to him about it afterwards, but he shook his head dubiously.

"It's too much," he replied sadly, "but if only I could!" *[This is the first of a number of references Goodwins will make to the fact that Chaplin wasn't "over there" doing his part in the war effort. Here he tackles the issue head-on by portraying Chaplin as an agent of peace because of the universal appeal of his art. It's a brilliant and touching bit of public relations. Chaplin would need all the good press he could generate in England to counteract the negative press that he was getting in some quarters.]*

We ranged ourselves around a long table, and disposed of the excellent lunch he ordered for us. It was a gay little party—utterly different from the usual moving-picture luncheon—and chatter throughout the meal was the order of the day. What is more, there was plenty of cause for genuine laughter, too.

After dessert we called upon Charlie for a speech, whereupon he rose, amid vociferous applause, and rendered us, as only he can do, a ridiculous little character-sketch of an after-dinner speaker delivering an address in an absurd mixture of French, Italian, German, and what not. There was nothing in it particularly, yet everyone present listened in amused silence until he finished, "And can anybody kindly tell me what the blazes I'm talking about?" whereupon the whole room burst into an unrestrained roar of laughter and applause. *[This is the first recorded instance of Chaplin's uncanny ability to speak in fluent, authentic-sounding foreign language gibberish, which he would make good use of in* Modern Times *and* The Great Dictator.*]*

As our party rose to leave the most wonderful thing of the afternoon happened. That orchestra of German musicians, without a dissentient note, played "God Save the King" until our party was out on the sidewalk once more!

The remaining days the comedian had our lunches at his home, and the way we disposed of those meals was at once a compliment and a surprise to his Japanese manservant, who had prepared them with wonderful culinary skill.

We found much to amuse us about that picturesque home during the times the camera was not busy. One day Charlie produced a violin from the music-room, and as we sat over our coffee he began to play. A hush fell over us all as the strains of that threadbare ballad, "The Rosary," floated down the long drawing-room. I had often heard Charlie play, and knew him to be an expert, but there was more than mere playing in the room that afternoon.

I detected possibly a dozen false notes, yet they didn't count, for in the rendition lay the soul of the musician, the true artiste. As the last long note died away, we seemed to wake up from some sort of trance and all those boys—even the manual workers, who knew the comedian, with his faults and virtues from A to Z—applauded frantically until he gave us an encore.

It was all extempore and unaffected. There he stood in his grotesque costume and eccentric make up, devoid of stage-setting or pretention, surrounded by none of the atmosphere of the recital-hall. Yet I verily believe I enjoyed those two selections more than anything the Albert Hall has ever had to show me. And that is not encomiastic "press-dope," but the honest, spontaneous truth. I hope that some day you may have a chance to verify it for yourselves.

One afternoon I took a walk through the orange-and-lemon groves in the company of Vincent Bryan, who affords Charlie such invaluable assistance in the writing of his scenarios *[Bryan was an important member of Chaplin's creative team at both Essanay and Mutual, contributing scenarios, gags, and possibly assisting in the direction as well]*.

"Vince" it was that gave us "Bedelia," "Down at the Old Bull and Bush," "The Cubanola Glide," "We All Had a Finger in the Pie," "Don't Take Me Home," and a score of other ditties that have made his name famous wherever modern music is known. A charming and interesting character himself, he has the fullest appreciation of Chaplin's merits, and his great sorrow is that the latter doesn't appreciate himself enough.

"I have the darn'dest job making that boy realise just who he is and what the world thinks of him," he complained. "Only the other day I had to stop him from going across the room at Levy's Restaurant to shake hands with some rough-necked desert-rat, much the worse for liquor, who had sent the proprietor to fetch Charlie over to him. He'd have gone, and let himself in for a perfectly boring time of it as a consequence.

Then, again, before Sir Herbert Tree came to Los Angeles to start on this Griffith picture of his, Charlie spent days wondering if Sir Herbert would consent to meet him! Can you beat that? I told him to sit tight and wait until Sir Herbert asked for him. He couldn't convince himself that that eminent gentleman would really want to meet him, but I knew, and I fastened Charlie down to his seat.

Sure enough the first person Tree sought was Charles Chaplin, and Charlie has been his most frequent guest ever since. *[In his* Autobiography *Chaplin gives a humorous account of how tongue-tied he was to meet Tree, until he finally managed to blurt out that he had been a huge fan since the age of fourteen, and was simply dumbstruck in the presence of his idol. Naturally, this broke the ice, and Chaplin relished the time spent with Tree and his brilliant, bohemian young daughter Iris.[8] One of the most celebrated actor-managers on the British stage, Tree founded the Academy of Dramatic Art—later the Royal Academy of Dramatic Art—in 1904. Noted for his Shakespearian roles, he had come to Los Angeles to play Macbeth in a 1916 film produced by D. W. Griffith. Tree's illegitimate son Carol Reed became a highly regarded film director (*The Third Man*), and Reed's nephew was the actor Oliver Reed.]*

I spoke to Charlie about this as he was dressing for dinner that evening, and he pleaded guilty.

"I can't overcome it," he told me. "I started so badly in life and went through so much that I get to feeling my position deeply. A chap of my position ought to have a certain amount of assurance, I know, but it's no good, old man."

"Well, it's got to be, "I told him. "You'll just have to overcome it, Charlie. You're fifty miles ahead in every way of 90 per cent of the people you shrink from meeting. The fact that they seek you ought to teach you that."

"Well, you see," he continued, a little more brightly, "I've been cooped up so long in this burgh"—Los Angeles—"ever since I left the stage and made a name for myself that I don't see like you have done what they think of me back East and away home in England. That's why I am taking this two weeks' holiday. I'll find my level alright once I see for myself where I stand."

"That's the right stuff!" exclaimed Bryan, entering at that moment. "Brains and talent are the only true aristocracy."

But Charlie only laughed a little awkwardly, and led the way out to the car.

Charlie Has to "Flit" from His Studio

March 4, 1916

Immediately following the happenings chronicled in my last notes we of the Chaplin organisation awoke one morning to raise our window-blinds and gaze out upon a heavy downpour of soaking rain which made many of us homesick for our Old Country.

During the majority of the year in this Southern California the sun shines with a persistence that is almost cruel. Often in the dog-days we have sat in our stifling dressing-rooms gazing out onto a sun-baked earth, with the atmosphere visibly quivering before our eyes, and at such times we have longed for rain—just one good, hearty, heavy downpour to remind us that there is such a place as Great Britain on this little old planet of ours!

But when rain does come in Los Angeles it comes with a vengeance, and, as if to prove its ability to emulate the climate under which Charlie and we others were born, it doesn't let up until the streets resemble a series of cultivated mud-bogs, to which one's feet fondly cling, until by the exertion of considerable strength one finally succeeds in removing them, to the accompaniment of a mighty sound of suction forcibly reminiscent of a New York department store girl chewing gum.

[It's rather remarkable how Goodwins spins the simple fact that it was raining into several paragraphs of magazine copy, in which he also reminds his readers that Chaplin and his cronies are homesick Brits, stuck in a land of crass American gum-chewers.]

It rained then, and when it rains the order of the day among us "shadow actors" is to pull down the blind once again, carefully muffle the telephone bell with a piece of paper, and return peacefully to resume our interrupted slumbers.

For four solid days the heavens continued to pour without cessation— something of a record even for these tropical regions—and there was nothing for it but to make life as cheerful as possible. Work, of course, was utterly out of the question, and therefore play had to come to our rescue until such time as Odin should cease his fury. Of some of the things that happened during those days of enforced idleness I cannot but hold my peace and refuse to tell, but the sun mercifully shone once more on Thursday of the week in question, and Charlie was able to think motion-pictures again.

Then, just as we were able to resume our duty to society as aides to the world's jester-in-chief, there came down upon us a disturbing gentleman, to whom the studio rented by the Chaplin-Essanay Company belonged, and reminded us that our lease had expired, and that if we were to stay upon the grounds we must take out a fresh one for a further period of six months!

Needless to remark, there was "nothing doing." We packed up our belongings, and by the courtesy of Colonel Wm. Selig took up our abode in a small corner of the Selig Company's plant which is situated in the heart of a vast menagerie. *[Movie pioneer William Selig specialized in films featuring wild animals, and by 1913 had installed them in a large public zoo.]* Therein we are now finishing up our picture—there is but a little more to do—and within a week or so the connection between Charles Chaplin and the Essanay Company will terminate.

The staff, which is, of course, part of the latter organisation, and has no relation to Charlie, except by the Essanay Company's behest, will take its departure in a body to Niles, the Californian headquarters of the Company, while Charlie, with but a select few of his actors and assistants, will remain in the Southern City until such time as he is ready to start on his own account, furthering the good work he has begun for the amusement of the whole civilised world.

There is an old saying in the theatrical profession that "wherever there is mud there is actors!" It probably originated from the fact that the stage doors of theatres invariably open out upon the dirtiest spot around the building, also possibly because the dressing-rooms are generally the grimiest and most dilapidated places inside it. If the saying be true, however, we were certainly in our element when we stepped into the Selig Zoo.

Beyond the animal-houses we passed through a rough wooden gateway cut into a high palisade, built presumably to cut off the curious gaze of the general public. A hazardous journey through a lane of pure, unrelieved mud in automobiles, which skidded merrily from side to side, finally brought us to the new scene of our labours, and we started in upon them.

Charlie was not in his merriest mood. He loves a studio to himself, wherein he can concentrate his mind upon the work in hand, and, as there were a half-dozen other "companies" working upon the stage, there is much truth in his remark that the place "inspired him not!"

On one side a "crook" drama was being produced; on the opposite side another; while in yet a third corner of the stage they were putting on a story concerning a society pickpocket—and ours is a crook comedy! It was the crookedest atmosphere I was ever in.

"I can't think with pistols going off all around me," Charlie complained. "Let's all go to lunch."

So we removed our several moustaches and other hindrances to comfortable eating, and after climbing sundry miniature mountains and jumping over diverse small rivulets and ponds finally arrived at a big wooden structure imposingly labelled "Cafeteria."

For your amusement I have transcribed a special oration in description of the place delivered by the comedian as we sat at our depleted table that afternoon. I have revised it as little as possible:

"The Cafeteria is an American imposition—I mean invention—which reminds me of the Salvation Army soup-kitchens at home. It is run on the 'serve-yourself' method, thereby doing away with the expense of waitress' salaries. The place is built like a complicated cattle-pen, with a 'cute' little run-way, which leads its victims—pardon me, patrons—past a pile of trays and boxes containing knives and forks. You pass in, seize your table weapons; then you move—or are pushed—along to where an inviting array of eating material, in various stages of over-cooking and coldness, lies for your delectation.

"You demand whatever looks least likely to give you chronic indigestion, and then by easy stages the 'bread line' passes on, by way of the coffee urn, to where the dessert—the last cruel blow!—is spread out in merry little soap-dishes. The dessert lady hands you a check, and you discover that for the privilege of having been allowed to run wild among all those delicacies you have contracted liabilities amounting to roughly double an ordinary meal at the Carlton!"

There is no particular point in my quoting this little after-dinner dissertation, but it is so typical of Charlie's good-naturedly cynical view of things that I felt tempted to repeat it.

Some wonder may exist in the minds of my readers that these anecdotes of mine are so out of accord with the comedian as the world knows him, but it should be remembered that I am writing of Chaplin as he is and as I see him every day, and Charlie Chaplin of the screen is as different from the Charlie Chaplin of real life as chalk is from cheese.

From his personal demeanour in everyday life right through to the depth of his heart and mind Charlie is a sentimentalist and a thinker—one of the most serious-minded men I have met in all my wanderings around the world. A buffoon upon the screen—although an exceedingly clever one—he is the absolute antithesis in his true personality. Even in his ever-present readiness for a joke or a bit of frivolous story-telling his depth is always apparent. Had Chaplin been raised in another and better walk of life and given the opportunities of early and thorough education, the world might have been the possessor of a man immortally great in brain and achievement, and may yet, for the matter of that.

Before I close my article this week I am going to give you a side-light upon just how deep a nature Charles Chaplin (low-comedian-in-chief to the world) actually possesses by quoting as accurately as my memory serves me a conversation we had over late supper at the local restaurant here. It shall come presently.

Charlie is in a very preoccupied state of mind these days. I understand there is some little hitch occurring in New York in the formation of his new syndicate, and also that the final settlement of his affairs under the old contract is causing him a little mental unrest, but he never for one moment forgets, with all his little worries, that he is Charlie Chaplin and "one of the boys," as the saying goes on your side of the Pond. In that spirit lies the secret of the deep and sincere regard in which we of his company and of his list of friends staunchly hold him.

With all his seriousness of mind Charlie is nothing more than a wonderful big "kid"—a temperamental, lovable youngster—who, like Barrie's "Peter

Pan," has never grown up, yet has to bear upon his shoulders responsibilities from which many a strong and experienced man of business would quail. *[Goodwins here puts his finger on one of the necessary paradoxes in Chaplin's personality—retaining the boyish sense of play that was at the heart of his screen character while maintaining his position as the head of a complex and rapidly expanding business empire. Chaplin was acutely aware of the duality, and of the need to keep his inner-imp alive and well.*

Naturally, Goodwins puts a positive spin on the "kid" side of Chaplin—that was his job. But while many observers were delighted to witness the offscreen antics of the "world's jester-in-chief," others found them tiresome. He particularly irritated many in the small community of Niles, California, where he made four of his Essanay films.[2]

As to Pan, Chaplin fantasized about playing him, and five years later he came close by flying in a heavenly Never Land in The Kid's *dream sequence. When Chaplin met Sir James Barrie shortly after* The Kid's *British premiere in 1921, Barrie criticized the sequence and many other things about the film. Far from being offended, Chaplin was deeply flattered to be discussing dramatic structure with the legendary playwright. Before long the two were enthusiastically suggesting ideas for each other's future projects, and Barrie asked Chaplin to play Pan in an upcoming film adaptation. The role eventually went to Betty Bronson.[3]]*

Imagine a boy who is little else but an infant prodigy having to cope with the problem of keeping up the most widespread popularity it has ever been the lot of any man to enjoy; who has to write, direct, play the lead in, and piece together every picture he turns out. Add to this the ceaseless pestering and the endless stream of callers and telegrams with which he is visited, and you have a fair idea of how much balance of mind the little artiste has to exert, particularly when he still retains the comradeship of the men who work under him.

A deep-thinking man has to admit that, when all is taken into consideration, the life of a prominent public character like Charlie Chaplin is no sinecure.

What Charlie seems to deplore most of all is that his success lays him open to much unsought publicity; that it brings him into contact with bores the likes of which he had never credited with being upon earth; and, most of all, that his privacy is utterly gone.

He is a public "poppy-show" here in town, both on the screen and off, and if he can sit through a meal in a public restaurant without being accosted by someone he never met in his life before he has achieved something wonderful.

Laudation and recognition have a pleasant ring to the man in the street, but my association with Charlie Chaplin has shown me with convincing clearness the fact that the rose-strewn path of popularity conceals its relative number of thorns.

I remember having asked him once why he didn't grow a real moustache on the lines of the one he puts on for his screen work. It struck me that, since so many men have been wearing that very type of lip adornment for many years past, the comedian might just as well adopt it himself, and so avoid the unpleasant sensation of the artificial moustache, with its gum and constant irritation. It was his reply to this suggestion that gave me the first inkling of how dear his privacy was to him.

"Good Lord!" he exclaimed, in something akin to panic. "Do you think I want to be followed by every kid in Southern California? It's quite bad enough now."

But to go back to the happenings of the week—for I seem to have strayed off into a vivisection of poor Charlie and his character!

On Monday morning the sky became overcast again, and before we had left our houses the rain began to fall once more. Work, of course, had to be abandoned again, for the interior scenes are, you must understand, taken in the open air, the sunlight being diffused by huge strips of linen stretched across the tops of the stages. This is done for economy and effectiveness.

On Tuesday the rain let up, and we hurried on with our work. There is little to record of the latter. It consists of just the cleaning up of old scenes—a short entrance here, an exit there—just those little connecting links that go to make up the continuity of a big picture upon which the important scenes have already been taken.

I am not, of course, at liberty to tell the story of the picture until it is on the market, by which time it will have told itself, so you must forgive me if I content myself with saying it ought to be the funniest thing Chaplin has ever done since he first went before the camera two years and a month ago.

The rain has prevented my speaking much of the work we have accomplished, for the very good reason that it has reduced that work to practically nil, and has carried the finishing of this last Chaplin-Essanay story into another week, in which I hope to be able to tell of a really busy winding-up of his affairs with the Company in question.

As I look back over the events of the week, my mind goes back to my promise to relate to you that little conversation in Levy's Restaurant, and, since I appear to have told all there is to tell, my article shall close this week with an account of it.

I had just taken to her home my lady friend, who was suffering from a headache or something, and when I returned to the restaurant I discovered a solitary figure sitting at my table. Investigation showed it to be Edna Purviance, and in response to her invitation I sat down, skilfully and tactfully removing as I did so the card which bore my name.

"Where's Charlie?" I asked.

"Oh, he's nervous and fidgety, so I told him to go and walk around the block a few times," she smiled.

So we talked for a while about everything in general, and nothing in particular, until the comedian presently showed up, dragging with him Herbert Rawlinson, of Universal fame, who greeted us and sat him down.[4]

"I'm mighty glad Charlie spotted me," he said. "I've got the blues tonight. I don't like being a bachelor" (his wife, be it said, having gone back to the stage for a short tour). "I was just going to drive back home and go to bed."

For possibly an hour and a half the conversation passed mostly between Edna, Herbert, and myself, Charlie remaining in his preoccupied state, and taking but little part in it, until suddenly, during a lull in the talking, he leaned on his elbow and said—

"Isn't joy a wonderful thing? I've been looking at all these people here tonight. They come here to shake off their little worries and woes, yet each one of them is trying to make for the happiness of others. It is only the poor beggar that's alone that shows his true self, and that is only because he hasn't anybody to please at the moment but himself. Happiness is not of the individual; it's only a thing existing in our relation to others. In short, without the people we meet in life we are nothing. The individual for himself doesn't count."

"But nearly all philosophy teaches us that man should be self-sufficient," I reminded him.

"Then philosophy and I don't agree," he answered, without a moment's hesitation. "I consider the happiness of the human mind a grand and glorious thing—a thing to be striven for above all else, and the only true happiness is contentment of the mind."

I must confess that this brought down upon him a somewhat involved argument, wherein it was proved and disproved that contentment was another name for decay, that we should and should not be self-sufficient, that (by Schopenhauer's contention) all pleasure is temporary, and pain the only positive and enduring thing, and so on, ad libitum, all of which has nothing particular to do with my story. *[Goodwins is not bragging about Chaplin's erudition here; although Chaplin had little formal education, he became an enthusiastic autodidact, and discovered Schopenhauer's* The World as Will and Idea *when he was touring America as part of the Karno company.*[5]*]*

But when it was all in its most confused state Charlie arose and laughed.

"Well, when we start on a thing like this we might go on for ever. It's an endless, bottomless pit, in which you keep falling, and never arrive at any real conclusion. It's trying to solve the riddle of life, and it can't be done. Let's go home."

And so we went.

3

Charlie Chaplin Sends His Famous Moustache to the *Red Letter*

March 11, 1916

The picture which marks the termination of the old contract of Charles Chaplin with the Essanay Company is completed at last, and the Company—meaning that branch of it—is no more.

After many weeks of inclement weather—so many that they created a precedent in the matter of rainfall for the city of Los Angeles—the clouds finally passed away from our horizon (in more senses than one), and we were able to set to upon the long-delayed cleaning-up of *Police*, as Charlie has decided to title the story.

I am not sure that the title fits the subject as aptly as it might, although the whole story does deal with the persecution of the little comedian by officers of the law. It is such a beautiful little story, with its touch of pathos and its love interest skilfully interwoven with the comedy plot, that I personally would have chosen a more descriptive name, but so many titles were proposed and rejected that I suppose the comedian finally settled on upon this one in order to dismiss the matter from his already overworked brain. *[Considering that Goodwins's avowed purpose is to eulogize Chaplin and his work it is rather surprising to find him criticising a film's title. And he's right; aside from their usual omnipresence on the slum streets the police have little to do with the action until the final scene, when they make their way in leisurely fashion (a clear parody of the frenzied Keystone Kops style) to thwart a robbery. Incidentally, one of the film's working titles was* Nine Lives, *an interesting choice considering Chaplin's creative reuse of the* Life *footage.]*

On the morning when work was resumed there seemed to be an instinctive feeling in the air that we were in for a busy day, and, despite the fact that it was fully noon before we shot the first scene, we certainly were.

Faithful to instructions, we put in our appearance at 8.30 a.m., and, Charlie not having shown up, settled ourselves to our various methods of passing the time away.

I am afraid the majority of the boys are smitten with an excessive love of card-playing, for there was never a "school" smaller than eight players, and the games were wont to start with the arrival of the first three, irrespective of the hour! Others, however, preferred to chat on different topics, or to read the heterogeneous lot of literature which happened to be lying around the office. And thus it was on the day of which I am writing.

As the hours wore on, and there was still no sign of Charlie, we telephoned out to his home. The result was a little amusing, for Charlie's Japanese manservant, with the wariness typical of his race, would only make the most noncommittal replies to our enquiries as to Charlie's whereabouts.

"Cannot say," he kept repeating. "He gone, I think."

And with that we had to be content so far as telephoning was concerned. But that picture had to be finished, and as none was more anxious to see it done than the comedian himself, we feared all kinds of automobile accidents and what not. So one of the automobiles was despatched to the house—some five miles from the studio—and within half an hour a telephonic message came through that the chauffeur had located the comedian. He was getting up!

Charlie laughed when we told him of the manservant's diplomacy, and, while making up, told us that "Harry O'Brien" (as he has facetiously christened the Oriental gentleman) is an endless source of amusement to him.

"He inspires me sometimes," he said. "The other morning he dropped a lot of kitchen utensils to the floor and smashed the teapot to smithereens. 'Ah!' he grunted, sweeping up the wreckage. 'Musical teapot!' I ask you, what's the use of getting your rag out with a fellow that pulls that stuff?" *[Toraichi Kono was Chaplin's invaluable factotum, acting variously as household manager, butler, valet, and chauffeur from 1916 to 1934. He appears as a chauffeur in both* The Adventurer *(1917) and* A Day's Pleasure *(1919), and as a member of the audience in* The Circus *(1928). Kono was the primary source for an unauthorized 1940 biography of Chaplin.[1]]*

With time getting so short and the end of the picture so near, I knew I was in for a hustling day with my camera if I was to get enough illustrations to see me through during Charlie's absence, but fortunately the comedian was in his best mood—his Sunday morning "lie-in" having apparently benefited him beyond measure—and offered to pose some special pictures for me exclusively for the *Red Letter*.

Our make-ups completed, we journeyed through that fascinating morass which marks the bridle-path to the Selig stage, and began to "depict," as Charlie calls it.

I don't think I have ever known him to be in a more prankish mood than he was that day. From the moment we reached the stage until the sun finally deserted us he was never still a moment—alternately dancing, telling stories, directing, and clowning all the time. We made some wonderful scenes that day. He told me afterwards that he can always work better when he does his scenes spontaneously and without getting them set by repeated rehearsal.

"When I try to be funny I'm all wrong," he said. "It's when I begin to fool around in front of the camera and do the thing that first enters my head that I am at my best." *[Chaplin said very little about comic technique in interviews, evidently considering the subject too boring for his fans, so this is a good example of how unguarded he feels in Goodwins's company. Late in life Chaplin would tell Peter Bogdanovich that he didn't like improvising, but preferred to have his scenes mapped out in advance.[2] Given his highly choreographic form of acting and directing it isn't surprising that he needed to balance the need for precision with spontaneity. Luckily, many of the Mutual outtakes survive, and they vividly demonstrate his relentless quest for both technical precision and spontaneity in his performances, a balancing act that was necessary because, as he said, "in pantomime the technique of acting is so mechanical."[3]]*

In one scene he had the camera started, and just rushed into the set without the vaguest idea of what he was going to enact, yet he did some of the funniest things in the way of falls and eccentricities that I have ever seen.

Around the set were gathered several of the Selig Company, including Bessie Eyton, Wheeler Oakman, Jack Pickford *[the dissolute brother of Mary Pickford]*, and Tom Persons (general manager). It was something of a novelty to them to witness what the world is pleased to call "slapstick comedy" in the making, and their genuine unrestrained laughter was a tribute to the comedian's genius, even though actors are notoriously the best audiences in the world.

When he had finished the scene he turned to us, grinning, as he always does, and said,

"How's that? Am I funny?"

We assured him that he would do.

Charlie, with all his mental depth, is the veriest youngster in the world!

The work proceeded apace, but we were not destined to complete it that day, for the sun sank behind the mountains before we could film our last three scenes, so we returned to our dressing-rooms and cleaned up.

"To-morrow, then, boys," said Charlie, as he jumped into his car. Any of you going down town? If so I'll give you a lift."

That is the spirit of Charlie Chaplin!

The following morning he was up betimes and on the job before the majority of us had arrived. He took the final interior scenes, and then we all jumped into the car and drove out to Hollywood, where the last scene of the story was staged.

It has always seemed to me that a man's work and his conception of things are the surest indications of his character, and in a way this picture proves that I am right, for from beginning to end it is a most characteristic expression of all that I know to be "true Chaplin."

Its artful little turns of comedy, its little subtleties, its striving for sympathy, and at the last its big laugh, all seem to me so truly indicative of the mind that conceived them that I am almost tempted to say that this is the first real Chaplin story that has ever been given to the picture-goer. Unless I am very much in error, this story is going to finish what was begun by *Charlie the Tramp [British title of* The Tramp*]* and *Charlie in the Bank [British title of* The Bank*]*—the proof positive that Chaplin is an artist of emotion as well as the greatest of all comedians.

After passing through innumerable trials and difficulties the character which Charlie portrays goes out upon the highway full of the resolve to profit by the influence of the girl on whose behalf he had fought a hand-to-hand battle with a fellow criminal. With this in his mind he stretches out his hands to the heavens, swearing to stick to the narrow path of rectitude thenceforward.

But even as he starts upon his climb up the hill, full of his newborn resolve, the shadow of a police officer looms before him, and with the most absurdly comical expression in the world he glides out of the picture, leaving the policeman shaking his fist at his retreating figure in amused reproof.

RED LETTER PHOTOCARD.

(Charles Chaplin.)   Charlie Yawns.   (Charlie the Tramp.)

Charlie, Paddy McGuire, and Ernest Van Pelt in *The Tramp*.

After this scene had been taken the cameraman said—"Now, what about the finish, Charlie?"

"Eh!" said Chaplin. "Why, that is the finish."

"But," began the co-director.

"Oh, yes, I know it's unconventional to leave another actor occupying the scene at the close of the story, but that's what I'm aiming at—unconventionality. Besides, I don't see why the star should hog the whole picture to himself."

And that, too, is the spirit of Charlie Chaplin.

The last scene was taken at 4.30 p.m. and afterwards we piled back into our car and returned to the studio.

On the way back I spoke to Charlie about this article in *Red Letter*, and he was deeply interested in the idea. We discussed it for quite awhile, and presently he peeled off his little moustache, and handed it to me.

"Here," he said, with a grin. "Send it to the editor, with my regards, just for the fun of it, and tell him it's the last one I ever wore under the Essanay Banner."

Which, being a good journalist and true, I did.

On the way back he started to sing some of the old songs that were popular years ago, and before we knew it we found ourselves raking up our memories for the most aged of them. Neither of us being very mature, however (for

Charlie is but twenty-five, while I am a year younger), the best we could manage between us was "The Golden Dustman," with which classic we promptly proceeded to rend the Hollywood welkin [*archaic term for* sky] all the way home. The lines that pleased Charlie the most were:—

> "Asteratamachan around the bottom of me coat—
> A Piccadilly winder in me eye"—

which we both repeated ad nauseam until Edna begged us both to "dry up," and, as neither of us would hurt a hair of her golden head, let alone the drum of her shapely ear, we immediately did as we were told! [*"The Golden Dustman" (1897), popularized by music hall star Gus Elen, is a song about two garbage men who come into wealth when one of their customers dies, leaving them to "clean up" the fortune he's left behind. The singer imagines his future life of luxury. "Asteratamachan" is a cockney corruption of Astrakhan, a Russian city whose lambs provided distinctive black wool often used to trim coats. A "Piccadilly winder" is a monocle.*

The premise of a poor man assuming the airs of a rich one was a staple in comic music hall songs, and Chaplin sang one, "'E Dunno Where 'E Are" (1893) during his first stage appearance, at age five.[4] *The comic juxtaposition of wealth and poverty, of course, is at the heart of Chaplin's filmic universe, and scenes in the spirit of these songs would appear in such future Chaplin classics as* A Dog's Life, The Gold Rush, *and* Modern Times.*]*

It was nearly dusk when we arrived at the studio, and the evening chill common to the tropical winter began to settle upon the air, so we all, Charlie included, set to find some wood with which to make a fire in the stove.

"You break the wood," he said, "and I'll be stoker. I love these American stoves. They're specially designed to safeguard against giving any heat!"

There was, however, more poetry than truth in that remark of his, for within ten minutes he was clamouring for the window to be opened to let in some air! One by one the boys left the dressing-room, bidding the comedian goodbye—and I know they all felt the parting of the ways very keenly—until only Charlie and I were left in the room.

While we were washing up he started to talk about the past, the present, and the future, and such a multiplicity of subjects that I scarce know where to begin in recounting what he said.

I think the conversation began by my speaking of his doing falls. I asked him where he had learned them, and that got him going.

"Why, I just picked them up when I drifted into vaudeville. I saw they might be necessary to me, and I went ahead and taught myself to do them. I believe in going after anything that may be of material benefit to you, because versatility, so long as you're not a Jack-of-all-trades and the master of none, is the greatest asset in the world. I got the real body of my stage training from William Gillette and Mr Saintsbury in the old *Sherlock Holmes* days. What I did with Karno was just the ordinary routine of my stage career."

"Then you don't really regard the Karno days as the school in which you gained your experience for this work?"

"Heavens, no!" he exclaimed. "Although I naturally picked up something—everything teaches us at least that—and I also have to thank the turn of circumstances that sent me to America under his management, and brought me into contact with the motion picture people." *[Chaplin toured in Karno's companies from the age of eighteen to twenty-four. Given that Karno was almost certainly his most important theatrical and comedy mentor, it is very odd to find him vehemently denying Karno's influence. Since at this stage Chaplin was recycling a lot of Karno material in his films it may be that he felt the need to establish some distance from his old employer; however, the proof in the pudding is that he surrounded himself with Karno-trained actors. In later writings he acknowledges his debt.⁵]*

Presently we fell to talking about a certain Broadway star with whom I played last season in New York. I spoke of his having once admitted to me, that he did not consider himself to be a clever actor, whereat Charlie laughed—"You don't suppose he meant it, do you?"

I ventured to say that I certainly had done so.

Believe me," said Charlie, "the man who doesn't think himself clever never succeeds. He needn't be egotistic, but he's got to have supreme confidence in his own cleverness."

"Had you that confidence?" I asked.

"I certainly thought, and still think, that I am gifted. I'd be a liar if I said otherwise! The man who doesn't appreciate his own value stands forever at the bottom of the ladder."

I reminded him of his statement just two weeks ago to the effect that he always felt bashful about meeting the big men of the world.

"Yes, personally," he agreed. "But that doesn't hide from me the truth of whether I am superior or inferior to them in my gifts. I have a perfect sense of my position when it comes to that." *["You have to believe in yourself, that's the secret," Chaplin would later tell his oldest son, Charles Jr. "Even when I was in the orphanage, when I was roaming the street trying to find enough to eat, even then I thought of myself as the greatest actor in the world. I had to feel the exuberance that comes from utter confidence in yourself. Without it, you go down to defeat."*[6]

Many others would attest to Chaplin's supreme confidence in his own abilities, which occasionally came across as arrogance. His insecurities manifested in his stubborn refusal to acknowledge the creative contributions of others to his work, which earned him both lawsuits and bitter enemies. One such enemy was the celebrated director Robert Florey, a Chaplin idolater until he worked with the comedian on Monsieur Verdoux, *after which he wrote several scathing indictments of his former hero.*[7]*]*

The conversation continued at great length, while the comedian leisurely dressed in his street clothes, but I must, from want of space, reserve some of it for a future instalment. It is too good to miss outright, pointing as it does to the fact upon which I am laying so much stress—that Charles Chaplin is something very much more than a mere slap-stick comedian—that he has wonderful depth of character and a power of analysis that is positively remarkable.

Possibly the serious side of the comedian is not so interesting to the man in the street as his comedy vein would be, for it is in the latter that you have seen him—or his shadow—most frequently, but the fact remains that he is more often serious than he is frivolous, and if I were to say otherwise I would be losing sight of a great truth. Besides, by showing just how much there is in Charlie Chaplin, I may be able to make his pictures even more enjoyable to you, inasmuch as they are full of little touches which might otherwise pass by the average picture-goer, because of their unexpectedness from a "mere buffoon."

Look at it from whatever angle you will, Chaplin is a man of sentiment—not a sentimentalist, for there is a world of difference between the two terms—and in his sentiment lies the strength of his appeal as a comedian. The border-line between laughter and pathos is not very strongly defined, and Charlie, even in his most farcical pictures containing no actual vein of tenderer feeling, is always a sympathetic figure. It is more than just his outward personality. It is the truest index of his character.

Suddenly, as he was adjusting his tie, he asked me what time it was. I told him half-past five, and to my astonishment he ran out of the room without another word.

I finished my toilet, and followed him a few minutes later, just as he was leaving the office. "Goodbye," he called, jumping into his car. "I'm going to Chicago on the 6.40. Send the negative on by the next train. I'll be back within two weeks."

A puff of gasoline fumes, a little cloud of dust, and the huge car was speeding down the street.

That is another bit of Chaplin—his impulse. Without a moment's preparation he started off upon a 2,500-mile journey to the East, just because it occurred to him that he would save a day's absence if he left California that night. Where his trunks were I cannot say. Possibly he travelled just as he was!

So for two weeks we will see nothing of him, and I propose therefore to devote my next two instalments to a retrospect. There is so much to tell that has never been told—so much that will throw a new light upon the life of the real Charlie Chaplin and his work—that I feel I may be permitted to digress from the present (with which my article is supposed to deal essentially), and during the days that Charlie is in "Chi" arranging his plans for the future to go back into the past.

On the day following Charlie's departure the balance of the Company, with sole exceptions of Edna, Leo White, and myself, left Los Angeles on the boat for San Francisco where they rejoin the main body of the Essanay Company's staff. It was quite a business saying goodbye and godspeed to all of them, but they finally went on their way, and the same night I put Edna on the train for 'Frisco, where she will stay with her mother until Charlie returns.

As she stood on the observation platform of the departing train she waved her hand, and promised to write to me the moment she arrived.

For a patriotic American girl Edna is the most English-spirited thing that ever happened—a wonderful, lovable little woman, with a heart as big as her body, and a good fellow in the truest sense of the word.

As I drove back from the Southern Pacific Station an odd feeling of desolation came upon me, and I felt strangely alone.

The Essanay-Chaplin Company under the old contract was but a memory of the past!

4

Charlie Chaplin's "Lost Sheep"

March 18, 1916

I have applied that title to this week's article because I think it best fits us poor, wandering actors since our shepherd, in the shape of Charlie Chaplin, has gone to the Wicked East and deserted us. When you've heard what I have to tell I think you will agree with me.

As I told you last week, he rushed away upon a moment's decision, caught the 6.40 train from the Santa Fe Station, and sped from the scene of his triumphs at the rate of fifty miles an hour, leaving us behind him with nothing to do but pursue the Asquith policy. *["The Asquith policy" here means "do nothing." Herbert Henry Asquith, the British prime minister, had led the nation into war, but was increasingly perceived as indecisive, ineffective, and self-indulgent in his administration of it. He would resign in December 1916.]*

If you know anything about actors—as you probably do, considering how conspicuous we make ourselves in the public eye, both on and off the stage— you will know just about how long it took for this period of inactivity to pall upon us. But I don't believe that even you, good, kind, intelligent reader, will realise how true is the saying that his satanic majesty finds occupation for hands left in temporary idleness—particularly in regard to actors. Therefore, in a spirit of self-punishment I am going to commit myself and tell you.

On the day following Charlie's departure we were a very nice-mannered bunch of little fellows from the moment we arose—somewhere about noon, because it is seldom we are allowed to stay in bed so late—until we sought our humble cots. As you know, I saw Edna off to 'Frisco by the 8.15 p.m. train shortly after Charlie had gone East, but with the departure of Edna, who makes it her especial care that we behave ourselves properly and don't do anything she wouldn't, came the fall of all the good New Year resolutions of Billy Armstrong and yours truly.

I wandered down town rather aimlessly after I had returned the old "gasoline tank" to its garage, and was just beginning to think of turning in, like a good man and true, when who should I encounter but the incorrigible William, fresh returned from his day's labours at the L-Ko (with which organisation he is now connected). It was a long time since Billy and I had been "rounding" together, for with his change of habitat we had rather drifted apart socially, but we were none the less glad to see each other that night; and—well, there's only one place to talk over the past with any degree of zest, isn't there? As an old colleague of mine once put it—"I defy anyone to get up a political argument over a cup of cocoa!"

Charlie and Billy Armstrong enjoy their treats as Snub Pollard, soon to become a popular comedian in his own right, looks on aghast. *By the Sea.*

I shall draw the veil over part of our adventures that night. Suffice it that we sallied from the hostel where the tête-à-tête was held, and, minus some dollars which had passed across its shining bar, took our (then) righteous way to pastures new. I wanted to go back and fetch out the "gasoline tank" again, but Billy—rather prematurely, be it said—assured me that I was in far too "glad" a condition to be trusted at the steering-wheel, and pushed me into a taximeter cabriolet—vulgarly termed a "taxi," I believe. *["Taximeter cabriolets," French-made gasoline-powered taxicabs, hit the streets of London in 1903, and were obsolete by 1916. Here Fred playfully assumes the airs of a dissipated Victorian aristocrat, a staple of music hall comedy. Playing a drunken swell, of course, made Chaplin a star on stage, and he would return to the role in a number of films, including the Mutual films* One A.M. *and* The Cure.*]*

Here again the curtain must fall for possibly three hours, at the end of which time it rises upon McKee's Café, an all-night restaurant in the heart of town here.

Within ten minutes everybody had recognised Billy Armstrong as the chief Chaplin supporter of past pictures, and were begging him to give an exhibition of trick tumbling! In saner moments there is not a doubt that we would both have risen and made as hurried an exit as was consistent with dignity—for our English blood is still strong within us; in fact, it is undiluted, to be perfectly frank. Instead of which, before we knew what was happening, Billy was showing those Yanks something in the way of "cut-up" falls and "half-forwards" that they had never deemed possible on earth.

Of course, such goings-on were too much for even so genial a sport as McKee's, and the proprietor, with difficulty restraining his amusement, begged us to consider his license and desist. So, with many polite assurances that we were gentleman and knew when to stop (!), we settled our score, donned our hats, and prepared to depart to our homes. We lined up at the head of the aisle, and marched out in single file to the strains of:—"Left-right-right in the thick of the fight;

> It's a wonder I'm alive to tell the tale.
> They charge you left and right—
> They charge with all their might—
> They charge a tanner a pint for four-penny ale!"

I trow those American boys and girls had never heard the like of that ditty, which, being at least seventeen years old, evidences the fact that neither Billy nor I have forgotten much that we ever heard in the Mother-land.

For the rest, I will content myself with re-printing a paragraph which appeared in the *Los Angeles Times* a few days later—long after the incident had, as we thought, been buried in the obscurity of the past. It appears, however, that there is no limit to the resourcefulness of the American newspaper man in search of copy. Here it is:—

> Charlie Chaplin never put anything over in a photoplay that was any better than a couple of his actor friends got away with the other night on the occasion of Charlie's leaving for Chicago.
>
> Following the sad rites at Levy's, Freddie Goodwins and Billy Armstrong, of Chaplin's Company, started for home. It was 2.00 a.m., and by that time neither knew whether it was a celebration or a wake they'd been to. They knew only that they were consumed by a great thirst, so, halting a milk-man, they purchased a two-gallon can of milk, and . . . being the steadier on his legs, hoisted the can to his shoulder to take it home. But out in front of the Times Building a policeman arrested them. He was assured by both that the milk was duly and properly paid for, but nevertheless insisted on walking Freddy and Billy back four blocks in pursuit of the milk-waggon,[1] Freddie still bearing the can. Then the officer gave them a certificate to show to any other enquiring limb of the law:—"These men bought this can of milk from the Burr Creamery waggon, and are going home with it."
>
> "Did he think we were going to stop and do a Keystone with it right in the middle of Broadway?" demands Freddie.

It is not solely on account of this delectable little incident, however, that I have chosen to describe us actors as "lost sheep," for the other "remnant," to wit, Leo White, has shown symptoms of being similarly affected by the sudden inanition.

Being a respectably-married family man, with a charming better half and two very English kiddies, Leo, who is in real life the very antithesis of the formidable Frenchman he so often portrays in Charlie's pictures, never joins his single brethren upon their little convivial parties. He and his wife are chokeful *[archaic form of chock-full]* of the characteristic hospitality of the Britisher, and very excellent hosts at all times.

Imagine, then, with what alacrity I responded to an invitation to dine with them upon the Sunday following my little escapade with the redoubtable Armstrong.

After an uncommonly tasty meal, Leo and I took our cigars to the garden, where conversation naturally turned upon the subject most engrossing our thoughts—the future of the Chaplin affairs. He is Charlie's right-hand man, and I was sure that I could get from him even more information than my friendship with Charlie has given me.

Unfortunately, however, it appears that, at the time of writing, both he and Charlie are as much at sea as myself about just when, where, and how work will be resumed! It is in order to straighten out a certain deadlock in the arrangements that Charlie has gone East.

"If all goes alright," said Leo, "Charlie will put the preliminary affairs of the new company into shape, and either come back to California poste-haste or, if he thinks expedient, wire to me to bring you and Edna to New York and start work there. On the other hand, however, if any hitch arises, he has an offer to release under—" (Mentioning a big New York motion picture man.)

"You think he is likely to adopt the latter proposition?" I asked.

Leo shrugged his shoulders—a mannerism he has developed through having played so many Frenchmen all his life—and I gathered from that that I knew about as much as either he or Charlie on the subject.

During the afternoon I took a picture of him with his two kiddies. I had a lot of fun with the youngsters, whose appearance singles them out from the American children by the clear, full-blooded handsomeness of their features, and one of them handed me a good laugh by his reply to a question I put to him.

"What are you going to do for a living?" I asked him.

"Work for Charlie Chaplin," he asserted stoutly.

"Do you like Charlie Chaplin?" I inquired.

"No—I don't!" He exclaimed fiercely.

"Why?"

"Because he kicks my papa!" was the unexpected reply.

That is rather away from what I started to recount, but it leads up to it somewhat, so I may be forgiven for the digression [and also for the chauvinistic praise of the looks of English children over American ones!].

On the day following Leo and I drove out to Hollywood, where he wanted to rent a new bungalow for his wife and kiddies, and (should Charlie decide to return to California) for himself also.

But either the absence of the guiding hand was still upon us, or else there was a Jinx hovering over us, for after losing ourselves three times we finally located the street we sought, or thought we sought, as it appeared afterwards! Right in the middle of the thoroughfare was the "dog-gonedest" hill I have ever set eyes on. It was as much as I could do to get up it on my low gear. What is more, as luck would have it, the house we wanted was right on the top of this pretty little mountain, but we finally made it, and Leo hopped out and rang at the bell. It struck me that the house was rather a pretentious sort of place for a movie-actor to rent, but I presumed Leo knew his own business.

After a moment, however, he came back to me, cursing furiously. It appeared he had marked the wrong column of the news-paper. The house at which we had called belonged to a millionaire, who had advertised for a cook!

With more vigour than discretion I turned that gasoline tank around, and we disappeared down the hill at three times the regulation speed.

At the bottom, on Hollywood Boulevard, a friend hailed us, and demanded a lift back to town. We managed to pack him in somehow—for my machine is not exactly a Rolls-Royce tourer, you know *[Fred drove a two-seater]*—and proceeded homeward on high gear. Three blocks further on, however, with a report that reminded me of the 5th of November at the Crystal Palace,[2] my rear tyre blew out.

I alighted, took one look at a hole big enough to receive one of Charlie's shoes, and ran that car into the nearest garage without daring to vent my feelings on the twilight air.

It looked like "street-car for ours" then, but, as luck would have it (?), a big touring-car stopped by us, and the driver, with a genial smile, invited us to get in.

With many protestations of thanks we piled into the rear seats, and started off once more upon our home stretch.

Suddenly I noticed a big cardboard sign attached to the windscreen of the car, and asked the chauffeur what it was, dreading the reply I knew was coming, for I had come out without a dollar in my pocket!

"Why, that's my destination sign," he answered.

I gasped, as quietly as possible—

"Then you're—"

"A jitney-'bus? Sure!" he replied, smiling serenely.

I knew it.

A jitney-'bus is an American idea in the way of transportation. It is a touring-car which carries passengers at so much a head!

I conveyed the dread secret to my companions, feeling instinctively that they, too, had come out minus United States currency. They had!

It was a pleasant trip that. I foresaw giving the chauffeur an IOU, but I didn't altogether foresee his accepting it!

To cut the long story short, however, just as we neared Los Angeles I espied a friend from Universal City—Herbert Rawlinson, to wit—another English man. He was driving to the public danger, as he always does, having lived in America a good many years. But I managed to catch his eye as he passed us, and shouted to him, with as little noise as possible, to lend me a "two-spot" and trust in me. Without a moment's hesitation he handed me—perilously perched on the running-board of our "bus"—two honest American dollars, and thus were we saved the ignominy of an unpaid motor bill. I blessed Herbert fervently. Two dollars have seldom looked so good to me as those did!

This is the last bit of house-hunting I am going to do—with Leo White at any rate.

I have spent my time very quietly since then. Charlie has sent no news as to his plans, and there is nothing to do save cruise around town, see an occasional show, and—think.

There's a lot to think about, too, even though the present is somewhat empty for us. There is always the conjecture as to the future, and there is retrospection—the looking back over what has happened in the past.

It was upon the latter subject that I proposed to write this week, but somehow my machine seems to have rather run away with me, until I find I have talked more about myself and the others than I have about the great and only Charles. Yet perhaps you will understand. With the subject of my articles so many hundreds of miles away, I have found it difficult to nail down to the task of throwing my mind back over the days of *Charlie's Night Out [British title of* A Night Out*]* and the subsequent pictures. Somehow—and I suppose it is but another evidence of the power of Chaplin's magnetism—I continually find myself wondering what is afoot in New York City, just what is being done by that little man that holds our present destinies in his hand, the little man that holds the laughter of the whole civilised world between his finger-tips.

There he is, at the Astor Hotel, registered under the name of Charles Spencer, in order that prying busybodies may not interfere with the work upon which he is engaged.

Just what will the outcome of that work be? Will it spell further triumphs? Will it be the beginning of his end? What will it mean to the future of that great popularity that has set the whole world going?

Time alone will tell.

5

How Charlie Chaplin Got His £300-a-Week Salary

March 25, 1916

A little over a year ago—when the name of Charlie Chaplin conveyed practically nothing to even the British people, except perhaps as the brother of Sydney, who was then performing in Fred Karno's *Hydro* Company—there came to the managing director of the Keystone Film organisation a little man who had a proposition to make. *[Fred Karno was the most prolific and successful producer of comic sketches in British music hall history. He created dozens of sketches and had dozens of companies touring them. Sydney joined Karno in 1906 and quickly became one of his leading comedians, even coauthoring several sketches, including* The Hydro *and* Skating. *It took Sydney some time to convince Karno to audition his younger brother, but in 1908 Karno relented and hired Charlie, who rapidly rose in the ranks in his turn. In 1910 he was offered the chance to tour America as the lead comedian in a newly assembled Karno company, a tour that eventually extended to four years and led to his being hired by Mack Sennett's Keystone company.]*

His proposition was the outcome of a careful survey of what he had done in the past, and of what he saw coming to him in the future, although not he—not anybody, in fact—ever dreamed just how great that future was to be.

In short, then, Charles Chaplin, moving picture comedian of but one year's experience, reminded Mack Sennett that his contract with the Keystone Company was nearing its termination, and that it was high time that plans for the future were gone into.

The "Master of Laughs," as they called Sennett in those days, assured the little man that he was perfectly satisfied with his work, and that he was prepared to give him an increase in salary for the coming three years, rising yearly at the rate of one hundred dollars per week. But Charlie shook his head slowly and put the matter in front of the "Master of Laughs," as he saw it with his, more or less, prophetic eye.

His praises were just beginning to be sung by the public and the press, he said, and within a year, given only an ordinary amount of luck, he would guarantee to fill the place formerly held by John Bunny and Ford Sterling, in respective order, as the world's most popular picture comedian.

Sennett smiled diplomatically, albeit he knew there was a strong element of truth in what the little Britisher said, and asked just what Mr Chaplin thought was his just due for the coming contract.

"Give me a thousand dollars (£200) a week for 1915," he said. "Another five hundred a week for 1916, and two hundred and fifty dollars more a week for the last year." [*Mack Sennett remembered this conversation differently. In his version he offered Chaplin seven hundred and fifty dollars a week. When Chaplin declined Sennett offered to share his one-third ownership in Keystone on top of the salary.[1] Sennett, however, was never one to let the facts get in the way of a good story. Nor was Chaplin; in his* Autobiography *he repeats that he asked for a thousand a week, but states that Sennett counter-offered five hundred a week for the four months remaining in his contract, seven hundred for the next year, and fifteen hundred for the third, which would average out to a thousand a week. (Chaplin's math—or Sennett's—is a little off here.)*

Chaplin retorted:

> *"Mack," I answered, "if you'll just reverse the terms, give me fifteen hundred the first year, seven hundred the second year, and five hundred the third, I'll take it."*
> *"But that's a crazy idea," said Sennett.*
> *So the question of a new contract was not discussed again.[2]*

We cannot know at this juncture whose version is correct, but Chaplin's daring reversal of Sennett's offer certainly makes for the better story. For what it's worth, Chaplin repeated his story without variation over the years, including to his good friend Max Eastman.[3]]

Rumour has it that Sennett, aghast at the little man's temerity, begged him to give the matter more sober consideration and report within a week whether he had a more reasonable proposition to put before the firm.

"I am likely to get other offers any day now," Chaplin warned him. "Are you going to take first refusal of my services, or shall I grab the best offer that comes along without consulting you?"

"I'll take a chance," replied Sennett.

"Do you want me?"

"Sure, I do."

And thus the first interview closed.

Ten days later came a dozen propositions from various firms, and Charlie, exercising a diplomacy very creditable under the circumstances, kept them in his pocket and again went into conclave with the big chief.

What actually happened at that final interview is not public property, but within a week Charlie Chaplin, suit-case in tow, departed from the plant, armed with a telegram from the Essanay Film Company, wherein the latter agreed to pay him fifteen hundred dollars (roughly £300) a week for the year 1915. *[Chaplin's salary with Essanay was $1,250 per week plus a $10,000 signing bonus, the equivalent of $1,750,000 for a year in 2016 dollars. Sydney helped to negotiate this contract, which made Charlie one of the highest-paid actors in the industry. Sydney was in America because Charlie had urged Sennett to hire him, just as Syd had earlier urged Karno to hire Charlie. Sennett was only too happy to oblige, the Chaplin name having become big box office. In addition, he may have thought that hiring Sydney would ensure Charlie's loyalty. If so, that hope was soon dashed, for Sydney immediately began acting as his brother's business manager, negotiating not only the Essanay contract but the two precedent-setting contracts to come. At the same time Sydney established himself as a highly successful screen comedian in his own right. The brothers appear onscreen together for the first time in Charlie's last Keystone film,* His Prehistoric Past. *Syd would go on to play important supporting roles in five of Charlie's First National films (1918–1923). But his greatest contribution to Charlie's work, aside from his skill as a contract negotiator, may have been his behind-the-scenes work as a gagman and story collaborator, as we will see in later articles.]*

A few days later he was two thousand five hundred miles nearer his Homeland, formulating his plans for the new engagement at the Chicago plant of the new company.

His first picture under that contract was appropriately titled *His New Job*, and he set about getting together his cast for the production.

For two years there had been a young Englishman in the stock company there, hailing from Manchester, by the name of Leo White, and a little cross-eyed fellow, even smaller than Charlie himself, who gloried in the cognomen of Benjamin Turpin. White was playing in one of George Ade's "Fables in Slang" when Chaplin arrived at the studio. Turpin was "kinder hanging around," as he puts it. *[Turpin had appeared in the first Essanay film, An Awful Skate, in 1907, but had since then been languishing at the studio. Co-starring in Chaplin's first two Essanay comedies proved to be a huge boost for his career, and he went on to star in a series of highly successful comic films with Sennett, who capitalized on Turpin's goofy looks by casting him against type as a he-man or romantic hero in parodies of current popular films.]*

As it always has done, and doubtless always will, work on everything else ceased summarily with the arrival of the little star, and he was given his pick of the company for the purpose of the new release.

"Oh, just give me all the comedians you can spare," he said. "And I'd like to have Mr White." Then he caught sight of Ben Turpin. He has told me since that Ben was so cross-eyed in those days that one never knew what he was looking at!

"Come here," he said. "I want you to play opposite me."

So that was the basis of the first Chaplin-Essanay picture; Charlie as star and director, Leo White as "straight foil," and Ben Turpin as second comedian.

On your side the picture was called *Charlie's New Job* (they always stick the word "Charlie" in front of our titles at the London office), and it was an instantaneous success. For the first time, I think, the public was let into the secret of who the curly-haired bundle of trouble that had afforded them so much amusement in the past was by name and nationality. *[Keystone comedies in 1914 didn't include cast credits on either their films or their posters, so Chaplin's first audiences got to know him by sight alone. His name was used in the trade press, but newspaper reviewers had to make up names, such as "Edgar English" or simply "the funny man." Essanay and an eager world press—including the* Red Letter*—would soon remedy that.]*

After a couple of weeks of "cutting loose" in the Windy City, however, the call of the West—an odd feeling that assails one during an absence, yet doesn't prevent one saying unkind things about the West when one is there!—began to enter the comedian's heart. He often says how he used to miss the sunshine, the everlasting warmth, even on rainy days, the great palm trees with their welcome shade, the tall eucalyptus trees forever dropping their bobbin-like cones, pungent with the scent of oil, and, most of all, the flowers that grow as plentifully as weeds on every hand.

Back there in Chicago, he said, the place began to pall, with all its metropolitan attractions, and so, within a week of the finishing of *Charlie's New Job*, he was speeding back to San Francisco, accompanied by Ben Turpin, Leo White, and his family, and G. M. Anderson ("Bronco Billy"), who was until February of this year partner of the Essanay Concern.

Arrived in the big city of the West, the party spent a day in seeing the San Francisco Exposition—easily the most wonderful of its kind that has ever been held, by the way—afterwards journeying to a little town called Niles, which, until a few weeks ago, was the western headquarters of the firm.

The second picture was begun without delay, and was, so Charlie says, founded on fact—possibly he means that it was suggested to him by some of his experiences in Chicago. It was titled *A Night Out*.

Up to that time Charlie had no leading lady, but one day, while wandering around the lot in search of inspiration, he happened to catch sight of a beautiful blonde girl who had strayed there from pure curiosity. It didn't take long to persuade her to try-out in the picture, and so came the entry into the motion-picture field of Edna Purviance. The story of how she came, and the circumstances which led up to Charlie's engaging her as his leading lady, have already been accurately related to you by the lady herself in a recent issue of the *Red Letter*. [*Edna Purviance was Chaplin's leading lady from 1915 through 1923. They made thirty-six films together, and we watch them meet and fall in love again and again. So the story of how they met in real life, already of interest to readers in early 1916, remains a subject of interest to Chaplin fans. Goodwins's articles were preceded in the* Red Letter *by first-person articles purportedly written by Edna (November 13, 1915) and Charlie (June 26, 1915). These articles, written in a more stilted style than Goodwins's breezy prose, were almost certainly ghost-written by someone else in the Essanay publicity department. While both contain elements of truth, they also contain some whoppers, so we have chosen not to reprint them in this book. As to how she came to work for Chaplin, in the* Red Letter *article Edna claims to have been visiting a friend of hers who had been hired by Essanay. The friend was showing Edna around the Niles studio when Chaplin spotted her and hired her on the spot. Goodwins published an interview with Edna in another magazine in May 1916 in which she repeats the same story.⁴ In his* Autobiography *Chaplin gives a different but more plausible account. He reports that he had gone to San Francisco with G. M. Anderson to look over the chorus girls who worked at Anderson's Gaiety Theatre. He didn't find any of them suitable, but one of Anderson's cowboy actors suggested a pretty woman he had seen several times at the Tait-Zinkland Café, which was right next to the theatre. A meeting was arranged at the St. Francis Hotel in San Francisco, after which Edna was engaged.⁵*

Recent research reveals that the two versions are not entirely incompatible. David Kiehn found that on January 19, 1915, the day after Chaplin arrived in Niles, Essanay advertised in the San Francisco Chronicle *for "THE PRETTIEST GIRL IN CALIFORNIA to take part in a moving picture." On January 21 Edna and another hopeful registered at the Belvoir Hotel in Niles. Edna may simply have responded to the advertisement, or been asked by an intermediary or Chaplin himself to travel to Niles. Kiehn also found evidence that Edna was working as a waitress at the Tait-Zinkland Café, not, as she claimed in several of her interviews, as a secretary.⁶*

In the few interviews Edna gave to outside reporters she comes across as modest and relatively truthful about herself. But when she moved with Chaplin to Mutual someone in the company decided that she needed a more distinguished background than being a mere secretary or waitress, and this was left to the new Mutual publicist, Terry Ramsaye. Ramsaye quotes her as saying that she went to Vassar, had come to San Francisco to do "charity and settlement work," and that she and Chaplin met at a playlet put on by a charitable organization, in which she had the leading role. All this is manifestly untrue.⁷]

Then came the difficulty of getting a big, burly man to play the other husband—of course, you have seen the picture of which I am writing—and Charlie was again in somewhat of a quandary. Big men there were a-plenty, but they "weren't the character," and Charlie was particular. So work was hung up for a couple of days until a suitable actor could be found.

That night Charlie went down into 'Frisco to spend the evening, and, dropping into a café, chanced to espy a huge fellow, obviously quite young, with a good natured smile. He was one of the singers at the café, and Charlie, in order to get an idea of the fellow's personality, sent up a dollar and a request that the big comedian should sing Billy Merson's "The Spaniard That Blighted My Life."

Another motive for his request was a bad fit of home-sickness for England that assailed Chaplin that night. Merson's song always brings back certain memories to him, he has since told me. But all that is by the way.

The fat man's rendering of the song pleased Charlie, and he got into conversation with him. His parents were Scottish, it appeared, hailing from Dundee, where he was born only twenty-one years ago. Charlie formed quite a liking for the personality of the boy, and had him come out to the studio next day, where he, too, made his debut into moving pictures as the jealous husband of Edna. His work was remarkably good, and so he became a member of the stock company, playing with Charlie right up to the end of the comedian's term. That was the coming of "Bud" Jaimison.

For the rest, the principal cast was composed of Charlie, Sadie Carr, Ben Turpin, and Leo White, the latter in the character of the French Count, by which he is now known the world over.

There was no particular incident in connection with the picture to warrant my dwelling on it, so I will pass on to the next, *In the Park*, which was filmed in the famous Golden Gate Park of San Francisco.

Charlie told me once that it was a desecration to film a comedy in that park, for it seems still to bear the atmosphere of the days when it offered camping ground for the many thousands of families rendered homeless and destitute by the terrible San Francisco earthquake and fire of 1906. But that was mere sentimentality, which is not business, and so he went ahead and it formed the locale of one of his funniest pictures. *[Many of Chaplin's Keystone films took place in parks, of course, and in his* Autobiography *he reports that during their contract negotiations he told Sennett, "All I need to make a comedy is a park, a policeman and a pretty girl,"[8] a comment which has been much quoted. But parks also had powerful and melancholy associations for Chaplin. When he returned to England in 1921 driving past the familiar parks of his youth prompted him to write, in his account of the trip, "How depressing to me are all parks! . . . One never goes to a park unless one is lonesome. . . . The symbol of sadness, that's a park."[9]]*

In this picture Charlie stood by his original cast of players, except that Edna had gone away to her home for a while, her place being temporarily taken by Leona Anderson, sister of the aforementioned "Broncho Billy." *[Goodwins seems to be saying that Edna does not appear in the film, which is odd, since she is very much in evidence as Chaplin's love interest. In fact, David*

Kiehn observed of In the Park *that "Edna is relaxed and natural for the first time onscreen, and Chaplin can't take his eyes off her. Something was going on here. That something was love, and it changed the way Chaplin treated her character. She came through unscathed while everyone else was knocked about and manhandled."*[10]]

In the Park served to accustom the comedian to the people with whom he had to work, and showed a marked improvement, in the matter of teamwork, upon his first two subjects.

Then Turpin was requisitioned to play in the series known as "The Snakeville Comedies," and thereafter Leo White became for several pictures the second male player in the Chaplin Company.

Rumour has it that there was an ulterior motive in the transfer of Ben, some hinting that his size formed no contrast to Charlie's, others (less charitable) declaring that Charlie was afraid that Ben was becoming too popular. Such state-

" . . . a park, a policeman and a pretty girl." *In the Park*. Note the people watching in the background.

ments as these, which were circulated not only from here but in Great Britain as well, are manifestly absurd, for Charlie in his Keystone days had to work side by side with men who rank among the world's finest motion-picture comedians. Surely the fact that he not only held his own, but outstripped them in the race for popularity is proof positive that he had no cause for fear from lesser men, particularly Ben who is the least envious man in the wide world. *[Speculation continued through the years about why Chaplin stopped working with Turpin, with jealousy being cited as the most likely motive. But Chaplin found his inspiration in playing loner characters. His comic pairings—with Roscoe Arbuckle and Chester Conklin at Keystone, Turpin at Essanay, Syd at First National, Jack Oakie in* The Great Dictator, *Martha Raye in* Monsieur Verdoux, *and finally Buster Keaton in* Limelight, *were all memorable but short-lived.]*

So, with Ben Turpin out of the Chaplin ranks, Charlie was left with little else but "straight" men to support him, but he formulated a story around himself and them that, to my mind, has never been equalled for pure fun by anything he has since done. I refer to *The Champion*, which was called in Europe *Champion Charlie*. *[Turpin, almost unrecognizable without his brush moustache, actually does a small bit as a cigar vendor in the film, which proved to be his last appearance for Chaplin.]*

For days before the actual taking of the picture Charlie and "Bud" Jaimison practised incessantly with the boxing gloves, and by the time the scenes were enacted they pretty well knew each other's little idiosyncrasies in the matter of sparring, although I am not trying to suggest that Bud, in a real "scrap," could not have put the goodbye upon Charlie Chaplin with a single blow!

The boxing ring was erected, then, and the fun began. Every male on the premises was put in the "audience," and if variety was Charlie's aim, he certainly succeeded in getting it by this method, for the crowd of onlookers was composed of property men, carpenters, wardrobe men, actors, scene-painters, and any casual visitors that happened to be around, while right in the foreground, seated beside Leo White, who played a stage villain, one can easily distinguish the inimitable G. M. Anderson himself.

The floor of the ring was covered with a tarpaulin, beneath which were pads of felt to break the heavy falls that were expected—and realised—in the ensuing scenes.

Of the fight scenes themselves I can say nothing that the screen has not shown you, except that Charlie told Bud to go right in and knock him all around the ring. There was hardly any rehearsal of those scenes, and the comedy that resulted was nearly all invented on the spur of the moment. *[Slapstick violence, of course, had to be carefully rehearsed, and Goodwins admits three paragraphs above that it was rehearsed. The preparation is evident in the highly choreographed patterns and the many inventive gags. Chaplin wanted the public to know that he worked hard for his money; but he also wanted them to think that his comedy flowed effortlessly from him, so Goodwins is at pains to show that life at the studio is fun as well as work.]*

Perhaps the funniest incident of all was where Charlie makes a profound bow, and is knocked flat in the act by Bud's huge fist. The bow was really the signal to the camera-man for the end of that particular scene, but Bud, in a fit of excitement, swung up and landed Charlie on his neck just as the camera ceased to turn. They were not sure whether or not the camera had caught that particular little bit but when the film came to be developed, there it was in all its realism. So they kept it in the picture. *[Since both Chaplin and Jamison repeatedly bow to the spectators after they've knocked each other down it seems unlikely that Chaplin bowed as a signal to the cameraman to cut. Nor do any of Chaplin's knockdowns end with an abrupt cutaway. So once again it appears Goodwins is being a bit creative in his narrative. See chapters 7 and 18 for more on Chaplin's approach to comic violence, and several actual accidents that occurred.*

Chaplin would return to the ring fifteen years later for the hilarious boxing scene in City Lights, *and one can see the germ of many of its ideas in* The Champion's *bout, notably when the adversaries dance together and the referee is drawn into the action.* The Champion, *in its turn, borrows its basic plot device from* The Football Match, *the first Karno sketch in which Chaplin appeared. In the sketch a melodramatic villain attempts to bribe the star goalie to throw the match. On stage Chaplin played the villain; in the film the role is played with brio by Leo White, sporting a waxed moustache even more comically wide than the one Chaplin wore in the sketch. Never one to waste a good idea, Chaplin reworked the bribery angle for the boxing scene in* City Lights.*]*

At just about this time Charlie met his brother Syd, who was then working for the Keystone Company down here in Los Angeles, and Syd told Charlie of a boy who had been playing for him in London in the *Hydro* Company. Charlie, taking Syd's advice with the exemplary obedience of the younger brother, told the Essanay Company to send to London and fetch the boy in question. There

Leo White and Charlie in character. . .   . . . and out.

was some demur at first, but, as usual, Charlie won his point, and a cablegram was despatched to England to find the comedian and send him to California.

Work meanwhile proceeded apace, the comedian turning out both *The Tramp* and *Charlie's Elopement [aka* A Jitney Elopement*]* within the next six weeks; and then came our friend from London. He was just about "all in" from his fourteen days of travelling but he had a smile up his large and youthful visage, and his distinct London accent was good to hear. You would never believe how one misses those little things when one is seven thousand miles from home! So there became established yet another Britisher in the Chaplin-Essanay forces in the person of Mr Billy Armstrong.

Then suddenly Charlie grew tired of his surroundings, and told the company that he could get no more inspiration from the North of California. He must have the hot sunshine, the beaches, the sea, and the association of his old friends. In short, he must have Los Angeles.

During the time he had been working under the Essanay banner he had sprung from the status of a mere popular picture comedian to the height upon which he now stands—the most famous man in the world, and consequently his word was law. A little more humming and ha-ing, and then the Chaplin section of the organisation moved five hundred miles farther south, to the city from which I am writing—Los Angeles.

Just at this time a theatrical company which had been run by Mr Anderson in 'Frisco disbanded, and a number of its comedians were drafted into the Essanay ranks. Among them were two Australians and an Irishman. When the boat sailed from San Francisco it bore with it seven people, all of the Chaplin company, who were born under the British flag.

And here begins my own connection with the Chaplin boys, although I have, of course, known Chaplin for many years. The tour of a Broadway show, with which I was playing, closed in Los Angeles just at the time the activities of the little comedian began in the same city, and so I, seizing my opportunity—although it was an odd jump from an old romantic play to the ranks of slapstick picture comedy—accepted Charlie's offer, and became one of his "boys."

It was, as I say, an odd thing to do, and I started on it with some misgivings as to the wisdom of it, but whatever doubts I may have harboured then, my next instalment will show how much my association with the great little fellow has taught me. I do not mean essentially that it has been of great professional value to me, but of the moral value of Charles Chaplin's attitude in all his success I can truly say it has been an education and an example to be emulated—a thing to be borne in mind in all my dealings with my fellow-men for all time to come.

6

A Straw Hat and a Puff of Wind

April 1, 1916

When the Chaplin Company arrived in Los Angeles the weather was at its best. The torrid sun blazed down without cessation throughout the day, and the palms and flowers seemed to be nodding like sleepy mortals under its tropical heat.

The first job was, of course, to find a place to work. There were several studios vacant, which had belonged to various small ventures, since defunct, and Charlie, accompanied by his co-director, Jesse Robbins, made a careful survey of the situation.

They all had their advantages and disadvantages, and Chaplin's decision finally rested on one situate[d] in the grounds of what had once been a grand mansion. It was built upon the highest piece of land in the whole city of Los Angeles, and seemed to offer the best locale for the purpose; furthermore, there was a flat building right opposite its doors, and therein the entire company distributed itself, in singles and pairs, until the place was half full of Chaplin people. Since those days they have drifted away to spots that better suited their whims, until now there is but one remaining within its doors—the writer, to wit. This is however, not to the point.

The next picture was already overdue, whereas it had yet to be commenced, so Charlie, after looking once at the chaos that reigned among the scenery and baggage of the company, which was dumped in wild and inextricable heaps all about the stage, said—

"Come along, boys! Make up as 'squidges,' and pile into the cars."

The word "squidges," I should mention, is one he has coined himself, and it is most apt, for it means nothing at all—and that is precisely what he meant to convey! So we slipped into whatever make-up and costume happened to first come to our hands and minds, and within a few minutes we were speeding toward the coast in big touring cars.

"Where are we going, Charlie?" asked the chauffeur.

"Venice," answered Charlie, then thoughtfully (unconsciously giving the place its full geographical name) he added, "Venice-by-the-Sea. That'd make a good name for the picture wouldn't it?"

Nobody offered any comment, for we assumed that he was merely talking while thinking of something else, as he often does: but it seems that for once he meant what he said, for the picture we began that day was finally called *By the Sea*.

Arrived at Venice, we found the wind howling like a tornado up and down the promenade, and Charlie was somewhat lost for an idea. He walked up and down the asphalt for a few minutes, his trousers ballooning in the most ludicrous fashion in the world, while the camera man set up his tripod and awaited instructions.

Presently Billy Armstrong joined Charlie in his career, and the two began to talk, until suddenly the wind carried off Billy's straw hat. He recovered it after a short chase, and fastened it on with a piece of string. Charlie, in his kiddish way, was not content until he had imitated Billy, and so the two stood there with their hats blowing out on the ends of strings, until suddenly, as was inevitable, they became entangled. This seemed to give Charlie an inspiration.

"Come on—shoot!" he called to the camera man, and he and Billy (without the suggestion of a rehearsal) started to fool around before the camera, trying to untangle their hats. Then Billy gave Charlie a "stage" blow *[a fake punch]* and began to run. Charlie followed, and the camera man stopped.

That was the story of how *Charlie by the Sea* came to be commenced, and from it the ideas rapidly developed in the comedian's mind, until the picture, just as you have seen it, was completed—all within three consecutive days—and shipped to Chicago, whence it is distributed to the world at large. *[Only fourteen months earlier Venice had been the site of another Chaplin quicky,* Kid Auto Races at Venice, *which marked the debut of the Tramp character. That half-reel film reportedly took only forty-five minutes to shoot.]*

Charlie and a friend in *The Champion*. Original release poster.

After each day's work we would take advantage of our trip and go for a dip in the sea, which, although it was the middle of March was as warm as the sun itself.

There was nothing of particular interest about *By the Sea* to distinguish it from the other pictures—unless it was the speed with which it was finished, for Charlie takes, on an average, seven or eight weeks to turn out a picture, as a rule.

It was during this story, too, that news came from Niles that the big British bulldog which attacked "Bud" Jaimison in the fight scene in "Champion Charlie," had been poisoned by some mischievous brute, and had died. Poor Bud was awfully grieved for quite a while, and told me at great length how he had trained the dog to hang on to a pad fastened in his boxing shorts, prior to the filming of the story in question. *[As Goodwins points out in later articles, Chaplin made sure the animal actors and mascots at his studios were treated with great care. But he couldn't prevent some mishaps. Perhaps the saddest one occurred in 1918, when Scraps, the canine star of* A Dog's Life*, whose real name was Mut, became so bereft when Chaplin left on a Liberty Loan bond-selling tour that he stopped eating and died a few weeks later.[1]]*

It was just as well that Charlie did start making that first picture without delay, for within a day or so the sunshine disappeared, and the rainy season set in again, although it was not nearly as bad as it has been this year.

All the time it was pelting down Charlie was fretting around in his hotel, staring out of the window and (somewhat after the fashion of Canute[2]) muttering—

"Let up, will you? Let's do some work—work—work!"

And out of his impatience another title was born—*Work* (called on your side *Charlie at Work*).

Between the intervals of rain the scenes employed in the picture were hurriedly erected and a few scenes taken. It was working under difficulties with a vengeance, but soon the heavens smiled again, and we saw no more rain until very late in the year 1915.

At just about this time Charlie engaged two character people—a man and a woman—respectively Charles Insley and Marta Golden. (It was Insley, you will recall, that we were unable to find for the filming of the balance of Charlie's last Essanay picture.) At first we thought that Charlie had secured them for *Work*, but, although they both played prominent parts in that story, the secret was revealed after it had been despatched to Chicago—Charlie was going to make a six-reel feature!

Of course, there was a lot of excitement in the company, and not a little amusement, particularly over the prospect of our being cast for big parts. Egotism—the weakest link in human nature—asserted itself on every hand: one declared Charlie had promised him the second part, another that he was to play the juvenile lead, which latter remark led to a furious argument between him and another fellow which ended in both putting on "pretty" juvenile make-ups in order to prove that each was individually the more suited to the part.

In the midst of it all Charlie arrived at the studio, and inquired, with a grin of amusement, what was afoot. I explained the situation to him and he laughed uproariously.

"You chumps!" he said subsiding. "This isn't going to be an ordinary feature. It's going to be called *Life*. And it'll consist of six episodes, all more or less distinct from each other, showing my rise from the poverty in which I am supposed to live to wealth and position, and then back again to the depths. How can I have any individual big parts for you, running right through the six reels? Each episode takes place in a different walk of life. You'll each play a different part in each episode of course."

He went on reading his stack of mail, while the quandam *[the word should be* quondam, *meaning former]* "juveniles" stealthily retired to their dressing-rooms to hide their diminished heads.

It was for this projected "feature," I afterwards discovered, that Charlie had engaged me—he apparently remembered me as a portrayer of English dudes back in the old country, and had a part in the most important episode which would have suited me down to the ground. So that is why I came to be associated in a business way with Charlie.

I say "would have" essentially, for, as I explained a week or two back, the feature, *Life* was never finished. It took up so much of Charlie's time, and thereby starved the market of his regular short-length pictures that he finally put it on the shelf. It only came out after many months to form the basis of his last story, *Police*, of which I have spoken at such length in my previous instalments.

I cannot describe the story of it to you, for it may be used after all in the course of Charlie's picture career, but it would undoubtedly have been his greatest triumph, had it been completed. *[Goodwins's account here, sketchy as it is, along with what he says about* Life *in chapter 1, provides what little information we have about Chaplin's aborted feature film project.]*

Time passed while he was making scenes upon the feature, then, until the time drew near for another short-length release, and *Life* was put by, the problem of just what was to be his next story engaging the comedian's exclusive attention.

The idea dawned upon him suddenly while we were watching a picture in one of the down town theatres a few nights later, and he has to thank Miss Lilian Gish for having (unconsciously) given him material upon which to start.

"Funny way Griffith makes his leading ladies walk," he remarked, looking up at the screen. (His intentions were, of course, none but the most friendly, for Charlie is not capable of harbouring a mean thought.) *[Waifish Lillian Gish was already a major star by 1915, her popularity rivaling that of another Griffith protégé, Mary Pickford. Gish would go on to star in many Griffith classics and enjoy a long and distinguished career.]*

Knowing Charlie and his ways, I seemed to scent something in his observation, and I was right, for the next day he started on the preliminary scenes of *The Woman* (*Charlie, the Perfect Lady*), in which you will remember he made the most charming "female" imaginable. *[The film was released as* A Woman.*]*

The Woman, starting as it did in a spirit of good-natured burlesque, was really a brilliant thought on the part of Chaplin, but, if I may be so frank as to say it, the subtlety of it all went right "over the heads" of most of his audiences. They saw nothing in it but "Charlie, dressed as a woman." I suppose; the cleverness of his burlesque of Miss Gish and his little thrust at the inimitable Griffiths [*sic*] was lost. *[It would be nice to know which Gish film they had seen that night. Chaplin was known throughout his life for his ability to do wickedly accurate impersonations, once bringing the dancer and actress Louise Brooks to tears by lampooning the way she walked as a Ziegfeld Follies girl. However, Goodwins's attempt to chide Chaplin's audience for its ignorance here misses the mark, for a year earlier Chaplin had done a virtually identical female impersonation in* The Masquerader, *indicating that his sexy-demure characterization was probably in his repertoire from his music hall days.]*

And yet another thing—a mere incident—which evaded even his most ardent admirers who had seen every picture in which he had appeared, was the scene in which he sits at the table and, picking up a ring-shaped doughnut, nudges the girl (Marta Golden) and makes a motion of wrapping something around his wrist. Yet how many millions who saw *Charlie, the Perfect Lady*, must have laughed at Charlie when, in *Dough and Dynamite*, he made doughnuts by wrapping the pastry in that very way! *[Chaplin's pantomime in* A Woman *of his unorthodox way of making donuts from* Dough and Dynamite *is quick and very deft, and it is nice that Goodwins draws his readers' attention to it. Yet it may seem odd that he's doing it by putting Chaplin's audience down for a second time, in this case criticizing even "his most ardent admirers" for not making the connection between the two films. In actuality Goodwins is anticipating what would become a prevalent theme in Chaplin commentary through the teens and twenties, namely, that Chaplin's films had depths of meaning inaccessible to the common herd. Such an attitude, of course, implicitly flatters readers by presuming that they are among the select few who share the author's refined sensibilities, if only because they're clever enough to be partaking of them. Chaplin's highbrow admirers particularly evinced this attitude, and we'll encounter one of the most important of them, the actress Minnie Maddern Fiske, in a later installment.]*

After the film had gone to the factory Charlie made one last effort to get started on *Life*, but before any appreciable progress had been made the public was waiting for a new picture, and *Life*, which had already cost several thousands of pounds, was shelved.

7

A Bombshell That Put Charlie Chaplin "on His Back"

April 8, 1916

I should have mentioned last week that after the completion of *Charlie at Work* the Hill Street studio began to show its disadvantages. The sun would set upon it all too quickly, rendering photography out of the question after 3.30 p.m., and so the Chaplin-Essanay organization moved to Brooklyn Avenue, where we occupied a studio which had been especially built for D. W. Griffith, but which, for some reason, he had never used. We knew soon enough what the reason was, for with the coming of the afternoon sun that spot became a second inferno for heat! But the place had been taken for six months, and we had to stick it out.

Insurance was the title of the story upon which Charlie had proposed to work, but when the office scene came to be erected on the studio floor it looked so massive and imposing that Charlie decided that the scene would detract from the action, and promptly sat down to think out a plot strong enough to overtop the scenery. How well he succeeded is evidenced by the result, *Charlie at the Bank [aka* The Bank*]*, voted by all (on this side of the Atlantic at any rate) as his finest piece of work since the day he first began his career as a motion picture actor.

At just about this time, *Charlie, the Perfect Lady* was put on the market, and just as he was about to start upon *Charlie at the Bank* there came a bombshell that, to use an expressive vulgarism, "put him on his back." The critics declared that the former picture was full of all that was bad. For a while we

58

saw but little of Charlie. He shut himself in his dressing-room, as we thought, sulking. But when he reappeared and started on the bank picture even the densest of us began to see what had been engrossing his mind. For *Charlie at the Bank*, best of all his efforts, contained throughout its length no suspicion of anything that could lay the comedian open to criticism upon the score of impropriety. And that has been the policy of Charlie Chaplin ever since.

[During the early years of his film career a small but vocal chorus of film critics, schoolteachers, moralists, and religious leaders assailed Chaplin for the violence and sexuality in his pictures.[1] A Woman, Chaplin's third and final female impersonation on film, became a particular target because of scenes in which he uses a pincushion as a false bosom, inspires the lustful advances of several men, and perhaps most of all because his impersonation of a seductive female is so disturbingly convincing.

Chaplin was well aware that the violence, cruelty, and sexuality in his films were among the things that made them so popular, and the persistence of these elements in his films proves that he had no intention of abandoning them entirely to please a few stuffed shirts. But he didn't allow the chorus of disapproval to be drowned out by the laughter of his audiences either, for it coincided with his desire to expand the boundaries of silent film comedy by infusing his films with serious and romantic content—in short, by making them closer to the morally uplifting "real" art demanded by his detractors. As we now know, of course, he succeeded beyond his wildest dreams, transforming the humble art of slapstick comedy into something sublime, and ultimately disarming even his most puritanical critics. Goodwins was both a participant in the process and a privileged observer, and his comments about The Bank *show him to be an enthusiastic supporter of the new direction in Chaplin's work.[2]*

He is more specific about the critical "bombshell" that greeted A Woman, *along with Chaplin's reaction to it, in another article, published in* Pearson's Weekly *magazine:*

His fame was at its zenith here in America when suddenly the critics made a dead set at him. . . . They roasted his work wholesale, called it crude, ungentlemanly and risqué, even indecent. . . . The poor little fellow was knocked flat. But he rose from his gloomy depths one day, and came out of his dressing room rubbing his hands: "Well, boys," he said with his funky little twinkly smile, "let's give them something to talk about, shall we? Something that has no loopholes in it!" Thus *began the new era of Chaplin comedies—clean, clever, dramatic stories with a big laugh at the finish.[3]]*

When I say that this was the best piece of work he has done I should also mention that it was to a large extent made up of spontaneous and unpremeditated thoughts. *[That may be, but the plot* The Bank *was reworked from one of Chaplin's best Keystone films,* The New Janitor. *However, pointing out Chaplin's recycling would have subverted Goodwins's more pressing purpose, which was to deflect outside criticism and praise the new direction in Chaplin's work.*

During this period Chaplin coolly discussed his desire to upgrade his work with several magazine interviewers. Goodwins's accounts of his dressing room retreat reveal that he wasn't just paying lip service to his critics, but was genuinely upset by their criticisms. It's worth noting, however, that The Bank *did not represent Chaplin's first attempt at a "clean, clever, dramatic" story—he was already doing that in films like* The New Janitor *and* The Tramp, *the latter being the one most often cited by later writers as the watershed film that anticipated his mature work. What has not been recognized previously was how much the negative response to* A Woman *may have spurred his movement in the new direction.]*

For example, the picture *[The Bank]* was already due for shipping, and on the last day there was yet half a reel to be completed, which, considering that he had not the ghost of an idea what the finish of the story was to be, might have scared most men. Not so Charlie, however. He gave the matter half an hour of serious thought, and then gave us our instructions. So four of us hurriedly made up as "gun men," and came down upon the floor of the studio. Then began the fights that constituted the dramatic element of *Charlie at the Bank.* The whole of the last half-reel was completed on that Sunday afternoon, and I had several days' leisure for reflection upon the matter of a very tender left ear, contracted (through no fault of Charlie's) when he "laid me out" in the vault scene at the foot of the stairs.

[Goodwins notes in passing that The Bank's *final scenes were shot on a Sunday. During his Essanay and Mutual years Chaplin worked at a furious pace to fulfill his contractual quota. At Essanay he was initially expected to produce a film every two weeks. As his films grew more ambitious in scope, that pace inevitably slowed, but he still managed to produce fourteen films for the company in 1915. Since he was writing, directing, and starring in all of them himself,*

the pressure on him was enormous, and everyone in the studio was expected to work late into the night and on weekends as required, without the overtime pay and other benefits that would accrue to actors and crew today.

However, as Goodwins makes clear throughout the series, it was a price that most of Chaplin's coworkers cheerfully paid. It was both exciting and prestigious to be associated with the wildly popular comedian. In addition, although no one was paid overtime, they were kept on salary during the frequent periods of downtime, when rain, or the absence, exhaustion, or lack of inspiration of their "chief" prevented filming.

Some members of the cast and crew, however, did not thrive under these conditions, or simply left for greener pastures. These include Chaplin's memorable Essanay foil Billy Armstrong, whose departure Goodwins related in chapter 1 and elaborates on below; and cinematographer Billy Foster, whose lavish going-away party Goodwins describes in chapter 27.]

The picture which followed was entitled *Charlie Shanghaied*, and for the purpose of atmosphere he chartered the big cargo boat *Vaquero* at a cost of £30 a day, and took us all to a distant Pacific island. But the seasickness was too much for him, and within five days he brought us back to California, so *Shanghaied* was finished just off the coast of Venice.

It was a chapter of accidents that picture.

Edna has already told you *[in her autobiographical* Red Letter *article from 1915, which we have omitted]* how we were marooned until the next morning, because the sea was too rough to admit of our launching boats to take us ashore, and what with sea-sickness and accidents and some of those ordinary little incidents that go to make the lives of us movie-men so enjoyable, we were all—and Charlie most of any—heartily glad when that memorable picture was finished. It took us over seven weeks to make.

At the end of that story both Billy Armstrong and myself resigned from the company, the former to take up a featuring contract with another firm, while I had temporarily lost my nerve on account of a misjudged dive which followed a gentle thrust from Charlie's foot. I decided that the stage offered less hazards, and went back to it, only to return, as I have already related.

[In his Autobiography *Chaplin boasts that "no member of my cast was injured in any of our pictures. Violence was carefully rehearsed and treated like choreography."[4] Goodwins doesn't precisely rebut Chaplin's later assertion, but he has now described two injuries he sustained, the second of which spooked*

him enough to quit the company for a while. Goodwins is careful to mitigate these incidents, both by absolving Chaplin of responsibility and by recounting how distressed Chaplin would become when anyone got hurt. His concern extends even to a goldfish whose bowl he accidentally smashes while shooting One A.M. *(chapter 23). And when Billy, the studio's mascot goat, is hit by a piece of fallen scenery Chaplin makes sure the beast receives the best veterinary care and a pampered convalescence (chapter 28).*

The human injuries were perhaps inevitable, given the breakneck speed of production and the fact that the actors were expected to do their own stunts. Late in the series Goodwins mentions one exception: Albert Austin gallantly takes the place of Charlotte Mineau for a drop through a trap door in Behind the Screen. *Years later Kevin Brownlow revealed a second instance in his documentary* Unknown Chaplin. *An outtake from* The Cure *shows a stunt double taking the dangerous headlong dive from a wheelchair into the spa well for Eric Campbell. We can be certain that the daredevil in the well is a stunt double, for one of the people pulling him out is Eric himself.*

Goodwins and the critics were not the only people concerned with the violence in Chaplin's films. During this period there were persistent rumors that Chaplin had been injured or killed doing one of his stunts, and fan magazines had to reassure their anxious readers repeatedly that he was still alive and well. In actuality, he appears to have hurt himself only twice, once when the metal edge of a gas lamp in Easy Street *fell across the bridge of his nose, requiring several stitches (described in chapter 37), and a second time when he broke his middle finger while shooting* The Great Dictator *(you can see Chaplin's splinted finger if you look carefully for it in the latter part of the film, particularly in the coin-in-the-pudding scene).]*

Charlie was very sorry to lose Billy. This boy was easily the best supporter he has had throughout his film career, and had Chaplin known of his contemplated departure the Essanay company would have done anything to have retained him, but Billy—all against my own advice, be it said—had already signed up for nearly two years, and was gone beyond recall.

"All right," sighed Charlie. "Good luck to him—God bless his heart. I had a good part for him in the next picture, but I'll have to play it myself."

That is how, in *Charlie at the Show [British title of* A Night in the Show*]*, he came to portray two characters—both his own and that of Mr. Rowdy, which was to have been Billy Armstrong's part. It came to be whispered afterward that

Charlie had determined to make no more "stars," and, be that the case or not, the fact remains that there was no part of any importance throughout the picture except those played by Charlie himself. Thus deeply does he take things to heart.

Yet, genius of geniuses though Charlie Chaplin is, *Charlie at the Show* was one of his poorest efforts in matters of plot and interest. Wherein lies the proof of a statement he once made to me—"it is not our own selves that are great—it is our greatness in relation to others that counts and makes what the world calls greatness."

No, beyond a question, *Charlie at the Show* was not Charlie at his best.

[This is Goodwins's most damning criticism of a Chaplin film. The reason may be that the film somewhat contradicts one of the most important characteristics he attributes to the "genius of geniuses," namely, his originality. Many in Britain—and indeed the United States—would have been familiar with the uncredited source of the film, Fred Karno's Mumming Birds, *the most popular and longest-running sketch in British music hall history, which was still going strong in 1916. The sketch, featuring a drunk heckling a variety bill of bad music hall performers, became Chaplin's signature role in America, where it was retitled* A Night in an English Music Hall *(in these articles Chaplin calls it* A Night in a London Music Hall*).*

RED LETTER PHOTOCARD.

(Charles Chaplin.)   Unrequited Love.   Charlie at the Show.

Charlie takes Bud Jamison's hand by mistake. *A Night in the Show.*

However, it is worth noting that Goodwins's criticism of the film—that is, that it failed because Charlie didn't give himself a comic adversary—isn't true; he tangles with members of the audience, the orchestra, and all the performers. Further, Goodwins offers no such criticism of One A.M., *to which he devotes several upcoming articles and high praise. It may be that the word had come down to strike a more uniformly positive tone.*

Whether that's true or not, the articles are filled with small revelations that appear nowhere else, such as the account above of how Chaplin came to take on the role of Mr. Rowdy in A Night in the Show. *This explains why he wears the type of "brush" mustache that Billy Armstrong favored. Armstrong would return for* Police, *as Goodwins noted in chapter 1, for which he turned in a brief but memorable performance as a crooked preacher. He remained active in films until 1924, when he died of tuberculosis.]*

During the making of this picture the film of *Carmen*, featuring Geraldine Farrar, and another featuring Theda Bara, were on exhibition in town, and Charlie went to see them both.

Each seemed to thrill him in a different way, he said, and I noticed when we discussed them together that a whimsical smile invariably played about his mouth. Considering how utterly devoid of comedy is the story of "Carmen," I ventured to ask one evening, "why the amusement?"

"Wait and see," was his statesman-like answer.

It turned out afterwards that he was about to start on a travesty of the story, which at the time of writing the Essanay Company is holding back for some reason. *[After Chaplin left Essanay the company padded the film to twice its length by using Chaplin's outtakes, turning it into a repetitive muddle. When Essanay released it in April 1916 Chaplin immediately sued to prevent the butchered version from being distributed further, but the court promptly ruled against him. Essanay then countersued for supposed breach of contract, and that case dragged on for years. Emboldened, Essanay proceeded to release a stream of "new" Chaplin films, including* Triple Trouble *and several features they similarly cobbled together. From that point onward Chaplin made sure that his work was contractually protected from such interference. He makes a coded reference to the lawsuit in chapter 20.]*

My business prevented my visiting the Chaplin studio during the making of this burlesque of his *[presumably this is when Goodwins quit because of his injuries, since he returned for the completion of* Police*]*, and so I, like yourselves,

Essanay was still profiting from Chaplin's *Carmen* in 1920, as indicated by this sheet music spinoff from a re-release of the film.

must wait to see it on the screen, but I have gathered from odd corners and from various of the people who took part in it little bits of information that lead me to believe that *Charlie Chaplin's Burlesque on Carmen*, as it is to be called, will be really representative of the mind that conceived it.

Burlesque is Chaplin's strong point, as those who saw him in *Casey's Court*, the vaudeville sketch of his early days upon the English stage, will know. *[As mentioned earlier, the name of the sketch was* Casey's Circus, *a sequel to* Casey's Court. *Chaplin was in the company from May 1906 to July 1907.]*

Thus our ramble through the past brings us back to the place whence we started, for immediately on the finishing up of *Carmen* came the incidents mentioned in my first instalment of this article—the filming of *Police*.

For the rest I could write at indefinite length, analysing the personality, the mannerisms, the life and the work of my friend, Charles Chaplin, but my allotted space is rapidly running out, and not this entire issue, nor, indeed, forty like it, could half-way suffice to contain all there is to tell about him.

Suffice it that I have never, in the whole course of a restless and varied career, come across a man in whom—all apart from his "place in the sun"—I could find so much to interest me, or upon whom, as a personality, I could find so much to write.

Imagine, if you can, a man of a hundred different moods, yet through whose individuality runs a definite vein of sterling and solid worth; a man who has achieved the greatest of all greatness; whose name has been mentioned by more people than that of any man in the annals of time; a man whose success has left him unchanged from what he was ten years ago, and in whom human sympathy, lightness of heart, knowledge of things as they are, amazing commonsense and versatile gifts beyond compare are his strongest characteristics—imagine these, I say, and you will have a basic idea of what kind of a man is Mr Charles Spencer Chaplin, the world's jester-in-chief.

I find on looking back through what I have written during these past few weeks that I have dwelt much upon the serious side of Chaplin's nature. Yet, predominant as that phase of him has always been, he still, oddly enough, always seems to me the living instance of Dryden's proverb—"Men are but children of a larger growth."

Charlie Chaplin, the greatest of men, is yet the greatest child of all.

[Goodwins's glorification of Chaplin in these last paragraphs may seem excessive, but is actually very much in line with the worshipful prose that filled

newspapers and magazines in 1915. The world had gone Chaplin mad, a phenomenon that one perceptive writer dubbed "Chaplinitis."[5]

With this testimonial Goodwins appears to be bidding his readers good-bye. Chaplin left L.A. in February 1916 to negotiate his new contract with Mutual in New York, and in all probability Goodwins wasn't certain whether he'd be retained when the comedian returned. As it turned out, Chaplin retained Goodwins, Edna, and several other members of his Essanay stock company and crew, and there was only a one week gap before Goodwins's series resumed. Three anonymous articles describing Chaplin's activities in New York appeared in the magazine in April, and we have reprinted them as appendixes.]

8

When Charlie Chaplin Cried Like a Kid

April 22, 1916

I was reading the other day a singularly clever little article by an English writer, entitled "Charles the Greatest," wherein the author described how apt we all are to create clay idols and set them up for worship. By that he meant that so scarce are the real geniuses nowadays that the great public, ever eager to fall down onto its knees before something or somebody, has to make shift with very spurious articles until the real honest thing comes its way.

Our friend went on to say that he has found in Chaplin the real thing for which he had sought all his life; that Chaplin is one of those rarest of exceptions that only "happen," as we say in America, once in a while; and that when Charlie is no more—be it either professionally or in the mortal sense—no idol can take his place until the complete passing of the present generation.

I mention this piece of literature because it so closely expresses what I have striven to convey throughout my past stories in these columns—that Chaplin, the greatest genius of his age, has, by a remarkable stroke of luck, been recognised as such by the great human race, and that nothing can supplant him until there shall spring up one greater. It will not be in your time or mine.

I often regard Charlie somewhat in the nature of a star—not as we professional men accept the term, but as one of the constellation in the heavens, chiefly because in his greatness he has so many satellites forever around him. The greatness of Charlie Chaplin has been a gold mine of unprecedented richness to many, many thousands throughout the world. Radiating from the

WHEN CHARLIE CHAPLIN CRIED LIKE A KID

centre—himself—it has made him practically a millionaire, it has straightened up and fortified the tottering fortunes of more than one firm—apart from the Keystone and Essanay companies, to whom he has, of course, brought more money than to any individual.

Furthermore, his greatness has given a new lease of life to low comedy, not only on the screen, but on the stage as well, for he has created a vogue of slapstick humour that has enabled smaller and less talented men to sell their comedies in markets which are unable to afford the real Chaplin pictures. In proof of this, there are nearly four times as many slapstick comedies [sic— comedians] turning out pictures for the public as there were before Charlie gained recognition. True, he stands like a moon among the lesser lights, but those lesser lights are borrowing some of his radiance, just as the satellites owe their lives to their planet.

To spread the circle still farther, he has given lucrative employment to many whose glory, but for the greatness of Charlie Chaplin, would have waned long ago; he has replenished the coffers of countless hundreds of al- most bankrupt picture theatres—in a word, he has given a big chunk of the world a new lease of life.

When Charlie started off to New York to see what the future was going to hold for him I trow he never imagined for one moment just how great a thing he was going to pull off. In a way, I am almost tempted to think, he felt that he himself was on the wane.

I remember how he used to fret and fidget and wonder, while we were completing his final Essanay picture, just what was being done by his brother Syd in New York. Weeks before Sydney had gone east, to carry out on Char- lie's behalf the business negotiations for the coming year's contract. There were a dozen offers to be gone into and a thousand things to be figured out, and Sydney, with his business brain, was undoubtedly the man for the job. So East he went, and for weeks nothing was heard from him except for a short note written on a postcard, assuring Charlie that everything was O.K.

Syd knew Charlie. He realised that, whatever was afoot it was wisest not to convey it in detail to the younger boy, for Charlie, with his abnormal temperament, might misconstrue the gist of the matter and go up in the air completely, as the saying is. But it so happened that Charlie had other views. He was impatient, poor chap! and who shall blame him! In those days Charlie Chaplin came nearer to being irritable than I have ever seen him. Lengthy telegrams and night-letters were shot to New York in volleys, but still Syd's answers were noncommittal, and, to Charlie's highly-strung mind, unsatisfactory. *[This correlates with R. J. Minney's account of what happened, discussed in appendix B, although none of the telegrams are known to survive.]*

He grew terribly restless as the days passed, and tried a hundred and one different ways to occupy his mind with something outside the business of the future.

He would drop into Levy's Café evenings, and sit a while with us over a glass of wine. Then the fidgets would get him, and he would get up and walk around a block a couple of times. Sometimes again a reaction would set in, and he would come to us in hilarious spirits and would take a couple of us out on some mad party or other. To him at that time it was a choice between diversion and nervous breakdown.

But finally the breakdown got him, in a mild form. The day's work was done, and he had run me into town in his car. He wanted to run up to his offices on Broadway, he said, to see if there was any fresh word from New York. A disappointment awaited him once again; no message was there.

For a moment he stood staring out of the window like a child who has been disappointed about a visit to a theatre. Then, as if to complete the illusion, he sank into the settee, and burying his face in his hands, cried like a kid.

You all know how dashed awkward a man feels when a thing like that happens. We fellows kind of wished the floor would open and drop us all into the music store below.

But fortunately there was one woman there—Edna, it was—and she did precisely what any woman would have done in the same circumstances. We heard him complaining that "everything went wrong with him." That "the whole world was against him all the time."

It was soon all right again, and I suppose it did him good. But within less than a week he had left for New York.

You have heard something of Charlie's doings in New York, of his appearance at the Hippodrome when he conducted Sousa's Band *[see appendix B]*. The next afternoon he slipped quietly into the offices of the Actors' Fund of America and dropped a cheque for 1,300 dollars on to the secretary's desk.

"It's half my fee for yesterday," he explained, and backed out of the office hurriedly. His name stands first on the list. A few days later New York learned what had become of the other half. It had gone to the British Actors' Fund. That was typical of Charlie.

After that he was besieged with visitors, invitations, and offers, until there was nothing for it but to get his business deal completed and return post haste to the western side of the Rockies.

You know, too, what happened. Charlie Chaplin signed a contract to release his pictures under the Mutual banner, and was returning to Los Angeles. At the time of going to press I have nothing to go on but rumours as to what his salary is to be. There is not a doubt that it is a huge one.

Some papers say that he is to get 670,000 dollars (roughly £134,000) a year; others that it is £2,000 a week, clear, but I refuse to offer any statement until I have seen Charlie. There is positively more poetry than truth in both announcements *[both figures are accurate]*.

The contract was signed in the office of the Mutual Movie Corporation. After Charlie had appended his name to the document—and I can almost see that nervous hand of his struggling through his signature, for he detests writing!—the President handed him a cheque for 150,000 dollars (£30,000) as an advanced bonus.

Charlie looked at the cheque, then he turned to Syd.

"Take it, old man," he said. "It dazzles my eyes!"

It was not until afterwards that Syd found that he was expected to keep the cheque himself. Where is the man that started that yarn about Charlie being stingy? *[Charlie split his signing bonus of $150,000 with Syd.]*

A personal letter just to hand from Mabel Normand, who is still in New York, tells me that, after so many years, she has finally severed her connection with the Keystone Film Company for all time and has not formulated any plans for her future as yet. She adds that she has been with Charlie several times in the Big City, and that he seems deliriously happy.

I wonder if he really is!

Of course, out here Charlie Chaplin and his mammoth contract are being discussed in every café, and every cinema studio. Folks are already figuring out on the basis of £134,000 a year how Charlie compares with the highest paid men in the United States. Outside of Royalty, Charlie is about the highest paid public person. President Wilson hasn't a look in with Charlie so far as scooping in the dollars is concerned. He gets 75,000 dollars (£15,000) a year— about a ninth of what the famous comedian ropes in. The Chief Justice of the

Supreme Court—the most learned gentleman of the law over here—15,000 dollars (£3,000), so that dispensing justice—doling out hard labour and fining law-breakers, in fact, being "star" in the Court of Justice business, is a long way less profitable than the "star" in the cinema world. The Governor of Illinois is the highest paid of the U.S. State heads but he only gets £2,400 a year, which is the same salary as is paid to the Vice-President of the States, and each member of President Wilson's Cabinet.

So you see Charlie can drop a bit and still be well ahead. Someone has been studying the matter closely on the every labourer being worthy of his hire basis, and has come to the conclusion that Charlie has really earned his coin.

Wildly extravagant as a yearly salary of £134,000 may sound, he says it falls into its proper relation in the scale of receipts and disbursements when the profits made out of Chaplin pictures are considered. Recently the premier humourist of the shadow stage made ten pictures for Essanay, for which he was paid £15,600 salary and a cash bonus of £20,000, and for the first twenty-one days theatre use of these reels Essanay is paid £97,750. Eight of the ten reels have been released, and are still running—and being paid for daily at rates proportionate to those quoted: two are yet to be shown to the public. So there is money in it all around.

9

Excitement Runs High When Charlie Chaplin "Comes Home"

April 29, 1916

I had scarcely returned from mailing my last article, and settled myself to a perusal of the English papers when the telephone bell rang. It was Leo White.

"Come down to the office right away," he stammered excitedly. "Charlie gets in on the 4.30 train. There's a car waiting here to take us to the station!" And he rang off.

Charlie coming back! It sounded too good to be true, but I knew White too well to suppose he was "kidding," so I hastened to the comedian's office on Broadway. Outside was Charlie's big, seven-passenger touring car, containing eight actors and a chauffeur. They sandwiched me in somehow, and the way we cut by those cross-town streets was a caution.

Our haste was scarcely necessary, however, for when we arrived at the tracks and hurried into the station we were met by Harry Caulfield, the manager of the new Chaplin-Mutual Company, who had arrived from New York the previous day.

"What's your hurry, boys?" he questioned round the corner of a fat cigar, which was tucked, American fashion, "into his face." "She's not on time; you've got ten minutes to spare."

We breathed a sigh of relief and waited. I had had the foresight to snatch up my biggest Kodak before I left home, and was besieged with demands from sundry vain and ambitious individuals to "be took." I assured them there was nothing doing, and turned a deaf ear to their rude remarks about "Gaspard the Miser,"[1] &c. I had other uses for those six films, particularly as nobody else had thought to bring down any photographic apparatus.

While we were waiting I asked Mr Caulfield just how much truth there was in the rumour that Charlie was signed up for 10,000 dollars a week, and he explained the true situation to me in a way that left me no cause to doubt that he was drumming me straight goods. It seems that Sydney's silence during those weeks in New York had its method, for he was bargaining with might and main, playing off one against another, until Charlie's salary began to rise high in the thousands. Finally there were only two concerns left in the field, each offering him the 10,000 dollars (£2,000) a week, until Mutual finally closed the bidding by signing him up at that figure with the additional bonus of 150,000 dollars (£30,000) referred to last week.

Charlie Chaplin's salary for the year 1916–17 is, therefore, 520,000 dollars plus 150,000 dollars, making a total of 670,000 dollars (roughly £134,000) for twelve months' work, turning out twelve pictures during the year.

While I was trying to grasp the magnitude of this sum, which is far and away the most colossal salary ever paid to any actor in the annals of Time, Vincent Bryan stuck his head into the waiting-room.

"Here she comes!" he shouted and we rushed helter-skelter out of the room just as the big train with its huge engine steamed slowly into the depot.

All was hurry and rush.

"Here he is!" yelled one.

"No, he's in the Pullman at the rear end."

"Nonsense! That's a day-coach down there."

Right in the middle of it, a small figure, all alone, alighted from the steps of the end coach, 'way down the line, and strolled up towards us the station. There was no mistaking that quiet, thoughtful stroll or the neat hang of that nifty little New York suit upon his dapper frame. It was Charlie at last.

It was fully ten seconds before he realised that we had come down to meet him, but when he finally "came to earth" and saw us—say, didn't he let out a whoop!

"Hi!" he shouted, his high-strung temperament overcoming for the moment his habitual calm. "Hello, boys! Home again!" Then, as we started to run towards him, he greeted us all in rapid succession, "Hello, Leo!" "What, Fred!" "Good old Vince!" "Gee! But it's great to see you all again! Back to the old Californian sunshine once more—" But here he was interrupted by the volley of remarks that poured from his excited courtiers.

"Good old Charlie!" "Look at his New York suit!" "Little beggar, he's getting fat!"

Then suddenly I remembered the camera, and we picked him up bodily and stuck him back on the hurricane deck of the train.

"I've been doing this for four weeks in New York," he grinned as I snapped him for the fifth time. "Everybody seemed bent on seeing me photographed— as if it were a novelty!"

By this time, half Los Angeles seemed to be wise to what was afoot, and the crowd began to get in the way, so we bundled him headlong into the auto, and the party whirled back to town.

That night in Levy's the corks flew, and more than one of us drank a toast to the "10,000 dollars kid" once more within our midst. It was surely great to see his curly head bobbing around the table. He seemed to belong there so naturally that we found it hard to believe he had ever been absent.

Next day we took him out and showed him the new studio we had hunted out for him, one that had been especially constructed for the filming of *The Patchwork Man of Oz [actually, the film was* The Patchwork Girl of Oz *(1914)]*.

It had lain empty for years, but the location and environment had seemed to us so eminently suitable to Charlie's extraordinary temperament that we had not doubted that he would be "Tickled to Death with it," as they say over here. It stands directly opposite a huge grove of lemon trees, and is flanked by a plantation of palm trees. Within two blocks of it lie the Lasky Studios and those of the L.-Ko Comedy Company. The Griffith Studios are but a half mile farther down, towards Los Angeles, and facing them are the Kalem and Western Vitagraph plants. So you see we have plenty of company in our new field of work. *[Goodwins gets the neighborhood right but the studio location wrong. What became known as the Lone Star Studio, because Chaplin was its sole occupant during his Mutual years, was the former Climax Studio, located at 1025 Lillian Way, a couple of blocks from the Oz studio. In 1920 this would become Buster Keaton's studio.]*

The studio pleased Charlie beyond our wildest hopes; he was, in fact, quite in love with the place.

"Ah!" he exclaimed, as he stepped from the front offices on to the expanse of stage. "Air to breathe! Room to work! Fine!"

Dressing-rooms? Yes, there were plenty of dressing-rooms. In fact everything in the garden was lovely.

Presently someone came up bothering him for work, but he shook his head before the applicant had half begun.

"It has nothing to do with me at all, old man," he told him. "I am here to play my own part and direct my company. But everything else is left to the manager."

With which the applicant departed.

"And I'm mighty glad of it," added Charlie to me as we strolled up and down the stage.

"By the terms of my contract, I have nothing to think of except being funny and getting my stuff over. All the business and engaging and executive end of the joint is up to the other chap. I only have to 'comede.'"

He spoke as if "comeding," as he called it, were the lightest job in the world beside the other little worries that have been transferred to the shoulders of the new staff—an extremely competent one, by the way. But I wonder how many hundreds have tried their utmost to do one fraction of what Charlie Chaplin has done, with miserably ill success.

The art of comedy is not to be spoken of in the same breath with that of drama, for beside it the latter is child-play—at least, so far as pictures are concerned. The proportion of real comedians among all the would-be's is possibly one in ten thousand, while your good dramatic man in motion pictures may be picked up by the wayside in a day's march. The easiest proof of this is the number of good dramas on every programme by comparison with the painfully few good comedies.

Yet a few minutes later he himself bore out this belief of mine. Referring to the number of requests he receives daily for a dramatic picture, he said—

"I suppose I shall do it someday, just to satisfy everybody. It's little enough trouble, Heaven knows!"

That he meant it I am convinced, for his one real break into serious vein *Charlie at the Bank*, gave him less trouble than any picture he has yet produced.

"When do you figure on starting in, Charlie?" I inquired.

He looked at me with a comically serious expression.

"Right away," he answered. Mustn't delay a day. If I don't hurry up and put another picture on the market soon, the public will think I am on the retired list. Yes, indeed, I must get to work at once."

"Good!" thought I, for it has been several weeks since I have been able to record any current studio happenings for you, patient reader; and with my journalistic mind case, I took my leave for the day.

The next day I called up the studio.

"Is there anything moving? Do you want me to come out to-day?" I asked the clerk.

"Moving?" he repeated. I heard something that sounded suspiciously like a chuckle. "Nothing doing yet awhile, Fred; you can go and golf for five days."

"What are you talking about?" I demanded. "Isn't Charlie going to start work to-day?"

"Not a chance. He's gone to the mountains until next week."

I collapsed.

10

Charlie "On the Job" Again

May 6, 1916

It wasn't long before the necessity of getting started in returned to Charlie in full force, for he came flying back to Los Angeles within three days of his departure to the mountains.

I happened to be on the stage when he walked into the studio, and I began forthwith to "kid" him strenuously upon his broken vows.

"Did you take some good scenes up there, Charlie?" I asked.

He looked at me vacantly.

"Scenes?" he repeated. "Scenes?" Then he got me. "Listen!" he grinned. "Are you trying to kid me, or just show me a good time?"

"Neither," I answered. "But I like the way you 'start in right away,' Charlie."

He immediately felt he was losing his dignity, and tried to pull a solemn face.

"Really, Goody," he said, "I went up to the mountains in the sacred cause."

"Of charity?"

"Sure," he replied. "Harry" (his chauffeur) "was down with influenza, and I thought the trip would do him good."

A volley of incredulous jeers greeted his diaphanous statement, whereat Charlie proceeded to look very much hurt.

"You chaps don't believe I'm capable of doing a Christian act," he grumbled. But he couldn't keep it up any longer. That irresistible, twinkly smile came over his face, and he darted into his dressing-room.

During the afternoon he unlocked his trunk, with its multitude of labels proclaiming the fact that he had but a short while ago travelled over the "Western Vaudeville Circuit" with the "Karno Company." Other labels betrayed him as having stopped at the So-and-so Hotel—one dollar a night and up, with private bath one dollar 50 cents, in most of the big cities of the U.S.A. between here and New York City.

I began to get into that pensive mood of mine then, wondering what it must feel like to rise in two short years from the necessity of living in dollar-a-night hotels to a state of affluence that enables one to walk into the palatial Los Angeles Club and demand "The best suite you've got."

I was suddenly brought back to earth by a yell from the comedian, and turned to see what was doing.

His shoes had disappeared! High and low we searched in that wardrobe trunk, throwing shirts and collars and papers indiscriminately around the room until some genius finally discovered that those mighty and famous pieces of footgear were snugly tied up inside a roll of music! Delicacy forbids that I should record the obvious joke that was immediately pulled by every individual member of that coterie. *[Presumably everyone held their noses, the joke being that Charlie's old shoes were as pungent-smelling as fish, which were often wrapped in newspapers in those days. Goodwins is also acknowledging the public's fascination with the elements of Charlie's costume; cartoons and songs of the period attest to the talismanic powers many ascribed to it, as though the comedy were inherent in the clothing rather than the man wearing it.]* Suffice it that Charlie was as relieved as if he had discovered a long-lost relative.

He began to give his outfit the "once over," and the result did not quite please him.

"These togs are getting all out of step," he mused, examining the filthy little brown coat, so dear to the hearts of all motion-picture goers. "See those stains around the shoulders? I don't know whether they're ice-cream, from that *By the Sea* picture, or the soapsuds we used for paste in *Charlie at Work*."

He turned up the tails and examined two huge burns in the lining.

"Reminiscences," he said, reflectively. "Remember where I burnt them in *Charlie the Tramp*? Poor old coat! She's been through the mill properly. Here take it to a tailor and have it sewn tighter together."

The property-man departed on his mission to the sartorial gentleman's establishment, and Charlie picked up the shoes again.

"More old warriors!" he said, turning them over thoughtfully in his hand.

We could see what was running through his mind. How little had he dreamt when he donned those shoes for the first time, over two years ago, with apprehension in his heart, that they were ever destined to encase the feet of a "10,000 dollar kid!"

But did he cast them aside? Had he been anybody but Charlie the Sentimental he possibly might have done so. Instead, he handed them to his dresser.

"Get 'em patched up nicely, and a one-piece sole and heel put on. Just one strip of leather from end to end—and tell them not to make it thick or I'm ruined." *[Chaplin preferred flat soles with no heels—like ballet slippers—for his oversized Tramp shoes.]*

Then he proceeded to unearth a number of photographs from the recesses of his trunk. Many of them were from famous folk. All of them were signed. In particular, I noticed one from Roscoe Arbuckle ("Fatty," of the Keystone Co.), which read, "To dear old Charlie. What would you have done without my trousers?"

I asked Charlie what Roscoe had meant by that, and he told me how, when he first "broke into" the picture game, he had been compelled to gather up bits of wardrobe from various members of the company, because they needed him in a hurry, and he had no time to go down town and make a careful selection at the second-hand dealers. Thus from a heterogeneous armful of old clothes sprang the costume that is more famous throughout the world than any that has ever been devised or worn.

Presently back came the property-man. He was laughing to himself, and when we inquired the cause of his mirth he told us the Jewish tailor had insisted that the coat needed dry cleaning. It had taken some strong and masterful arguments to prevent him doing it.

"That would have been a tragedy!" said Charlie as we walked out on to the stage.

His first Mutual picture is to be laid in a dry-goods store (or, as we would call it, a draper's shop), and some massive and wonderful scenes were in course of erection upon the stage.

Besides the pillared walls and the long run of counter, there is a practical lift, an escalator, and a porcelain ice-water fountain, from all of which Charlie proposes to get a lot of funny "gags."

As we walked through the "shop" Charlie beckoned over a big, important-looking man, who was exercising a little dog on an adjacent grass plot.

"This is Mr Eric Campbell," he said, and we shook. "Another Englishman. Ah, and here comes Austin"—as a tall, young man, with a mass of frizzy, blonde hair approached. *[While in New York to sign the Mutual contract Chaplin and Sydney had spotted their old Karno colleague Eric Campbell performing in a show and hired him on the spot. Campbell became arguably Chaplin's most memorable movie foe, appearing in eleven of the twelve Mutual comedies. He would have gone on with Chaplin if not for his untimely death in a car accident in 1917. The ferocious bully of the Mutuals is invariably reported to have been a gentle man in the Chaplin literature, but it is only in Goodwins's articles that we get such endearing details as his incongruous preference for small dogs and, in a later article, small cars.*

During his years in England Campbell had performed in the Karno company, but not as long as Albert Austin, who toured with Chaplin in the American company from 1910 through 1913. Austin has the distinction of being the only actor besides Chaplin himself to appear in all twelve Mutuals, and he went on to appear in most of Chaplin's films through City Lights *in 1931, in which he also got an assistant director credit. He was active through the mid-thirties as a writer, director, and actor, but reportedly spent the last two decades of his life as a studio guard at Warner Brothers.]*

"Say, we seem to have enough Englishmen here! There's us four, and White, and Lloyd Bacon" (a Cornishman who played with Charlie in the early Essanay days, and has rejoined him since), "and—"

He rambled on through the names of the staff, and we found we had two carpenters, one stenographer, and one property-man among the British element at the new plant.

"We ought to fly the Union Jack here," he concluded—and but for certain American laws I imagine he would have given orders for it to be done.

During the next three days the weather was misty and rainy, and work was out of the question, but the sun broke through at last, and the company, for the first time in eight weeks, donned grease-paint and crape-hair,[1] and once more the wheels of a Chaplin comedy factory began to revolve.

At first Charlie was out of his stride. He was in the best of humours, but eight weeks of idleness had left him somewhat staled, and he found himself at a loss for "snap" in his ideas.

But after an hour or so that powerful mind of his began to operate more smoothly, and the gags came thick and fast.

I love to see Charlie "stuck" for a good, smooth-running gag. It is such an education to see how, bit by bit, his mind gets over the difficulty. At first he will struggle with the action—the "mechanics," as he calls it—then, as he goes along, a better move will suggest itself here and there, and he will finally get the thing boiled down until it has that facile, well-shaped continuity of action that has made the Chaplin comedies dear to all lovers of life's funny side throughout the world. It is the real psychology of a "gag."

The sets were ready, the cameras were primed; around the stage we principals stood intermingled with the "extras"; Charlie picked up his hat and cane and set his coat in shape.

"All right," he said. "Let's break the ice."

I don't think Charlie really intended to do anything in the nature of creating a record that day, but nevertheless he did so, for the first scene we shot—his entrance and preliminary gag—was 310 feet long, without a cut or break. Considering that this will run five minutes and ten seconds upon the screen when it comes to be shown, the average picture-goer will agree that this is probably the longest continuous scene that has ever been taken.

But the gag is a cracker-jack, and, to my mind, fully justifies that the length of time it takes. Just what it is, diplomacy forbids my recording. It does not do to spread advance information anent Chaplin's notions, for the very good reason that there are hundreds of picture-men in this little world of ours who would eagerly seize upon them and shoot them onto the market before Charlie's pictures had a chance to be released.

Friend Albert Austin shared my dressing-room, and during the waits between the scenes he related to me quite a lot of little anecdotes concerning Charlie, with whom he toured in the Karno days for nearly nine years [*Goodwins exaggerates here, as Chaplin spent only six years in the Karno company*].

Upon the second day Charlie's energy seemed to have taken a relapse, for he was unable to concentrate without sitting down and smoking a cigarette before every scene he shot. That cigarette trick of his is not a vice—indeed, it could scarcely be termed a habit, since he smokes less than five a day, and never carries any about with him; but when he is stuck for an idea he flops down into the nearest chair, demands a cigarette from the ever-watchful "Scotty," and puffs at it until the tangle is straightened out.

Sceptics may declare that there is but little work connected with the making of a comedy, especially a Chaplin comedy, where the comedian's own personality and acting are the mainstay of the story. Yet the Lone Star Film Company's plant is perhaps the busiest, for its size, in the whole of this moving picture land of ours.

As I have stated in an earlier issue, stuff like Charlie's can hardly be turned on tap, like water, and neither does consistency play any large part in its making. A whole story will probably turn upon one chance thought of Chaplin's, and that thought may not come until the story is halfway through. Consequently an army of men has to be always on hand, ready to execute the bidding that may come "from headquarters" at any moment.

Expensive? You bet it is; but there are more Chaplin comedies sold throughout the world than any other make of picture, so that a few hundred dollars more or less makes but a little difference in the huge turnover represented by each picture we send off the plant.

But I am wandering again.

On the morning I speak of Chaplin was rather inclined to be in that mood that causes him to have all superfluous people sent away from the set. He says it detracts from his train of thought. Yet on another occasion he will welcome an audience of any kind and care not how much they laugh or comment upon his work. He is essentially a creature of moods.

On the day in question, work finally "got his goat," and after lunch he shook his head and abandoned himself to the inevitable.

During the afternoon he gave us an exhibition of the most extraordinary breaks in Lancashire clog-dancing I have ever seen. The whole studio gathered round him and watched. He seemed to be tireless, and the regularity of his foot-beats was a "thing of beauty and a joy forever." *[A little over a year earlier, on his first day of work at Essanay, the entire staff and a large number of reporters crowded into the studio to watch the newly minted star go through his paces. Chaplin startled and amazed them by warming up with a clog dance to put himself into a proper comedy-creating mood.]*

I recalled suddenly that this newly-discovered talent must be the result of his early—his very early—training with the Eight Lancashire Lads. He told me that he had joined that famous troupe when he was but a child of seven, and that they had to rehearse, for all the world like a school, every morning of the year. *[Chaplin joined the company when he was nine and toured with it for two years.]*

I could not help adding this to what I already knew of his early life, and feeling strangely gratified that such an existence of hard struggling and discipline should have met its due reward. From what Charlie has told me from time to time, I know that each and every one of those little quips and gags that have endeared him and his work to the whole civilised world has been paid for by hours of practice, and not a few infantile tears.

Again, I began to realise what a many-sided man he is in his talents. The very quintessence of comedy, a born dramatic actor, a brilliant musician, a tumbler in no mean way, a gifted dancer, and the possessor of a clear and excellent singing voice—it is small wonder that Charlie Chaplin is recognised among the few geniuses of this twentieth-century day.

But the greatest tribute of all, and one that must be paid to him, is the concession that whatever Charlie has achieved, or even had thrust upon him, is his just due; that he has worked and fought for his recognition through countless set-backs, innumerable privations, and the handicap of a gentle and sensitive nature, that has reached, and over-reached his goal, and that not even his most jealous rival (for he has no enemy) can begrudge him a thing in the world.

11

Rehearsing for
The Floorwalker

May 20, 1916

The name of the first Chaplin Mutual picture is to be *The Floorwalker*, and it is going to be placed on the market with a speed that will probably constitute a record, for Charlie has had no release for over four months at the time of writing!

Consequently everything is being done to expedite the completion of the story; we even have two camera-men taking simultaneously in order that we shall have a duplicate negative, one copy to go to New York, for America and the Western hemisphere; the other to go to London, for distribution in the East. *[The Mutual films marked the beginning of Chaplin's practice of shooting with two side-by-side cameras so that he could produce separate negatives for foreign and domestic release. These "A" and "B" negatives utilized Chaplin's first-choice takes. The two versions differed slightly from each other in camera angle and also in speed, since the cameras of the day were hand-cranked.[1] When he moved from Mutual to First National in 1918 Chaplin also began assembling a "C" negative as a safety, using his second-choice takes. This proved to be a wise precaution, since eventually the A and B negatives deteriorated, and he had to cobble together new release versions using the C negative and his outtakes.[2]]*

But while this is a matter of vital importance to the executive part of the business, we ourselves have enough to do to get *The Floorwalker* out within the stipulated time, and still make it a story worthy of Charlie's first release under the new 10,000 dollar contract. New York must attend to the rest.

Speaking of this gigantic salary of Charlie's reminds me that I was amusing myself to-day with Vincent Bryan (co-director of the Chaplin comedies[3]) by doping out ad infinitum what 10,000 dollars a week roughly amounts to. Here are the conclusions at which we arrived:

—Ten thousand dollars a week, allowing the comedian an average working day of five hours, and a six-day week, figures out at (excluding all decimals) roughly 1,666 dollars a day, 333 dollars a working hour, 5.33 dollars a minute, or 88 cents a second. Taking the fairly accurate rate of one cent being equal to one halfpenny, Charlie Chaplin thus earns on his new contract about 3s 8d for every second of his working hours.

This sum represents 98 per cent of the gross combined salaries of the whole United States Congress (equivalent to our Parliament), which is probably the most powerful law making body in the world.

Before I leave this subject and go to my real task, I ought to record what Miss Ruth Roland, a favourite of the screen for many years, has to say about the meaning of this handful of dollars.

"I tell you," she declares jokingly, "I simply wouldn't be Charlie and earn all that 'kale' for anything. The Government income tax takes away from 520,000 dollars a year no less than 26,070 dollars. To be separated from that much money would surely kill me!"

[Chaplin's tax rate at the time of this article would have been 7%, not the 5% that Ruth Roland assumes, but a raise in the rate in September placed Chaplin in a 12% bracket for 1916, as the U.S. girded for entry into the war. In the years to come he would run into serious problems with the IRS, the FBI, and other elements of the U.S. government.]

So far as the Chaplin studio is concerned, it has always been one of the chief attractions of the low comedy end of the business that one does not have to rise with the sun and put on grease-paint at an hour when most actors are just about to retire to bed. But those early-rising and industrious creatures, the dramatic picture-actors, have nothing on us little fellows in these days of hustling against time, for we are expected to be ready made-up by eight a.m. If we are not, there are inquiries.

Yet it is still out of the question, apparently, to put on a picture without wasting an awful lot of time; although we were all right on the job at the stipulated hour, Charlie was often so lost for the exact routine of a certain situation that he would sit sometimes for hours each day thinking it out. In just such a pensive spell I have caught him with the camera, and although the attitude he has adopted is far from being a dignified one, he apparently derives a lot of comfort from it. *[In the photo, not reprinted here, Chaplin, in full costume and makeup, lies with his legs jutting up at a sharp angle and his heels hooked over the top rung of a wooden chair, giving his hamstrings a great stretch as he ruminates.]*

The character immediately behind him is Lloyd Bacon, made up as a double of Charlie, while the other man in this particular snap-shot is George Cleethorpe, the head property-master, nicknamed "Scotty," to whom I referred in my last week's notes. "Scotty" is one of the few hold-overs from the old Chaplin-Essanay ranks, and is a native of the South of Ireland. It was at "Scotty's" suggestion that I mapped out the article which constituted the first instalment of this series—the *Red Letter*, oddly enough, having commissioned me to write just such a story, while I was halfway through it.

I don't think I have ever seen Charlie so undecided and fickle as he has been during the past few weeks. He will sit, oftentimes, resting his head on his knees or playing with some trivial toy or other upon the counter at the scene, what time his brain is working at a furious rate. In Charlie's most trivial moments he is thinking his hardest, just as he has an odd way of walking up to anybody who happens to be talking to a friend and saying "Eh?" without having the faintest desire to know what was being said. It is but a way of his and his mind is far away when he does it.

On the evening of which I am writing he "called off" for the day, and sent us all to our respective dressing-rooms to clean up. Yet when I returned to the stage he was still perched on a chair, his knees under his chin, in full make-up.

Presently Albert Austin came out with a handful of photographic post-cards, which he showed to us. They were taken as long ago as 1910, and showed the record of the old Karno's *Mumming Birds* Company, with Charlie in the leading part, through the U.S.A. and Canada. One of them represented Charlie, standing in the middle of Market Street, San Francisco, clad in the first American suit he ever wore. It was in the days when those wide, peg-top trousers and the heavily-padded shoulders were the vogue here. And how he laughed when he saw it!

"The original 'Frisco kid!" he cried. "Look at that hat. And maybe you think I wasn't proud of it in those days!"

Presently he looked at the remainder, and each called forth some odd comment from him, such as "Get the hair cut! I look like an Italian waiter out on holiday!" "See us all hanging out of the railway coach window? That was near Sacramento—hot as the hobs of Hades, too! And we'd all been playing cards. Look at that English collar I've got on. It's as limp as a rag."

"Well, well, "he finished up. "Them *was* the days!"

I recalled the different state of his finances nowadays, and the fact that he had said only two days ago that the making of pictures had the stage "beat to a frazzle." Whereat he only grinned.

"Well, each has its advantages, Nat"—a new nickname he has stuck on to me, evidently on account of the likeness of my name to that of the famous Nat Goodwin. *[Goodwin was a comic actor as famous for five marriages as his long and distinguished acting career. During this period he owned a popular seaside restaurant in nearby Santa Monica, where Chaplin, who lived nearby, often dined. Chaplin found Goodwin charming and wise, and later recalled with great affection their twilight walks along the deserted ocean front.*[4]*]* "For some things I prefer the stage, though; I love the feeling of comradeship between the boys, which so seldom exists in this new industry. I love the old digs, back home, and the old landladies, and the fun, and—yes, in a way, I love the poverty."

"Do you remember these?" I asked him taking a two-shilling piece from my pocket.

"Great Scott!" he ejaculated, taking it and turning it over in his palm. One would have thought he had never seen one in his life before. "That brings back memories, doesn't it? Remember how we used to go to the manager of the company and ask him to lend us two bob? Then he'd say 'Sorry, Charlie, I've only got a half-a-jimmy myself. Won't a shilling do?' And then we'd say 'Go on be a sport! Make it a couple of bob. I want to take a girl out!'"

We all laughed at that; it was so natural to us professionals from Britain, and, what is more, his imitation of the attitudes of performer and manager towards each other was so realistic that we just couldn't help it.

"Can you imagine how far two bob would go in taking a girl out over here?" he commented presently *[at the time two bob (two shillings) would have been worth fifty cents].*

At this juncture up came the manager, bringing with him a man armed with a heavy case and tripod.

"This is Hartsook's representative," he said *[Fred Hartsook was a celebrity photographer of the day].* "He wants you to pose some portraits, Charlie."

Charlie sighed and rose to greet the visitor.

"'Chaplin in his hours of ease,'" he misquoted.[5] "Ease! There ain't no such animal."

That evening he posed something like fifteen new portraits, and I couldn't help remarking to myself how clearly he must be able to see just where his appeal to the great public lies, for he selected just those attitudes and facial expressions his admirers all the world over best love. Some of them accentuated his woebegone and hunted air *[Goodwins probably means* haunted*],* which has brought real tears to many in the midst of their laughter, while others were in the most ludicrous positions and situations his mind could conceive. It may seem nothing to the average man, yet a moment's thought will convince anyone that it takes a great mind to be able to grasp exactly in what way its possessor best appeals to his public.

During the week I have had quite a lot of chats with Edna, and during one of them she voiced a thing that has often come to my mind.

"Doesn't Charlie look nifty in his street clothes?" she said. "It's the funniest thing. When he gets into his make-up he seems to change completely. As long as I have known him I can never associate him with the character he plays. He is so normal and slick and keen on the street and in his home life, yet when he gets his make-up on, his whole being seems to change into a poor, unhappy, shabby-genteel creature without a hope in the world."

I agreed with her; although it might have been put more clearly, I understood what she meant to say. Charlie's make-up transforms him into another being in spirit, appearance, personality, and mind, and thus he remains until he removes it. Even in his conversation with us, he is, when made up, a different individual entirely from the Charlie with whom we dine and wine in private life.

But to return to Edna. As we sat over a box of chocolates in her dressing-room one afternoon she sprang something on me which I had been expecting for a long time.

"Fred," she said, with an air of a conspirator, "will you do something for me?"

"Anything," I vowed recklessly.

"Well, I want you to tell me what all that slang is that you and Charlie and Mr Austin and Mr Campbell are always talking?"

THE WORLD'S LEADING MOVING PICTURE MAGAZINE

PHOTOPLAY

15 Cents

READ
Julian
Johnson's
Review of
the Year's
Acting

September

Edna Purviance

AN AUTHOR
IN BLUNDERLAND
By CHANNING POLLOCK
A Sensation of Wit and Fact!

"SHELL 43"
A Tremendous Tale of the War, and
Other Great Short Stories

"CALIFORNIA'S BROADWAY"

Edna in a rare offscreen appearance as the *Photoplay* cover girl for September 1916.

It was minutes before I could talk coherently, for the idea of her wanting to learn cockney rhyming slang tickled my sense of humour hugely; she had always sworn that it "didn't interest her in the least, and that she would not speak it if she could."

But Edna is beyond the power of human resistance, and I couldn't help but give her a lengthy lesson in the art of twisting the King's English out of shape.

"Well, now, 'Fire,' for example is 'Annie Maria,'" I began.

"Why?" she questioned, artlessly.

"Oh I don't know. Just because it is, I imagine," I said vacuously.

"But why shouldn't it be—oh, anything else?"

"Because it isn't," I assured her, growing less logical every minute.

"All right," she said. "Go on."

"Well, 'Annie Maria' is 'fire'; 'plates of meat' means 'feet'; 'chalk farm' is 'arm,'" and so on I went through the gamut of our poetic vocabulary.

"I see," she said when I'd finished. "And will you write it out for me sometime?"

The sequel came two days later, when Charlie came up to me with a rueful expression.

"I say, Nat," he said seriously. "What have you been doing with Edna?"

"Doing?" I echoed, surprised, for the lesson in slang was all but forgotten by then.

"Nothing, Charlie. Why?"

"You bounder! You've been teaching her rhyming-slang. I just pulled some of it in the scene we've been taking, and the little son-of-a-gun answered me back in my own language."

Then came what might have been a sad blow. A notice suddenly appeared on the back wall of the office bungalow, which read—"No amateur cameras are allowed on the lot. Please note."

I foresaw all the little exclusive snaps I have been taking for these stories going up in smoke, but I knew my own weight enough to challenge the notice with Harry Caulfield, the manager.

"That?" he said, without a smile. "Oh, that refers to amateur photographers."

"I see. And I'm not a photographer, eh, Harry?"

"Possibly," he observed dryly. "At any rate, you're not an amateur, so what are you worrying about? That notice doesn't concern you."

I thanked him fervently and breathed more freely; but there was more thanking to do a little while later, when, in his dry way, he called me over and said—

"You're not doing enough for your living, Fred."

"Hello!" I thought. "Here's where I get called down."

"No," he continued, thoughtfully. "You have a lot of time on your hands which I think you can occupy better than you do."

"In what way?" I asked.

"I've been reading some of your articles to-day"—referring to the *Red Letter* which had arrived from London that morning—"and I want you to add the official duties of publicity manager to what you are doing now. It will carry with it roughly as much again as you are getting now. Do you agree?"

"I do."

Since I wrote the earlier part of this week's story, things have not progressed very much further. *The Floorwalker* appears to be causing Charlie a lot of trouble that he has never experienced before, and the crowd of actors and extra people who are engaged for the picture have stood around idle for days.

Charlie has changed his mind with the rapidity of a neurotic female. One man has put on six different make-ups within two days, and the camera-men have changed their "set-ups" from one spot to another, at Charlie's bidding, more times than they or I can count. With a thousand and one opportunities around him—there is no gainsaying it—Charlie, for the first time in his career, is temporarily flummoxed to a standstill.

Yet withal I have known that colossal brain too long to feel an apprehension about the upshot. When the tangle is at last unravelled the resultant gag will assuredly be worthy of the difficulty it has involved. Charlie doesn't waste time on trifles.

He has got to the stage where his chief amusement is bowling a hoop around the studio. A stage of childishness you venture to suggest. Not a chance! I have explained it earlier in these very notes. In Charlie's most trivial moments he is thinking his hardest.

The outcome may be wonderful, whatever else it may be. Mark me!

12

Charlie Chaplin Talks of Other Days

May 27, 1916

It is, I suppose, an unusual thing for anyone in the motion-picture industry to feel any cause for satisfaction when the failure of light holds up work upon the picture in hand. Yet when the camera-man reported one day this week that he "wouldn't give fifteen cents" for the sort of photography that could be obtained in the prevailing light, I was secretly elated, for Chaplin was in narrative vein that day and I scented the prospect of obtaining some interesting copy. Nor was I disappointed, for although I could have wished his trend of thought to have been a little less reminiscent, he talked of many things that I feel will afford amusement to my readers.

Contrary to all "property" rules, Charlie curled himself up on one of the heavily upholstered chairs that graced the set in which he has been working before old Sol went back on us, and called his henchmen around him.

There were possibly twenty of us, including Eric Campbell and Albert Austin, co-workers of years gone by, and we ranged ourselves in divers positions of ease that were quite out of the usual in this busiest of all studios, and then Charlie began—

"This weather reminds me of Chicago. Whenever the sky is cloudy it always makes me think of the day I signed my last year's contract."

He smiled reflectively, evidently comparing the latter document mentally with the magnificent one he is now fulfilling for the Lone Star Film Corporation, with its unprecedented salary and its remarkable provisos.

"It was on such a day as this, too, that I took the train for Los Angeles in company with Leo White, Ben Turpin, and the manager of the old concern. *[Dissatisfied with the working conditions and icy weather in Chicago, where Essanay had its main studio, Chaplin headed west for the company's studio in Niles, California. In addition to the cast members, Chaplin traveled with the producer assigned to his films, Jess Robbins, on board to mollify his unhappy new star.]* I remember there was an English actor in our Pullman—a very nice chap, too, named Roland Bottomley—and soon we became acquainted and got to playing poker to while away the tedium of the journey West. *[Bottomley (1880–1947) was a successful stage actor who appeared in many Broadway productions and a number of silent films.]*

"You know Ben and his funny personality, so you can imagine the sort of looks he began to throw around when the luck persisted in flowing in every direction but his. It was a very polite little party—for, of course, we scarcely knew Mr Bottomley at the time; but it was altogether too polite for Ben. With a perfectly good 'full house' being smashed by a mere 'four sixes,' he would have preferred to chastise somebody. But presently the cards began to come his way, and he held an undeniable fist of unbeatables. Then the betting began.

"'Twenty-five cents,' he ventured.

"'Pass me,' I replied, throwing in.

"'I'm with you,' said the manager.

"'And ten cents bettah,' murmured the Englishman.

"Ben looked at him; a hush fell on the assembly, as they say in the novels.

"'Ten bettah!' he echoed. 'Ten bettah!' He paused, surveyed his cards again, and threw in two more counters. 'And "ten bettah" than you, ole fellah,' he said.

"We nearly fell off our seats with laughter.

"Ben was a great source of amusement to us chaps. I shall never forget the first time Leo White came to the Western plant to work with me. Ben was working busily in overalls and a painter's cap, and when White sailed on to the stage in a tight-fitting New York suit, immaculate laundry, and carrying a swagger-looking cane in his hand, Ben paused with his mouth open.

"'For the love o' Mike,' he gasped, surveying the resplendent vision, 'what the heck are you made up for?'"

*[Chaplin often enlivened his stories with uncanny vocal and physical imper-
sonations of the people he was talking about, and it's tempting to believe he was
doing that here. But while* Red Letter *readers couldn't experience this aspect of
his talent, they could easily imagine Ben Turpin's doltish character mocking
the polite Britisher's posh accent, and later naively assuming that Leo White's
dapper street clothing was a costume.[1]]*

Presently the conversation drifted back to the days of Chaplin's early stage
career.

"It's a funny thing," he mused. "People always connect me and my work
with my training under Fred Karno, the vaudeville manager on the other side;
but, as a matter of fact, I owe more to the tutelage of a Mr Saintsbury, who
gave me my first legitimate engagement as Billy, the boy in *Sherlock Holmes*,
than to anybody in the world.

"Saintsbury had a director named Quentin M'Pherson, an exacting, particular sort of man, who used to run out of town, and give the company the
'once over' regularly every three months or so. Two weeks' solid rehearsals
would invariably follow these little trips of his, and I remember how they used
to strike terror into my heart, for I was little more than a child at the time.
Yet even in my awe, I couldn't keep my sense of humour in check—there was
always something irresistibly funny about it all that would cause me to laugh
at the very moment he was showing me some piece of business he wanted
interpolated. Then he would glare into my face and say, 'Don't be rude; don't
be rude! Leave the stage at once, you naughty boy.' That would make me feel
terribly hurt, for I was always a sensitive kid, and I would go and cry in a
corner of the theatre.

"But I suppose I had more genuine fun among the Karno boys than I did
in those infant days, with all their trials and struggles.

"There was one old fellow, a brilliantly clever pantomimist, who used to
play the 'drunk' in *A Night in a London Music Hall*—the show which brought
me out to America—and he was forever at loggerheads with the youngster
who played the boy in the box. Both were pretty good disciples of Bacchus,
and neither was ever particularly flush with money as a consequence. They
would quarrel regularly every week and ignore each other until one ran out of
money completely. Then he would go up to his bête noir and extend the olive
branch with a show of diplomacy that was worthy of a better cause.

"'Jim, old man,' he'd say, with an imaginary lump in his throat, 'don't want to quarrel with you, old fellow. Been pals for a long time, you know. Hurts me here'—banging his heart—'to have a—difference with you.'

"'That so?' the other would comment, jingling his money in his pocket. 'All right; I accept your apology.' Then more jingling of coins.

"A long pause would ensue and then the affluent one would generally say—

"'Well, I'm going to get a little refreshment. Would you—?'

"'Oh, that's not really necessary,' the other would say. 'I—er—I didn't—'

"And so on; but finally they would both get beautifully lit, either on cash or credit, and turn up to the show in a disgusting condition of inebriety.

"But one night Karno was in front, and there were these two; one playing a drunken swell, but in such a sloppy state of intoxication that he was literally a 'mess'—the other, supposed to be an angel-faced boy in a schoolboy collar and suit, hanging out of the box on the stage nearly oblivious to his own existence. Of course, Karno fired them both in spite of their protestations that they had both been sick from heart-trouble and had gotten out of sick-beds in order to save the show.

"The sequel came a few days later, when I met the fellow who played the 'drunk.' He assured me that he had been to see Karno, who had begged him to stay, and this was his account of the incident. 'I said to him, "Mr Karno, you placed upon me last night a stigma from which I might never have recovered, but for my position as a master-professional. You accused me of being under the influence of liquor, whereas I was sick. I had risen from my bed, all against my medical man's instructions, in order to save your show—your show, sir, and I am abused for my pains. No, sir; I shall not stay." And I went to the wall where there was hanging a playbill. I tore it in halves and wrote on the back my notice of resignation, which I handed to Karno. "There, sir," I said, "is my notice," and I strode towards the door. "Come back, Jim," said Karno. "No, sir," I replied. "I am finished with you." Now, young Chaplin, you know the kind of man I am.'

"The next day," continued Charlie, "we heard what had actually happened. It seems poor old Jim had gone up, meek and tremulous, to Fred Karno's office, and the moment he put his head inside the door Karno seized a book and shouted, 'Get outside!' whereat Jim had fled precipitately down the stairs.

"But he was a great old boy, and a wonderful pantomimist. I even feel I'd like to fetch him out here, if only for the sake of the amusement he'd afford us all.

"The last I saw of him was just before I left England, six years ago. He was on top of a street car, and he saw us down in the street. He stood up, shook his hands together, threw an imaginary kiss, and made an imitation of sea waves with his hands, by which we gathered that he meant, 'God speed you on your journey across the sea!' Yes, a great old boy.

"Then there was another chap in the crowd, who was never known to disburse a cent that he could possibly avoid spending. He suddenly decided to take unto himself a wife, and we boys all framed it up to talk in stage-whispers while he was around concerning what we proposed to give towards a wedding present for him. It wasn't long before he got wind of it, and (presumably to clinch the matter) invited us all out to take a little drink with him. The drink grew into several, the majority of which he paid for; but when Saturday came and all we offered him was our congratulations—Good-night! That was the cruellest blow of his life."

Charlie smiled reminiscently.

"But they played the same trick on me when I was leaving for America. I was one of those original 'never-buy-any-grease-paint' boys, always borrowing somebody else's, you know, and after kidding me unmercifully about it for months they finally gave it up; but on my last day with the company I received a neat little box. I opened it, expecting to find some nice souvenir from my brother artistes. All it contained was five short ends of grease-paint!" *[Chaplin repeated this story in his* Autobiography,[2] *but in that telling he is at the end of his American touring years rather than the beginning, leaving the Karno company to head to Hollywood to make movies. There is a further discrepancy; according to Stan Laurel, who was there, one of the other company members thought Chaplin cold and haughty, and he intended his gift-wrapped brown greasepaint stubs to represent lumps of excrement. However, following the last performance the would-be prankster saw Chaplin slipping away for a private cry, after which he took the company out for farewell drinks. The "gift" was put aside. Later that night Chaplin came upon it and drew his own conclusions.[3]]*

As the afternoon drew to its close we fell to singing the choruses of a few of the songs of other days, and this seemed to please Charlie hugely, for he continually demanded more, until we must have unearthed from the cobwebs of our memories some twenty or thirty old choruses, each of which seemed to bring something back to his mind—for Charlie is essentially a dreamer, although a very practical one.

Then finally, Eric Campbell brought to light one which was new to us all, and which he declared he had heard sung by a street vocalist years ago. It ran:—

> "In a cottage in the country,
> Where her poor old parents live,
> They drink the champagne that she sends them,
> But they never can forgive."

This fairly convulsed Charlie, and he demanded that it should be repeated to him until he had learnt it by heart.

"I'll spring that at the next dinner party I go to," he declared. And as by this time the light, such as there was of it, showed more tendency to wane than to wax, the party dispersed until the morrow.

Work was resumed the next day and Charlie surpassed himself. His fertile brain never seemed at a loss to find something new to do in the way of gags, while the pressure at which he worked beat all previous records. Within two days the last scene of the story was taken and Charlie, with a sigh of relief, turned round three times for luck, and then went to his dressing-room to change.

Soon afterwards I found him in a thoughtful mood, sitting on the steps of the office, and as I approached him I noticed he was chewing something. I was just about to ask him what was his staple diet that day, when he saw me and plucked a nasturtium which he held out to me.

"Did you ever chew these?" he asked. "They're fine!"

Presently one of the boys came out with his bicycle, which seemed to afford Charlie food for thought.

"What a craze those things used to be at one time," he remarked. "It was the greatest ambition of my life to own a bicycle, yet now they're all but obsolete." (This is the fact, so far as America is concerned.)

"I haven't ridden one for over six years. Let's have a go!" He got up from the step and mounted the bicycle, which he gingerly proceeded to pedal along the sidewalk; but the machine had a coaster hub, and when he tried to back-pedal the brake brought the bicycle to an abrupt standstill and the 10,000 dollar comedian fell off. He anathematised it heartily, and mounted again, and this time the back-pedal brake gave him no trouble. In the small things, as well as the big, Charlie seldom had to try more than twice.

After cruising up and down the sidewalk a while he became more adventurous, and he went up the street to Santa Monica Boulevard, where the street cars and automobiles fly thick and fast. The first thing he did was to run within a foot of a passing car, and for the moment a million-dollar life was in jeopardy; but he recovered himself and turned the corner. For ten minutes we saw nothing of him. Then, he suddenly appeared in the distance, "scorching!" He pulled up outside the bungalow that serves as the offices of the company, and dismounted, breathing heavily.

"Gee!" he panted. "I never dreamt it possible for my bicycle muscles to get so slack with all the exercise I do. I'm all in."

So saying, he sank down on the step and chewed some more nasturtiums.

Then his mind began to turn back to business—though I suspect that he was thinking of nothing else all the while he was on his cycle trip—and he spoke of gags.

"I think I've tried everything and done everything in pictures there is to do," he said. "Yet they still come."

Therein lies a big truth in regard to the Chaplin comedies, and one that is largely accountable for their success—the gags "still come." Often I have looked back over the numberless bits of business, the jokes, the gags, and the situations that Charlie Chaplin has presented to us, and I have wondered if there is left anything under the sun; if, indeed, there is anything that he has not done already? Yet with every new picture comes a hundred new situations and as many new ways of handling them. The scope of Charlie's brain seems to be limitless.

The Floorwalker, then, is finished, and that night, at nine o'clock, he commenced to "cut" it—that is to say, to weed out all the unnecessary scenes, join up the film in its proper order, and then cut the whole negative down to the requisite length of two thousand feet—or, as the posters say, two reels. This is a long and tedious job, a difficult one, and one that requires a lot of mental concentration, and possibly that is why Charlie prefers to carry it out in the still watches of the night.

Celebrating Charlie Chaplin's Birthday

June 3, 1916

The Floorwalker was shown in the projecting-room of the studio shortly after I had despatched my last week's notes to *Red Letter*, and a screamingly funny picture it is. There had been no official notification that it was to be "run," but we saw the head camera man sneaking from the dark rooms to the miniature-picture theatre wherein each film is given the "once-over" by the critical eyes of Charlie and those in authority before it is shipped to New York for distribution to the world at large. That is how we kind of got wind that there was something stirring, and we made excursions at odd moments into the vicinity of the theatre, until the whirr of the projector told us that this, Charlie's first picture under his Mutual engagement, was really being flashed onto a screen. Thereupon we slipped into the room as unobtrusively as possible and seated ourselves behind the critical committee.

We had not intended to betray our presence—for it is not customary to admit even the members of the company to a trial run of any picture—but whatever our good resolutions may have been *The Floorwalker* scattered them to the four winds. Within five minutes we were laughing ourselves to death at the conceptions of the inimitable Charles, while he himself was so tickled that, if he were actually aware of our presence in the room, he was too busy laughing to comment on the fact.

To merely say *The Floorwalker* is funny is to give but the mildest expression of what it really is, but when it comes your way—and it should be there very soon after these notes are in print—you will have an opportunity of judging for yourself whether the Chaplin Mutual pictures are going to be funnier than those of other days or not.

During the run we received a visit from Marie Dore [*sic*—Doro], the eminent American actress, who created such an impression by her work in *Diplomacy* at the Wyndham's Theatre, London, recently. She was accompanied by her husband, Elliot Dexter, and the English playwright, W. H. Hulbert, both of whom were reduced to a state of helplessness by the ludicrous situations Charlie has embodied in his first picture.

After the run the party declared *The Floorwalker* to be the funniest thing Charlie has ever done, and invited the comedian to take luncheon at the Dexters' beautiful palm-girt residence near the studio.

[Chaplin was totally smitten by Marie Doro when, at age sixteen, he played the part of Billy the page boy in William Gillette's London revival of Sherlock Holmes *and she played the female lead. When he encountered her again in Hollywood she was thrilled to meet the famous Charlie Chaplin, but had not the slightest recollection of working with him a decade earlier. In his* Autobiography *he vividly recalls the agony of his unrequited teen crush, along with his delight at meeting her again, looking "as beautiful as ever."[1] Over the next few years the two spent several evenings together that Chaplin describes fondly, leaving to the reader's imagination whether anything more than friendship blossomed between them. Marie's marriage to Elliot Dexter was short-lived, and, evidently weary of the trials of both romantic and professional life, she retired to a life of seclusion in the mid-twenties.]*

Shortly afterwards I had a chat with Mr. Hulbert, who related to me a happy little incident in connection with Charlie's visit to New York, which I am going to recount for the benefit of *Red Letter* readers.

It seems that Mrs Fiske, America's greatest actress, is a most ardent admirer of Charlie's work, and made strenuous efforts to meet him while he was in the East, but business forced the comedian to return to California before the meeting could be arranged, and so, to the disappointment of both, Charlie and the great actress are still strangers, except across the screen.

But she heard that Mr Hulbert was going West, and this is her message to Charlie Chaplin—

"Tell the dear boy that Mrs Fiske thinks him the greatest in his own line the world has ever seen. I have seen each and every one of his pictures, and have laughed until I have cried; and then I have seen them over again in order to analyse him and his work. I have tried to find a flaw, and have failed completely, for he has unfailing technique."

And here comes the greatest tribute of all—

"Tell him that the greatest achievement of his career is this—that at twenty-six he has made the whole world laugh, while at fifty-six the Kaiser has made the whole world weep."

By which she meant to say that Charlie Chaplin, genius of a generation, has become a sort of antidote to the greatest criminal the world has ever known.

When I related to Charlie Minnie Maddern Fiske's beautiful tribute to him, his thoughtful blue eyes shone with genuine pleasure.

"'Unfailing technique,'" he repeated with a pensive smile. "That is wonderful—especially from Mrs Fiske."

Then I handed him a signed photograph, which the eminent tragedienne had sent by Mr Hulbert, and he held it in his hands, as if, deft as they are, they might injure it with their touch.

He read the simple inscription—"With love, M. Fiske!" and nodded mutely. His heart was too full for words.

[Fiske's comments in her letter are quoted almost verbatim from her article "The Art of Charles Chaplin," which was published on May 6, 1916, in Harper's Weekly. *The article was tremendously important to Chaplin's career, for it opened the floodgates of commentary by the artistic and intellectual elite of America, making him and his work a part of the national conversation in a way that no amount of newspaper and fan magazine coverage could ever do. From this time forward Chaplin's films would be seen by opinion makers as something more than disposable popular entertainment; they would be seen as Mrs. Fiske saw them, as works of art. Chaplin relished the attention and eventual friendship of people from this exalted world, and there is no question that their acceptance inspired him to ever greater artistic achievements, starting with the stunning series of twelve films he was just then embarking upon for Mutual.*

This had already been a heady day for Chaplin, and there was more to come.]

Late that evening Lloyd Bacon and I entertained Mr and Mrs Albert Austin to a little dinner party at Levy's restaurant, and just as we had reached the liquor stage Lloyd espied Charlie and Edna at the entrance.

"Don't call him," I suggested, remembering Charlie's occasional preference for his own company. "He'll come down to us if he feels like it."

A few moments later I glanced up the hall again, and there was Charlie leaning absently against a vacant chair while Edna stood regarding him in silence, waiting, presumably, for his verdict on things in general or something in particular. Presently he straightened up and led the way down the aisle until he was almost level with my table. I signalled to the others not to speak, and, just as I had expected, he looked straight at me without the faintest sign of recognition. His mind was a thousand miles away!

But Edna happened to turn at that moment and see us, and her exclamation brought Charlie back to earth with a start. Instantly his face was wreathed in a smile such as only he can assume.

"Hello," he called. "Holding a party here, or what?"

"What," I answered, and he immediately proceeded to choke me.

I pleaded for mercy, and waited for him to sit down. It never occurred to me to ask him, for it has always been such an accepted thing. But still he stood up with Edna, and after exchanging a word or two with Mrs Austin whom he had not seen since the old Karno days, he stuck his hands in his pockets and inquired—

"Well, may we sit down with you?"

Might he sit down! Could a duck swim? It wasn't five seconds before he and Edna were ensconced at the table just for all the world as if they had been there all evening. Of course I asked him what was his pleasure in the matter of refreshments, but he shook his head.

"Drinks are on me this evening."

"But, listen," I began.

"Shut up," he commanded me. "It's my birthday to-day."

That was the signal for a storm of chatter. Everybody talked at once, and nobody understood anybody else, but the main idea seems to be that he was to see many returns of the eventful day, and when the noise had subsided I managed to ask him what anniversary it might be?

"Don't you know?" he asked.

"Your twenty-sixth, unless I am mistaken," I said.

He shook his head.

"You flatter me by one year," he told me. "I am twenty-seven this sixteenth day of April nineteen-sixteen."

And so we drank to the sixteenth of April, nineteen-sixteen, and for many a year after.

Charlie was in his best mood that evening, and everything was merry as a marriage bell. Of course, he and Albert talked of other days—that was inevitable among old cronies—but a lot of the conversation was of the present, and we were all able to participate in it. I suppose it was rather an odd party, for all four of the men were English and both of the ladies American, but there was no lack of bon camaraderie because of that.

"There's one thing I always feel sorry for when I look at Charlie," said Austin. "If you look just over his left eye you will see a scar."

Charlie grinned, and rubbed the spot reflectively.

"It was at a 'Chicken Ball' in 'Frisco, and Charlie and I were both about half-seas-over, but everything was all right until we started to do a dwarf dance, Charlie tucking his knees up his jacket and making himself look about three feet high, while I stood on tip-toe, which made me about six feet two. Then, as the thing made such a hit with the crowd, we both lost our heads and started a rough and tumble dance, and I, like an idiot, got hold of Charlie and another fellow by their necks and banged their heads together. I split Charlie's eye-brow wide open and it swelled up like a tennis ball. I thought I'd go mad when I saw the blood starting from it, but Charlie only dabbed it with a handkerchief and said 'Gee, Albert, you ought to be more careful than that!' and never referred to the affair again."

"All right, Al," interrupted Charlie, laughing. "Don't let's mention it now." So the subject was dropped.

As the evening went on we grew more talkative and Charlie presently told us the rough plots of some of his future stories. They were conceptions that can well be described as brilliantly clever, centring as they do around that woefully-cheerful, foolishly-clever character that he has set on the highest pinnacle of prominence in the world to-day. They are just the type of story that the world is wanting from him, but which, for some reason, he does not give. I refer to the sympathetic "heart-interest" theme set within a framework of his inimitable comedy, just like a vein of silver running through a piece of quartz. He started it gently in *Charlie the Tramp*; he gave his public a stronger taste of it in *Charlie at the Bank* a picture which, to my mind, has never been surpassed by him for all-round excellence; and now, if he keeps to his present resolve, he is going to give you, under his new Mutual contract, one heart-story alternated by one slap-stick comedy throughout the year, interlarding the rough with the artistic in order to cater to his wide and many-classed circle of worshippers.

I was thinking of *Charlie at the Bank* the other day, and it suddenly dawned upon me that what I have spent thousands of words in trying to express to you while I have been writing these articles could have been conveyed by a few lines and a visit to a picture theatre. The true Charlie Chaplin, and the spirit of Charlie Chaplin as he really is, has never been better indicated than in that one "close-up" where Charlie, peering through the doorway at Edna, the typist, places a finger in his mouth and turns a crestfallen eye to the camera. The wonderful sentiment; the sweet-tempered, sensitive nature; the wistful, child-like expression in those big, thoughtful blue eyes of his, yet with the irrepressible sense of humour lurking behind them, are just Charlie Chaplin, the man as he is, and as I see him every day. Perhaps that is why I like *Charlie at the Bank* better than anything he has ever done—it is he.

When J. M. Barrie wrote *Peter Pan* he might have had Charlie as his model, for he is in many ways just what every mother would like her boy to be, inasmuch as he has retained every one of those infantile characteristics that a mother loves in her first-born. She dreads the days when he shall grow up—possibly outgrow even her love—and become a sophisticated man-of-the-world, and that is what Charlie has never done.

RED LETTER PHOTOCARD.

(*Charles Chaplin.*)　　　Love Is Blind.　　　(*Charlie at the Bank.*)

Edna, Billy Armstrong, and Charlie in *The Bank*.

Yet the odd part about this is that it is many years since he knew the meaning of a mother's tender care, for his mother, as many of my readers are aware, is a permanent invalid at Hove, in Sussex, and Charlie has not seen her for goodness knows how long.

[Hannah Chaplin's sad fate was that she had been in and out of infirmaries and lunatic asylums from the time Charlie was six years old. The Chaplin boys were at pains to conceal their mother's condition because of the stigma attached to insanity; in some early interviews Chaplin even claimed that she was dead. Since 1912 Hannah had resided at Peckham House Hospital in London. While this was a humane institution, Hove, a genteel seaside retreat, would have been a much more appealing place for Red Letter *readers to imagine her living. And in fact, as the boys prospered they arranged for Peckham House to send her on extended, supervised visits to Hove and other seaside resorts, so Goodwins's comment above only stretches the truth a bit.*

In 1921 Charlie and Sydney brought their mother to America, where she lived out her days in a pleasant home not far from the homes of her beloved sons. She was cared for by a married couple, who saw to her needs and catered to her whims. Occasionally she would visit the studio, where she worried about the shabby state of Charlie's clothing—she couldn't separate him from his screen character. But at other times she was perfectly lucid, and would entertain visitors to her home by breaking into some of the very songs with which, years earlier, she had enthralled the impressionable Charlie.]

I seem to have wandered off again from the main object of my story, and the only excuse I can offer is the irresistible temptation to analyse my friend's unique character and personality, purely because they are unique. Let us return to earth.

Soon Charlie began to show signs of growing weary, for he had sat up several nights until the middle hours of the morning over the cutting of *The Floorwalker*, and so I proposed one final toast to him before we broke up the party.

This he acknowledged in due form, then shook hands all around, and took his departure for the Los Angeles Athletic Club, wherein nowadays he is domiciled.

Shortly afterwards we rose to go, and called to mine host for the bill. To our amazement the waiter assured us that there was no bill! Explanations followed, and it turned out that Charlie had secretly obtained the check from the waiter and had paid it unbeknown to us. Of course it was very nice for Charlie to have done it but it was our party after all, wasn't it? And we didn't feel as if it were altogether right.

The next morning Lloyd Bacon and I, as ostensible hosts of the previous night, tackled Charlie about what he had done and he placed a hand on our respective shoulders.

"Boys," he said seriously, "I hate to seem boastful, but I earn as much in a week as both of you do in a year." He drew out his pocket-book and showed us three buff-coloured notes. "You see?" he said simply.

They were the goods, sure enough, for each was drawn by the Mutual Film Corporation, and each represented the sum of $10,000 (£2,000) payable to Charles Spencer Chaplin!

Certain London newspapers may say what they will of the "inflated" reports concerning Charles Chaplin's remuneration, but what I have seen with my own eyes is good enough for me; and my word is as good as theirs. I say it in all egotism.

Had it been anyone else than Charlie I might have been worldly enough to stand in some awe of the magnitude of this figure, but the question of awe is as absurd in regard to Charlie Chaplin as is the supposition that his success has changed him one whit from what he was in the years gone by. It is his own doing too, and I sometimes believe it is deliberate.

Thus, for example, I asked him at luncheon to-day if he didn't think he ought to put on a somewhat sterner front against people who were unworthy, in the moral sense, of his notice. I quite expected him to laugh the suggestion to scorn, and, as he had one of his frisky moods on, he did that, and some more into the bargain.

Shall I tell you exactly what he did? Or are you going to think that what I have said about his serious side is all bunkum? I'll chance it.

He seized a handful of spring onions off the table and threw them up in the air, whence they fell all over the room!

I ask you, readers of the *Red Letter*, what is the use of talking about reserve to a man who does a thing like that?

Charlie's Wireless Message to Edna

June 10, 1916

In yet another picture will Charlie Chaplin be seen in garb other than that which he has made famous throughout the world, for the picture upon which we have been engaged since I penned my notes last week is to be called *The Fireman*, and deals with the adventures of the inimitable Charles in an American fire department—or fire brigade station, as we of Britain would call it.

Not Alfred Lester,[1] nor any other satirist of the flame-fighting fraternity, has ever conceived such weird and wonderful idea from a mere lay-out of common fire equipment, as Charlie Chaplin has done in this, his second Mutual picture.

If the pictures of other days have been funny, *The Fireman* is going to be a riot from beginning to end. It is of the same order as *Charlie Shanghaied*— a purely slap-stick, knock-'em-down-and-drag-'em-out sort of affair, but withal it is replete with subtle and original situations, the like of which have never previously been placed before the picture-going public.

I think Charlie first got the idea from a Sunday evening trip to Venice-by-the-Sea, for I was there myself, and chanced to see him walking up and down the promenade, all alone and wrapped in thought, somewhere in the vicinity of a dilapidated fire station which, although superseded, was not exactly useless, as the poster was wont to say. His state of mind was so preoccupied that I didn't stop to speak to him, fearing lest I might—to use his own pet word—"detract."

On the Monday then, *The Fireman* was begun, and a mediæval-looking fire-engine appeared from somewhere in the depths of the huge carpenter's shop which graces the plant of the Lone Star Film Corporation, followed by a smaller and less pretentious edition of itself, marked "Junior 23." These, Charlie informed us, were the chief pieces of paraphernalia to be used in the making of his next Mutual production. It seemed he had gone down to Venice in order to watch the modus operandi of an antiquated fire department, and that the engine and its smaller replica had been under construction for many days, all unknown to us mere players.

What Charlie Chaplin hasn't done to that larger fire-engine isn't worth doing. It has been a perfect horn of plenty, supplying everything and anything that happened to be needed at the moment. It has been everything, from a means of assault to a coffee-urn; it has cooked food, and it has gone out for runs upon the highway bearing eight lusty men upon its back. But the salient feature of the whole darned contrivance—to us actors, at any rate—is that it has no springs!

Can you imagine a fire-engine made of materials so light that three men could lift it with ease, but which has no axle-springs? If you think it is comfortable for eight good men and true to be borne down an ill-made road by two bucking bronchos attached to a contrivance of this description—why, you have another "think" coming, that's all. But it's all in the day's work.

With all its absurdity—and it is chock-full of that rare element—Charlie has managed to invest *The Fireman* with more than a little of genuine realism. His aim has been for an atmosphere of legitimate comedy interwoven with the absurd, and that is why he has insisted on the absence of things that would not for an instant be permitted to pass muster in even the most eccentric of fire brigades.

"Don't clown," he is forever drumming into the heads of his more dense supporters—and I am not leaving Fred Goodwins out of this class, except so far as certain occasions are concerned. "It's not funny to try and be funny," he maintained. "Be natural, and act every situation exactly as you would act it if you were the character you are portraying."

Easy to say, and (for Charlie Chaplin) easy to do; but, as a friend of his said to me recently, everyone isn't a Charlie Chaplin. The boy can do so much himself that he can't properly understand why others can't do the same, and once in a while that makes him difficult to keep pace with.

But I was speaking of his aim for realism and this reminds me of a little incident that happened in the taking of a short scene one day this week. It is amusing, in a mild way, yet contains an underlying tribute to the natural genius of Chaplin in his work that must be evident.

The situation was one where Charlie and Albert Austin are playing an earnest game of draughts, when the fire telephone rings. Up jumps Charlie, spilling the board, and rushes to the switchboard. In his excitement he pulls away the flexible cord connecting the 'phone to its base. That was the end of the scene, as rehearsed, but when it came to the taking, Charlie, as he so often does, put in a bit of additional business of his own. He seized the end of the flex, and stuck it back into the hole from which he had pulled it. As he did so he started back, his face twisted up in such a way that Austin rushed from his seat.

"What's the matter, Charlie?" he cried out. "Are you electrocuted?" Charlie gave him one look, and then collapsed on an adjacent bed, where he laughed himself blue in the face.

"Honestly," Albert said to me afterwards, "I never dreamed the little beggar was acting. I thought he'd stuck his fingers on a live wire."

That is something more than realism—it is reality!

All through this picture Charlie has worked at high pressure—a thing hitherto foreign to his method—and the evenings have consequently sometimes left him limp and fagged-out.

On just such a night as this I was sitting at my table in the local rendezvous of the bloods of Los Angeles—Levy's, mentioned in earlier issues—when I espied Charlie at a distant table. He was surrounded by a party which seemed to please him not, notwithstanding the fact that it consisted of many high-ups in the theatrical and motion-picture world. To put it bluntly, I, knowing his moods and his method of showing them, saw that he was bored! I stayed away from him, therefore, having myself a mood that would have done credit to the "gloomy Dane," and thus for an hour we sat apart—he all unconscious of anything but his own thoughts.

Presently the party arose to go, and Charlie for the first time since I have known him, I should imagine, stayed behind in solitude. Then it was that he caught my eye and beckoned me over. We chatted a while on trivial topics—for he was deeply engrossed in thought, and hardly knew what he was discussing with me—and presently we received an invitation to join a party at the other end of the room, consisting of William and Dustin Farnum, Courtenay Foote, and several others whose names would probably be unfamiliar to the majority of my readers.

I need not recount what followed during the evening. Suffice it that, at the witching hour one of the Farnums proposed that we all adjourn to a convivial meeting of "The Pals," a big social organisation of theatrical and picture folk which meets weekly in every big city of the U.S.A. for the purpose, it seems, of consuming a lot of honest brew and losing the best part of a night's sleep in so doing.

Charlie refused, with thanks! I had known he would. What is more, not I nor anyone there present could have changed him. There is only one thing in which Charlie weakens and cannot say "No," and that is when it comes to refusing to help a friend with either work or hard cash. In all else his negative is just what it seems to be, and nothing can construe it into meaning "Yes."

So the party left him at the door of his motor, and wended its way in several cars to the meeting-spot of "The Pals," minus Charlie Chaplin.

It has never been my idea to make these articles of mine into a sort of serial "John Barleycorn," although I did stray once into writing of a convivial evening with Bacchus, so I am going draw the curtain across the little party in question, which finished up at five-thirty in the morning.

My main object in mentioning this has been to impress the fact that Charlie, in this as in many other things, is, despite his gentle and sympathetic nature, a long way from being easily led from what he knows is best.

I am speaking of the Charlie Chaplin of to-day. Whatever you may have heard about him as an intemperate man may, or may not refer to other and less important periods in his life; I am not saying, for it is a matter of no importance to you or me.

It is not often that a note of even the mildest discord occurs to mar the harmony of this most genial of all studios, but when, from some cause, an occasional dissentient voice is heard in the land, Charlie Chaplin is invariably "there with bells on" to quell the argument. To him there is but one way to do it, and that is to make either one, or both, of the participants see the folly of their own ways.

Thus in the taking of a scene this week one of the extra-men (i.e., actors engaged for small parts and paid only on the days on which they work, usually a guinea a day) roared out in the middle of the scene, "Get out of the way,

So-and-So, you're covering me from the camera. Don't you think I'm in this picture, too?"

As a matter of fact, such is the lot of the extra man that he may be in a picture, but often nobody is aware of the fact, particularly when the picture is one featuring a big star. Consequently the objection was absurd, and Charlie, realising this, interrupted the lively argument which ensued upon our friend's plaint, by laughing at both of them.

"Tut, tut, children," he exclaimed, "don't be temperamental. I'm not that!" (I beg to differ, Charlie!) "Besides," he laughed again, "you'll be getting married to each other before the week is out."

The very absurdity of this last observation struck the two combatants forcibly, and in their amusement they forgot to get on with the war.

A singular instance of Charlie's affectionate nature even those for whom his relationship is only one of half-business, half-friendship, was demonstrated on this selfsame day. In case it may appeal to you in the same light as it did to us, I am going to recount it to you.

It was necessary to get a certain effect, that what is known as a "Life Mask" should be taken of the features of Edna, and for the benefit of the few to whom the process of this trying and sometimes painful operation is not known, I will describe it in as few words as possible.

First, a shallow tray of wood is made, and a hole cut in the bottom of it just large enough to admit the face of the subject. The entire countenance is thickly coated with cold-cream and the subject lies flat on her back, thus bringing the tray, containing her face, so to speak, into a horizontal position. The sculptor then inserts a rubber tube into each nostril to sustain the breathing, and pours into the tray a carefully-prepared mixture of plaster of Paris. This completely covers the face of the subject, the rubber breathing-tubes only being visible. The mixture slowly hardens—a twenty-minute plaster being used in the case of a woman because of its less violent drying-power, and consequent rapid change of temperature; while in the case of a man a two-minute plaster is not considered too drastic.

Just such a mixture as the latter was employed in the making of Charlie's life-mask several months ago.

As the time passes the plaster absorbs the cold-cream almost entirely, and the heat grows intense within the mould. Then, when the mask has been hardened right through, it is gently removed from the face, and a smooth, clear impression of the subject's visage, even to the eyelashes and dimples, is disclosed.

There was something that touched our imaginations in the sight of Edna lying upon the bed with her comely face totally obscured by a deep mess of plaster of Paris, and we all sat around silently watching, while the sculptor tested the heat of the mould from time to time. It was like seeing a dear friend placed in the grave in a way, for Edna could not talk or utter a sound, although she gripped her fingers into the bedding every once in a while as the heat became overpowering.

Then, all of a sudden, Charlie noticed what was afoot. In a flash he dropped his work of directing a scene and rushed over to the bedroom scene where the mould was being made.

"Ah, poor old Edna!" he exclaimed sympathetically, sitting opposite me on the bed. He took hold of her hand and asked, "Are you alright?" Of course she made no reply, and Charlie became much concerned. "How can you tell if they're alright?" he asked.

"Try wireless telegraphy," I suggested, taking her other hand, then to the "patient," "Are you alright, Edna? If you are, squeeze our hands." Instantly she squeezed, and we knew all was well within.

Charlie grinned like a kid who has discovered a new game. A few moments elapsed, and then—

"Are you alright?" he inquired again. This time there was no squeeze.

"Are you alive?" he asked anxiously.

A most decided squeeze, which left no doubt that her ladyship was very much alive.

"Isn't it done yet, Couderc?" he asked of the French sculptor.

"It would be bettaire to leave z'mould on a leetle longaire," answered the latter. "If Miss Edna can stand it."

"Can you stand it, Edna?" inquired Charlie. Nothing doing, apparently.

"Edna," urged Charlie, "it'll be better if you can stand it for another five minutes. Can you?"

An almost imperceptible squeeze gave reply, so we reduced the time to two minutes more, and then came the job of removing the mould. It had adhered slightly in places, and an occasional moan told us that Edna was very conscious of the fact. But Charlie held one hand and I the other, and by gripping tight she managed to allow the mask to be removed. It was a perfect success—

until Courderc accidentally ran into one of the carpenter's benches and shattered the whole thing to smithereens! And it all had to be gone through again!

But Edna didn't complain a single word. She just greased up again, and went to it once more. The second cast was all right, and did not adhere, but the smile which had graced the first one was conspicuous by its absence. Evidently the job of making two masks is no laughing matter.

The real point in my mentioning this is to show how deeply concerned Charlie really is for the well-being of those who work under his care.

Professionally speaking, we are all just his "boys and girls," and even Billy, our mascot, who is in person a very lovable and frolicsome little he-goat, comes in for a big share of affection from the greatest little man in the world.

So strong for Billy is Charlie Chaplin that if any of us became tempted to teach his goatship to butt us and indulge in rough and vulgar goat-play, we are severely called down for it.

"Don't make him butt," pleads the inimitable Charlie. "All goats butt. Let's be different in our goat as much as in our work. That's the true principle of success, provided you don't differ in the wrong direction. And butting is very wrong." This last was addressed to the goat, who promptly showed his respect for the world's most popular artiste by climbing all over his shoulders.

I suppose there are quite a few who would have liked to be "Billy" for just that moment?

15

Charlie Poses for
The Fireman

June 17, 1916

I don't think I have ever seen Charlie work at such a speed as he has done during the past week, and neither have I ever known him to be so impatient. His custom in other days has always been to take whatever length of time has happened to be necessary over his work, but on this *Fireman* picture he has been trying to make the work do battle with Father Time. The least delay has occasioned him displeasure, either with himself, or with the person who was responsible for it.

Consequently, for the first time since the early Keystone days he has completed all the interior scenes—i.e., the various rooms in the fire station—and has got halfway through the exteriors, which form the balance of the story, all within a space of twelve days.

Putting this side by side with his seven weeks' stunt under the Essanay contract—I refer to the making of *Charlie Shanghaied*—this looked rather remarkable and significant. So I ventured to approach Charlie upon the subject, quite expecting an unsatisfactory answer, be it confessed. But to my surprise he let me into the secret; he intends to get ahead of his stipulated time for the output of each picture till he is some week and a half to the good, and then he wants to cart the whole outfit—lock, stock and barrel—out into the middle of the Pacific Ocean for the making of something really new and original.

I don't mean that he is going to dump us all down into the sea, and start a story of Neptune and the sea myths; but there is a little spot away out which once belonged to the British Flag, but has now been annexed by the U.S.A., called the Hawaiian Islands, the capital whereof is Honolulu. That, if Charlie keeps to his intention, will form the locale of the story in question. He has mapped out the plot to me, and although it is a little reminiscent of a certain West End play I once saw in my London days, it has been Chaplinised—and will doubtless be Chaplinised still further before it sees a screen—until only the mere thread of the story of the play will remain. *[Goodwins is almost certainly referring to J. M. Barrie's* The Admirable Crichton, *an enormous theatrical success from 1902 about a butler who assumes the leadership role when he and his employers are shipwrecked on a deserted island. This, of course, set the template for the Jeeves-Wooster stories and many other film, stage, and literary variants featuring smart servants who must rescue their inept masters. A few months after this article came out Chaplin would use the resourceful employee–inept employer idea in* Behind the Screen, *which is set in a movie studio rather than on an island, and a few months after that he would stage shipboard antics (but no shipwreck) in* The Immigrant. *And in the end he did go to Hawaii, but only for a brief vacation after he had completed his series for Mutual.]*

Perhaps this is a little premature, however; what I set out to do was to give the explanation of Charlie's hurry.

After he had done talking to me about these future plans, he turned to his bouillon—for he has dropped the habit of eating luncheon now that the tropical weather is with us once more—and sipped it thoughtfully.

"How's the war going?" he asked presently. "I wish I had time away from my thoughts to read the papers more than I do. What's that you've got—a bundle of English papers?"

I removed the covering from a parcel I had just received from the office and opened it. His guess had been right; the parcel contained four illustrated dailies, six weeklies, and a monthly magazine, sent to me by a thoughtful mater.

I handed him one of the dailies, and he opened it with his disengaged hand. The contents appeared to interest him more than a little, particularly one large photograph of a Zeppelin which had been brought down by our boys at the front.

"Fine!" he exclaimed, and his eyes flashed. "What a lovely mess!"

For fully five minutes this picture engrossed his attention, and then he began to alternately imbibe his broth and turn the pages of the paper, what time I read a letter from home.

"Dear, dear!" he exclaimed presently, and I looked up to see what had gotten him now. He was gazing at a picture of the late Maurice Farkoa, a notice of whose passing away appeared beneath the illustration. "Poor old Farkoa—I knew him awfully well. Fancy his being dead!" *[Ten years earlier Chaplin had boarded with the Field family, and one of the other boarders, a schoolteacher, later told a reporter how he loved to entertain the residents with imitations of Farkoa and other famous performers. She also revealed another interesting experience she had with the budding comic: "One night I dressed him up in some of my clothes, and we spent an evening out as two girls without arousing the faintest suspicion"—an incident that Chaplin would resurrect in his Essanay film* A Woman.[1]*]*

"He was a foreigner, wasn't he?" I asked.

"A Frenchman, I think." answered Charlie. "He was wonderful in those little French characterisations of his." He paused a moment, then turned the page again. "We've all got to 'pass in our checks' some day," he said philosophically.

"You're getting sentimental," I warned him, as I had been wont to do when I saw him lapsing into a state of mind not consistent with the making of farce-comedy.

"No, I'm not," he said, "but there's no going away from it. Inside, say, fifty years not a beggar in this studio will be standing on his feet. No wonder the Japanese regard death as only the final adventure of life."

"Do you think that way?" I queried.

"I ought to, but I'm afraid I don't," he said. "It's the stuff real soldiers are made of. Even the Germans have lots of it in their ranks. That's why they're such daring spies."

We talked a while about the progress of the war, and presently he referred to the challenge that has been issued to him in various ways upon his absence from the front.

"I should be there," he said frankly. "I know I should, but I also know there are millions who ought to be there a great deal more than I. Think of what I have to give up if I go, think how little use I would be under a rifle, and weigh it in the balance with the question of whether I am of any use to the happiness of the world. Then is the time my critics will see where I stand. As a comedian I have—and I say it without undue egotism—achieved more fame and standing than any man in the annals of the whole profession of entertainment: as a soldier I would be less than a unit. It is a simple sum of arithmetic. Let my critics—the chief of them—take up arms in the struggle, however, and I will be glad to do the same, even giving up what I have fought a battle of life to attain." *[Chaplin is here trying to head off the negative publicity he was already receiving about his failure to enlist, which had been spurred by a "war" clause in the Mutual contract that forbade him to leave the country without the company's permission. On May 6* Red Letter, *which obviously had a vested interest in burnishing his public image, published an unintentionally ironic full-page cartoon strip—unrelated to Goodwins's article in that issue—featuring the Tramp abusing a posh, effeminate conscientious objector. Goodwins does his part by painting his boss as both saintly and brave in the remainder of the article. For more on the war clause, see appendix A.]*

I offer no comment for as a non-combatant myself I must necessarily hold my peace. To the critics be it said, however, whenever the Motherland calls specifically to us men in a neutral land she will not have to call a second time.

Charlie uses singularly few exterior scenes in his pictures of these later days, and, consequently, there are several hundred thousand inhabitants of Los Angeles who have never set eyes on their favourite in the flesh. But when the notice came that we were to take some material outside one of the local fire stations, I foresaw that we were going to give the natives a treat at the same time.

It takes about five minutes as a rule for a huge crowd to assemble whenever Charlie's camera men set up their equipment and begin to "shoot," and the day in question, far from being an exception to this rule, was a little more than usually the proof of it. It was a Saturday afternoon, you see, and the youngsters were on half-holiday—that is the explanation.

He worked like a Trojan in the morning, which was a beautiful sunny one, without a cloud visible in the blazing heavens. This, as a matter of fact, makes his industry all the more remarkable, for his strongest working days are dull, gloomy ones in which the light-diffusers have to be thrown back from the studio, leaving the natural cloud-light to fall direct upon the scenes. I suppose the explanation is not hard; he is an Englishman, you must remember, and a dull day is to us a natural one.

We got in a lot of fun that day, what with the kiddies and the real firemen with whom we mixed and Charlie's good spirits, which had been rather conspicuous by their absence during the past few weeks. And yet, as seems inevitable, there was also a touch of sentiment in some of the incidents; of these I shall tell you presently.

How those youngsters enjoyed the fun that day! No half-holiday had ever been quite so wonderful as that, for it was one that would never be duplicated. We never can duplicate that one, great epoch-making red letter day in our lives, can we? It may be a great moment of pride or one of pleasure in excelsis, or it may be some great love we have cherished and which has made us happy, but never, try as we will, can another such a one come to us again.

That is how it was with those kiddies; a whole afternoon of watching Charlie Chaplin act—for their especial amusement, as it doubtless seemed to them—was a thing apart from any event that ever had been or ever could be.

I have often tried to point out what a great amount of concentration is required to direct a Chaplin comedy, and consequently, I think, there was a great deal of credit due to Charlie in that he never once complained or gave sign of the slightest vexation at the incessant din that went on around him throughout the whole of that day. Those children kept up a running fire of remarks—some of them rather the reverse of well-mannered—interlarded with suggestions and irrelevant shouts, all directed at the head of their one and only idol. Yet he had a cheery word for all of them, and no really bright sally went by without drawing a smile from him.

It has always seemed to me, in my uncurbed youth, that there is nothing so absurdly funny as people who take themselves terribly seriously. Yet that is precisely how we ourselves must have appeared in the eyes of those children that day. They couldn't for the life of them see why we actors, who were enjoying the "Lark" of really taking part in the picture with Charlie, didn't laugh and roll on the grass whenever he conceived something really funny. To them it wasn't work, of course; it was just "movies"—the chief entertainment of their leisure hours. Yes, I imagine we must have been as much a joke to them as a super-serious person is to me.

The whole company was there on the location, for there were many exits from and entrances to the fire house, and all were likely to have at least one scene there. There must have been twenty of us, all told, including the stock company, consisting of Charlie, Edna, Eric Campbell, Lloyd Bacon, Charlotte Mineau, Albert Austin and myself, so that when a halt was called for luncheon it was a mighty concourse of people that wended its way towards a small and unoffending lunchroom that was hiding up a side street.

Space is too precious to allow of my describing at length the events of that lunchtime. Charlie was in his lunch-hour mood of frivolity—a rather remarkable thing since his broth diet compared so ill with our own mighty feats of trenchermanship *[hearty eating]*. He danced for us, kidded us unmercifully, kept changing the gramophone records, talked to the children who had strayed into the parlour; was, in fact, never still for a moment. But presently there came to him a child of but half-developed mentality. His vacant stare and hanging jaw were not pretty to behold, and some in this work-a-day world might have thoughtlessly ignored him after a cursory glance.

Not so Charlie.

The boy had brought with him an offering of a mere half-faded carnation, which he extended toward the little comedian with a semi-articulate greeting on his lips. Charlie took it gravely, and thanked the youngster with all sincerity in his tone. Then somebody laughed and made some reference to the effect that there was "nobody home"—a slang American expression meaning the subject is mentally deficient. In a trice Charlie turned his eyes upon the misguided jester. They bore an expression of mild reproach, untempered by any suspicion of real anger.

"Don't say that," he almost pleaded. "Poor little kid," and he turned back to the half-wit and kissed him on the forehead.

That is all there is of the incident. What there is speaks for itself.

The afternoon was even busier than the morning had been, but finally the sun went down behind the distant mountains and the time had come for us to pack up our goods and return to the studio. What a rousing cheer those kiddies gave as Charlie's car drove by! He waved them au revoir as we left them astern, and presently we turned the corner of the street. Our way led us past the little lunchroom wherein we had refreshed the inner man that day. The gramophone was still playing and the tune was aptly enough—"The End of a Perfect Day."[2]

For more than one infantile heart it had been a perfect day indeed.

Next day came the more serious side of the picture—that little touch of drama which Charlie proposes to incorporate in all his Mutual Productions this year. In this case the plot, which strongly resembles that of *Charlie Shanghaied*, deals with an incendiary father, who, after having set fire to his mansion (presumably for insurance purposes) discovers he has locked his own daughter up in the burning building. To cut a long story short, it is, of course, Charlie who finally effects the rescue of the maiden, who finishes up by eloping with him. *[Actually, they just walk off together.]*

That all sounds perfectly nice, quite Chaplinesque, and perfectly easy—on paper. But when it comes down to getting at it, why, that's a horse of another colour.

I suppose Charlie has to be original, and that is why he disdained to use any ladders or ropes in performing the rescue. But I can't for the life of me see why he chose to endanger his 10,000-dollars-a-week life for the sake of creating a thrill. Yet this is what he did.

The building which had to be burnt down, and which had been especially built for *The Fireman*, was three storeys high, and had a stuccoed front with several jutting ledges of masonry worked into its design. The object whereof, as it turned out, was to furnish foot-hold for Charlie, who climbed up the front of the building to the topmost floor, at times completely enveloped in smoke in order to create a thrill.

Of course, we tried to dissuade him from doing it. He has never had to stoop to mere "stunt" stuff in order to get his effects with the public, but for once he was quite beyond advice. He wanted to climb that building, and not all the King's horses nor all the King's men could have stopped him.

So the cameras were set up at a distance sufficiently near to just get the entire building. The fire and smoke was started up, Edna was placed on the top floor, and the cameras clicked.

He got up within a space of about seven seconds, as the picture will show when it comes your way, but when it came to making the return, with Edna clasped around his shoulders, that was a different proposition, I assure you, for Charlie weighs about seven stones and ten pounds, while Edna has fully two stones the advantage of him. *[Goodwins's claim that Chaplin weighs about 108 pounds to Edna's 138 is untrue as well as ungallant. Chaplin weighed about 125 pounds during this period, and he carries Edna with apparent ease in a number of films. Goodwins may have been trying to make Chaplin's rescue stunt seem more impressive, and he does scamper up and down the wall with great agility. But no viewer is likely to confuse Edna with one of the least convincing dummies in movie history. This dummy was obviously the intended recipient of Edna's life mask, described in the last installment; however, only the back of the wig shows.]*

Imagine, then, Charlie, nimble though he is, jeopardising his life and hers in that risky downward climb. Yet he seemed all devoid of trepidation. Even

Charlie rescues Edna in *The Fireman*.

when once he missed his footing and caught it again his heart-beat seemed more normal than ours. I don't mind confessing for my part that I was in what is vulgarly termed a "blue funk" throughout the whole business, but when finally he landed on terra firma, and handed his burden over to us, we couldn't help giving him a round of applause for his daring.

It pleased him, beyond a shadow of a doubt, yet, as I say, he doesn't have to do those things in order to make a hit. It reminds me rather of Caruso stooping from his pedestal and singing "Boiled Beef and Carrots," or something of similar classical pretension.

Yet—and the saying is older than the hills of California—"the King can do no wrong."

And who shall say that Charlie Chaplin is not, in his own line, the monarch of monarchs?

• • •

In a recent issue of the *Red Letter* I inadvertently referred to Charlie Chaplin's "co-director." This reference was noticed by Mr Chaplin, who has asked me to correct the mistake. The expression should have been "studio manager." Mr Chaplin has never had any assistance in either the direction or writing of his stories, and my statement was a pure slip of the pen.—Fred Goodwins.

16

Charlie Chaplin's Love for His Mother

June 24, 1916

After a strenuous two weeks *The Fireman* is at last an accomplished fact and the film is speeding on its way to New York City.

I have seen it run three times in the projecting-room here, and haven't a scruple in declaring it to be one of the most technically perfect—indeed, the most technically perfect picture—Charlie Chaplin has ever turned out.

Presumably a man has his "off" periods, followed by a reactionary spell, which enables him to turn out some flawless work, and that is how it seems to have been with Charlie, for *The Fireman* shows conclusively that he was well into his stride once more while it was in the making, and this is what, to my way of thinking, his previous effort, *The Floorwalker*, lacked.

He seemed, in the first picture, to be apprehensive, scared of himself, over-anxious not to make some blunder which would lead people to think him unworthy of his wonderful new salary, and, to my hypercritical eye it seems to show on the screen. But *The Fireman* was another proposition altogether. The effects of his long vacation in New York had worn off, and he was, as I say, into his stride—the keen, hard-thinking, fertile mind that has afforded joy to such countless millions in bygone days was itself again. Thus *The Fireman* has either a laugh or a thrill to every other foot of its length, and not once does the interest lag. *[Interestingly, while both films were rapturously received by the public at the time,* The Fireman *came to be considered one of the weakest of the Mutuals. Goodwins's negative assessment of* The Floorwalker *may have been influenced by his witnessing the way Chaplin agonized over it.]*

When I speak of Charlie having regained his old form do not misunderstand me by thinking that the making of *The Fireman* has been a cinch—or, to use a British slang expression with the same import, "pie-easy." It has involved every bit as much concentrated thought, as many sleepless nights, and the exercise of as much discretion as anything he has ever conceived. Only the situations came more freely to his mind, fell into shape with more precision, and so saved a lot of time that would otherwise have been wasted.

After the events of my last story, yet another specially-built house was set on fire for the purpose of certain scenes of the picture, and the results obtained by the camera men far exceeded the expectations of even the exacting Charles.

The cottage, which was built solidly of wood and decorated by experienced men, was a picture to look upon. Its light blue paintwork, clear crystal windows, and immaculate little front garden made it seem a pity that it was doomed to destruction merely to create an incident in a two-reel comedy.

But you cannot serve your scruples and the public as well, so the basement of the little home was filled with shavings and satured [*sic*—saturated] with petrol and turpentine, and the fun began.

At first, in accordance with the demands of the story, only a mere suggestion of smoke issued from the door and windows. Then out rushed the excitable Frenchman (played by Leo White) to whom the house is supposed to belong and telephoned to the fire station, the latter scene being, of course, photographed later upon another spot.

This left the building unoccupied and free to burn in Hadean fury. Bit by bit the flames increased as fuel was added to the existing fire, and then, for a final scene, the whole of the basement was touched with a brand, and burst into a pillar of flame which shot twenty feet above the roof. I don't suppose one of those present had ever seen a conflagration gain ground with such speed as did that one. There was not a part of the whole structure that was not enveloped in flame, and the heat was unbearable.

Those of us who were not working in the scene took a hurried leave from the vicinity while Charlie, shielding his face with his megaphone, stood by the camera-men until the lenses of the machine threatened to crack with the expansion. Then, unable to stand the heat any longer, he bolted, and the camera-men, seizing their valuable instruments in their scorched hands, dragged them back into a less torrid zone.

We couldn't help giving them a round of applause for their endurance, and that round was followed by another one next day when the result of the ordeal was shown upon our private screen. I dare swear that not one of my readers has ever been as close to an actual fire as the big conflagration scene in *The Fireman* will bring them.

As the fire died down somewhat, those of us who were playing firemen parts rushed in to enact a scene which shows us all industriously rushing about in front of the building, and doing nothing in the world. The film scene is a good deal funnier than the burns we sustained from falling sparks. But there was balm in Gilead even then, for, just as we were wondering how much longer we were to be kept between the camera and the flames Charlie turned the fire-hose on us. The first gush caused me to do a "cut-up" onto my neck, the like of which I shall never duplicate by trying as long as I live—and I certainly don't intend to try.

As may be well supposed, a soaking in hundreds of gallons of water with a pressure like the kick of a mule is no garden-party, but it was far preferable to the terrible heat of that fire, upon which it acted as a sort of antidote. Only I do wish they'd warn us when we're in for a soaking—just so that we can be sure there's a stray suit or clean underwear kicking around the dressing-room, you know. Still, I personally didn't bother long on this point. Charlie's underwear is not so small that I can't wear it!

All that remained after the burning of the two buildings was the "chase" faction[1] of the story, showing Charlie rushing away from the fire at the Frenchman's house, to the larger one at the home of Edna's father, and it was in this part of the story that we began to realise why springs are generally used in making vehicles. As I told you last week, our technical director had thoughtfully omitted anything in the nature of shock-absorbers from the fire-engine, and consequently the vibration of the latter as it tore along the road at forty-five miles an hour with two mettlesome horses at the pole was so violent that the whole landscape seemed to be oscillating to and fro.

But the chase was accomplished successfully, and without any serious in-jury to life or limb, and then came the great breakaway. This was where the engine, bearing the distracted father and driven by Charlie, is speeding to-wards the burning house of the former, when suddenly the whole conveyance is supposed to part in the middle, leaving the fore part of the engine, with its two occupants clinging to it, to go to the fire. This pleasant little incident was arranged by means of a spring-lock to which a wire was attached in such a way that, when Lloyd Bacon (who plays the father) pulled at it, it would release the spring and leave the boiler half of the engine behind.

In order to facilitate the separation of the two parts, and also to give some logical excuse for the accident, a stretch of road was chosen which had a miniature trench right in the middle of it.

The cameras were set up, the engine drawn back to several hundred yards behind them, and Charlie, perched on the box, gave the signal to "shoot"—an expressive Americanism, applicable to anything at all, which means "Go!" Simultaneously he whipped up the horses, and the engine, swaying and skidding from side to side, whirled past the cameras in a cloud of dust. All went well until it struck the ditch; we could see Lloyd Bacon tugging at the wire, and then, as the rear wheels crashed over the rut which preceded the trench, the vehicle parted. But the speed was so terrific, and the bump so violent, that the break-away justified its name in a way that was as thrilling as it was unexpected, for the whole boiler, with all its fittings, tore loose from the base of the vehicle and went hurtling through the air.

At first we all gripped our hands in terror, for the heavy metal boiler had fallen upon the very spot where, but a fraction of a second earlier, we had seen Lloyd tugging at the wire. The clouds of dust prevented our seeing whether or not our comrade was safe, but presently it settled, and we discerned with unmixed relief, the forward half of the engine careering away into the distance, bearing two very live figures with it. The camera-man ceased to crank, and, taking out a handkerchief, mopped his brow.

"Gee!" he exclaimed. "I sure thought Charlie and Lloyd had gone up that trip!"

And we all agreed.

When, a minute later, the dismantled vehicle drove round the corner with Charlie at the helm, so to speak, and Lloyd clinging casually to the back of the driver's seat, we gave them a cheer and a round of applause. But Charlie raised an eyebrow enquiringly.

"What's that for?" he grinned. "Are you kidding me?"

Neither he nor Lloyd had been even aware that the boiler had broken loose.

This incident, too, makes a wonderful showing on the screen, as my readers will have an opportunity of judging within a very few weeks after these notes are in print.

Then came a scene where the firemen, in a body, are tearing after the fugitive engine, having left the Frenchman's house to burn itself out! During this run the fire-chief, played by Eric Campbell (the huge English comedian whose work in a dozen pantomimes back home will be remembered by thousands of my readers), falls headlong down a pit which had been dug in the road.

But for a wonder Los Angeles—which some wit has named "the City of Torn-Up Streets"—hadn't a hole or pit of any description within miles of the studio. It became necessary, then, to overcome the difficulty by doing a little street-tearing on our own account, so various members of the company stationed themselves as spies and outposts at odd corners of the location, and our staff of manual workers, hastily summoned from the studio, dug a hole in that roadway that was at least eight feet long and four feet deep (as it needed to be in order to securely contain the person of the ponderous Eric!). The L.A. Council inspector might chance along that way at any moment, we feared, and we might be brought to account for ripping up without due authority a portion of the United States. But for once the law of cussedness, which usually brings the minions of the law proper upon a location at the crucial moment, was out of office, and we were allowed to "depict" without interruption.

That same night the last scenes of the picture were filmed, and Charlie, removing his fireman's helmet, threw it into the air and shouted, "Hurray! Another one off the fire!" But then he shrugged his shoulders and added, "And now I start worrying again about the next one."

There was as much philosophy as truth in that remark of his, for that has been his life ever since he became his own director. No sooner has one picture been completed and made ready for shipment to headquarters than he has had to start on another, so that his existence, well remunerated though it is, has never ceased to be one round of work and mental exertion. The winding-up of each picture always makes me think of the time-honoured proclamation in Great Britain, "The King is dead! long live the King!"

Charlie generally allows himself a little relaxation on the night of the finishing-up of each picture, so it was no surprise to me to see him that evening at the local prize fights. He is an ardent devotee of the fistic sport, and whenever a more than usually exciting bout is in progress it is amusing to watch him out of the corner of an eye. His behaviour seems to me to be so much a part of his art that I find in it the true expression of his genius for assuming with heart and soul whatever character he happens to be playing when at work.

At a prize fight his eyes never leave the ring for an instant, and so quick is his perception that he anticipates almost every blow that is delivered by the combatants, his clenched fists working convulsively into upper-cuts, swings, and jabs. Of course, he is totally unconscious that he is reproducing the actions of the fighters, but the spirit of the thing strikes his receptive brain, and he is oblivious to all else. It merely brings us back to what I said some weeks ago—that Charlie, when he assumed a character, either the one he has made famous throughout the world or any other, seems to pass through a complete metamorphosis, becoming for the time being the character itself.

A fellow of my acquaintance who knew Charlie long before I did once told me that, with proper training and a life that afforded better opportunities for regularity of living than the stage, Charlie Chaplin would have been a candidate to be reckoned with for the lightweight championship of the boxing world. His sprightliness and lightness on his feet would seem to indicate that there is more than a little likelihood in this statement, but what the world of sport has lost the world in general has gained, so there is no time for regrets upon this score.

Charlie did not go home until very late that night, for he wanted to tire himself out so that he might sleep far into the following day, arising in the early afternoon. This procedure was less eccentric than would appear, for the next night was set for the cutting-down and assembling of the negative of the picture, an operation which is invariably left for the still watches of the night, because they are still.

It was six a.m. before the cutting committee got through their arduous task, by which time the sun was rising above the treetops in the East. They all felt horribly stale, utterly silly—for hysteria invariably sets in on an all-night session of brain-work—and ready to sleep in the middle of the studio floor. The only bright living thing of the lot was Billy, our pet goat, who greeted the toilers with a cheery bleat and gamboled up and down the grass plot which is his especial domain, as if to say, "This is how you guys should feel first thing in the morning."

But the cutters all, from Charlie to the laboratory boy, were but ill-disposed to gambol, and so a couple of touring cars, hired from a neighbouring garage, bore them, fast asleep, to their respective homes.

Charlie did not show up until mid-afternoon of the same day, and the first thing that greeted him on his arrival was a large flat package. He opened it casually, but when his eyes rested on its contents he gave a perceptible start. It contained a picture of his mother—the only one in existence.

For fully ten minutes he walked around the office, looking at it from every angle, and then he sat down and looked at it some more. He had not seen his mother for many years, and the portrait, it was clear, brought back a world of memories to his mind. Just what they were none could tell, but shortly afterwards he took me down town to my residence, and then it was that I gleaned something of a side of him I had not seen before. He had never referred to his mother in my presence on any previous occasion.

The evening coolness was descending on the boulevard as we bowled along townwards, and he drew the motor-rug over his knees and threw the other end to me. In a few moments he, Edna and I, were snugly wrapped in its folds, but a minute later he let it slide from his limbs, and, leaning forward, stood the big portrait up against the footrest before us.

"There she is," he murmured affectionately. "After all those years, and in all my achievements, I've just got a photograph of her to look at. Do you know, I'd almost forgotten what she was like. Even with all those dearest to us we lose sight after a while of the outlines and expression of the face. This picture coming to-day brings it all back to me."

Neither Edna nor I made any comment, for we knew Charlie well enough to know he wanted to stay lost in his contemplation of the sick woman's likeness. Presently he spoke again.

"Lord, how you've suffered!" he said, half to himself. "Not I nor anybody else knows just how much, and not a fraction of it will ever be told."

I surveyed the picture closely in compliance with his request, and noted the striking resemblance he bore her. The likeness was a remarkable one, bringing out the character of the woman's face in a manner all unusual for such a primitive era in the photographic art—for it was taken fully twenty years ago.

Indeed, except for the difference in the character of the clothing, one might have thought it to be a picture of Charlie in one of the two female impersonations he has given during his motion-picture career *[He had actually done three,* A Busy Day *and* The Masquerader *at Keystone, and* A Woman at Essanay]. She had the same shaped forehead, the same expression of the mouth, the same contour of the chin. Only the expression of her eyes differed somewhat from Charlie's in that they were less thoughtful, less those of an habitual dreamer.

She was a woman of education and fine principles, Charlie said, one who had drifted into the profession more from force of happenings than from any actual ambition. And yet she had been clever in her art, and family affairs had tended more than aught else to drive her into such privations as she had endured at just about the time of Charlie's birth.

There is much that he told me that I may not recount, the kind of intimacies that one only writes of after the demise of the persons concerned in them, but what he said served to add yet another notch in the tree of excellent qualities I had already erected to my friend.

Every man who is halfway worthy of the name loves his mother, you say! Assuredly so, but the depth of Charlie Chaplin's love for his, together with the circumstances attendant upon that love, seem to me to make it different, a matter for intense admiration of the man upon this score alone—and yet one for a tender feeling of sympathy.

In years to come it will probably all be told, but not now.

17

Chaplin's Success in *The Floorwalker*

July 1, 1916

The Fireman was finished, but the days of idleness between the dispatching of the negative and the starting of the third Chaplin-Mutual picture lengthened into a week, and still the comedian made no move to recommence work.

I wondered at first why he was "stalling" and one day ventured to question him on the subject. I knew he was not lost for ideas. He always has at least half-a-dozen outline plots in his head. His answer explained the cause of his delay, but vaguely, as it seemed to me then.

"You haven't even ordered the carpenters to put up any scenes for your next subject," I reminded him tentatively.

"No," he agreed, "I know." A long pause ensued, then—"I'm waiting till Sunday." I looked at him quizzically.

"Going to work on Sunday, are you?" I asked.

"Work on Sunday?" he repeated, looking at me as if I were a brand of idiot quite new to him. "Of course not, chump. On Sunday we all go and see the first run of the first Mutual picture. It's down town at the Garrick."

So that was the reason, although at the time I could not quite see the connection between the release of the first picture which was, as you will remember, *The Floorwalker* and the inordinate delay he was allowing between his stories.

Sunday came and with it a morning of glorious sunshine. I don't think I have ever breathed the air of such a gorgeous day as that was. It was cool, despite the dazzling sunshine, for a gentle northerly breeze had sprung up with the rising of Old Sol, and served to temper the heat.

I sallied forth then with the air of springtime upon me. I was clad in a perfectly good new suit of Scotch tweed—for which, by the way, the enterprising American tailor had bashfully soaked me nearly eight guineas—and was at peace with the world. Motion pictures and such like horrible things were far from my mind at that time. I was, in fact, debating whether it was to be a trip to the beach or a round of golf "for mine." But fate settled the doubt for me by leading my steps past the Garrick Theatre.

Of course, you don't need to be told the rest. Being but human I fell. Inside forty seconds the sunshine and breezes were forgotten, and I was ensconced in a tenpenny seat in a palatial, but utterly sunless, picture theatre among a "capacity" crowd, which was yelling its head off at the antics which had cost Charlie such hours of patient thought.

I described to you in an earlier issue what an amount of trouble he took over the situations in *The Floorwalker*; told you of the hours and hours we spent in waiting around, killing time while he concentrated his mind (then all out of training) upon his points. But what I did not tell you, because you would not have believed me, was that waiting and stalling had so sickened us all, including Charlie, of the whole thing, that we got it into our heads it was going to fall more than a trifle flat when the public came to see it.

Believe me, friends, the only thing that was flat in the Garrick Theatre that afternoon was the floor itself.

I am a pretty good booster, you know, and, if certain people are to be believed, a pretty facile exaggerator at times, but I am ready to make affidavit before a commissioner that I have never in the whole course of my life heard such a riot of laughter as that which reigned in the Garrick on the morning of Sunday, May 14. Hardly once during the whole forty minutes of the run was there a lull in the mirth of that audience. *[A forty-minute running time for* The Floorwalker—*or any two-reeler—seems exceptionally long. It was standard practice in the silent era to speed up comedies, and the average two-reeler lasted between twenty and twenty-four minutes. While projection speed varied from theatre to theatre, at forty minutes* The Floorwalker *would have been shown at close to real-life speed. Seeing a Chaplin film that way is fascinating, but much of the humor evaporates without the extra kick that speeded-up action lends to his movement. We know from the shooting logs of* Modern Times *(1936), the first film in which Chaplin used a motorized camera, that at that time his preferred speedup for silent sequences was between 25 and 30 percent. Recent restorations of* The Floorwalker *run roughly 30 percent faster than real life and last around twenty-nine minutes.[1]]* Some of them were even screaming hysterically at times, and I couldn't help feeling a kind of thrill that I had in some small way participated in a picture that could sway thousands of people daily in [one] small city alone.

It will require a fellow-worker in the motion picture business to fully understand me when I say that the difference between *The Floorwalker* as I saw it privately run in the little projecting room at the studio, and *The Floorwalker* the public saw that day is like a comparison between the traditional chalk and cheese. It was to me like another picture, with all that audience around me laughing themselves into tears, and I began to realise what Charlie had meant when, many weeks ago, he told me that "it is not ourselves that are great; it is our greatness in relation to others that counts."

Oh, yes, I laughed as much as the best of them, even if I was perfectly aware of what was coming in every situation. In a way I may have enjoyed the picture even more than some of them, for my association with Charlie during the past twelve months has kind of educated me up to the spirit of his humour, and little points, subtle to a degree, past by quite a number of people that day, while their full value came home on me every time.

I don't mean that to sound like a pat on the back for my own perception; it is simply a proof of Chaplin's cleverness in that he is something to which a person has to be educated, in a sense, before he can appeal to them at his full value.

It was only eleven in the morning, yet the house, which has a seating capacity of over six hundred, was full to standing. I left there with a feeling of elation at the lovely come back I would now have at the jealous critics who are forever pointing out to me that "Chaplin is done." If being "done" means making 4300 people in one theatre of one town in one day laugh their heads off for forty minutes each, why, then I wish that I, too, were "done."

I spent the remainder of the day with Jack Pickford at the Athletic Club, and afterwards went to dine with a friend at Levy's Restaurant. Charlie was there in full regalia—at least, that is what it must have been intended for, consisting as it did of a silk shirt with a perfectly outrageous stripe, a black jacket, striped white trousers, brown shoes, and the need of a shave.

I rather wanted to avoid meeting him just for a while, for I felt I'd broken bounds in getting to the Garrick beforehand instead of waiting for the regular party, so I stood myself at an opposite corner of the big dining hall, leaving instructions for my friend to be sent there when he arrived.

But there's no rest for the wicked. As I made my way toward the door an hour and a half later Charlie caught sight of me and called me over to him. I knew what was coming and I was right.

"Have you seen the picture?" he asked eagerly.

I lied glibly, but softly, as if that extenuated my misdemeanour.

"Oh," he murmured, "I thought perhaps you had. I wanted to ask you how it was?"

"It's great, Charlie," I exclaimed, falling into it beautifully.

"Why, how do you know if you haven't seen it?" he fired back at me. I grinned like an ass, and suggested that we should all start off to the show since the time of our arrangement was nearly at hand. He nodded, and the whole party of seven strolled round to the theatre, for it is only one street away.

When we got there, a sight for the gods greeted our eyes. There was a crowd of over three hundred people waiting to get into the already packed house, and Manager Caulfield of our studio was dancing excitedly up and down the sidewalk with a camera man in tow, shooting flashlight pictures of the bunch from every available angle. It was a jubilee, and how Charlie laughed. But I saw his little chest swell up like a pouter pigeon as he beheld them. I wonder if he realised that they represented but a ten-thousandth part of his world-wide circle of worshippers?

Of course, a lot of them recognised him, for there is no face or head of shaggy hair like his in the wide world, and on various sides could be heard remarks such as, "There he is," "That's Charlie," "T'isn't; he hasn't got a moustache and Charlie has," and so on, all of which were lost on Charlie, who was waiting in his fidgety way for the manager to come and show us to the seats he had set aside for us. In a few minutes we were watching a public run of *The Floorwalker* for the first time (with the exception of one guilty wretch in the party).

No need for me to describe how Charlie received the picture. He always acts in one of two ways when he is at a first public showing. He either sits and smiles quietly all through (if the picture is flawless and is going strongly with the people) or, if it contains some errors or faults he tears his mane of hair,

Original release poster for *The Floorwalker*.

and anathematises moving pictures in general, and Charles Spencer Chaplin in particular.

But, since the first Chaplin-Mutual picture is from a public viewpoint a splendid success, he only sat and smiled. Even the yells and whistles of welcome that went up when he appeared on the screen, after a long absence from the public gaze, left him unmoved beyond a wider smile. He was still, as he evidently always will be, "Charlie," and one of the boys.

The next day he had to attend a big function at the home of a local society woman, which was given on behalf of the fatherless children of France. He seldom consents to giving his services for functions of this sort, partly because his calls are so numerous, and partly because of his natural bashfulness about publically exhibiting himself. But the mere mention of France settled the matter out of court, so to speak, for, without a second thought he said he would go.

And so the starting of the third Mutual picture was pushed along the calendar yet another day.

It seems that the way of the doer of good is as hard as that of the transgressor is supposed to be, for Charlie was bored to the verge of tears that day, so his secretary told me. He is no great admirer of the section of our social scheme which is known as society, and it was only the fact of the greatness of their cause that had enticed him out of his nest into the glare of personal publicity.

I remember his having spoken to me once about society as he saw it, and he has had a great deal of chance to see it since the world has hailed him as jester-in-chief. It was while we were dressing after the day's work on *Police*, that memorable day when he had such a long, philosophical talk with me before he took a hurried departure.

It isn't complimentary, but he said he didn't care who knew it, so here goes.

"They're cruel," he declared, speaking of fashionable folk as a majority. "They're cynical, bitter, hard as a grindstone, they turn everything to their own ends, irrespective of what it means to others. Even their charity is only a sort of fashion with them, and only does good incidentally and in a secondary way. I could accept their invitations if I wanted to. I could be feted and lauded and frothed over, but I've no desire to be a toy. And that's all I would be— something to amuse them while I happen to be Charlie Chaplin, the vogue of the day, and after that, rich or poor. What'd be the use even if I cared for it?

I'm greater than ninety percent of them, and I say it because I believe it. Why should I give off all my personal magnetism and fritter my brains for the tinsel of life? There's not a chance."

He did not speak in any personal sense, but that has been his impression, gathered from the examples he has seen of the world's upper half-million, or whatever they number.

On this event they feted him to rights. Thousands had flocked to see the greatest of comedians and to shake him by the hand, and thousands, it is presumed, radically changed their opinions of the great little star when they had gripped his hand and basked in one of those inimitably magnetic smiles of his. I judge so from the few remarks that were heard on various sides.

"Dear me," said one old dame, who was sitting in all her adipose glory at a pea-nut stand and studiously devouring those nourishing articles of diet. "Charlie Chaplin? Yes, yes, to be sure. I've never seen him, but I hear he's very vulgar." And she raised her lorgnette to survey the being who, "vulgar" though he was presumed to be, was evidently not too vulgar for her gaze. I imagine it would be hard to be too vulgar for such a female as that to gaze upon.

Charlie told me next day that there were many such remarks as those flying about, but he took them all with the fixed smile he had coined for the occasion. To him it had been merely a proof of what he had told me all those weeks ago. *[Skewering the snooty rich would play well with the working and middle-class readers of the* Red Letter, *but Chaplin's deep ambivalence about wealth and the wealthy was no mere pose, and his outrage over social injustice would permeate his greatest films.]*

Next day he had the motion pictures which had been taken of the event (for the benefit of the *Mutual Weekly*) run off for us to see.

What hundreds of youngsters there were! As Charlie put it, it seemed as if every man, woman and child in southern California had come there on purpose to shake hands with him, for his hand was aching and swollen by the time he had been able to slip off in his automobile.

"Oh, you thundering hypocrite!" he laughed as his vision flashed upon the screen in the projecting room. "Look at that wooden smile I've got on my map, and all the while I'm wishing them to the furthermost ends of the earth. I smiled for six hours yesterday, and my face felt too cramped to eat when I landed in Levy's afterwards."

Then, as he left the projecting-room, he added melodramatically, "But, thank Heaven I have done somewhat in the cause of charity!" And he flung his hat into the air.

That afternoon he intended to start work on his new story, which is to be entitled *The Vagabond*, and to deal with life in a Romany gipsy camp, ending up in the circles of the society that he regards so critically. But lunchtime brought to the studio no less a personage than his colleague of other days—to wit, Will Poluski, jun., and once again *The Vagabond* received a jolt. It seems that "Billy," as we always called him, is on a pleasure trip though the U.S.A. accompanying his wife (Rosie Lloyd) on her tour of the Western vaudeville circuit. He says "it is costing him the earth, and that it isn't worth it except for the sake of seeing old Charlie again."

Charlie was as pleased as Punch to see Will once more, and if there was a little vanity in his pleasure (for Will was doing fifteen-pounds-a-week stuff when Charlie was only supporting him at three pounds in the days of Karno's *Football Match*), why, it was harmless vanity, and as well meant as could be. *[The two performed* The Football Match *often between 1908 and 1910. The sketch was Chaplin's apprenticeship piece with the company, and while he didn't get along well with the lead, Harry Weldon, he and Poluski, who played the second lead, obviously bonded during their time together, as indicated by the red carpet treatment Chaplin extends. Poluski's wife, Rosie, was the sister of the celebrated Marie Lloyd, an enormously popular music hall star who was notorious for her suggestive material.]*

Be that as it may, he assuredly showed Billy a good time thereafter, and still is, for the matter of that, for at the time of writing Billy has not yet left town.

Wasn't he just glad to see us all, too! There are three Karno boys on our plant you will remember, viz Charlie, Eric Campbell, and Albert Austin, and several other Englishmen besides, so that after that tedious and rather lonesome tour through the Middle West of America, it was like coming into an oasis in the desert to suddenly burst in on a bunch of fellow-countrymen and colleagues like that.

Of course, nothing would do for Charlie but that Billy should come along with us to the canyon and watch us film the opening scenes of *The Vagabond*, and Billy, having nothing in particular to do, was mightily pleased to avail himself of the chance.

He is a wonderfully affable chap and he seemed to bring with him a breath of the old country—which I have not seen for two and a half years—besides which his unaltered London dialect sounded refreshing to our ears, long accustomed to the burr of the American accent.

So to-day he came out with us in one of the five automobiles, and joined in the fun of making a rustic picture, and it was rather amusing to watch him sitting in Charlie's car by the side of the gipsy camp, watching in wonder the doings of the boy who, so short a while back that it seems to us all but yesterday, was a mere supporting comedian to him, but who now has attained the greatest heights of fame in the history of show business.

Elsewhere I have spoken of Charlie's talent as a musician, and to-day he gave such an exhibition of it as he never did before. When he was not working—and he did not so much in that line, as a matter of fact—he was strolling up and down the lane beside which we have built our gipsy camp, dreamily playing, left-handed beyond all hope.

He was playing Mendelssohn's "Song of Spring."

The air must have gotten into his blood methinks, for it was springtime such as only California can produce. In other words, it was what London would call "deucedly hot."

This remark reminds me of something Charlie said when he came back from New York.

"Do you fellows realise," he asked, "that what we call a cold day out here would be considered furiously hot in England? Do you realise that when we go back we are going to feel as cold as ice half the year round, after being in the heat of California so long?"

He thought a while and unconsciously shivered.

"When I go home," he propounded, "I'm going to take the Californian climate back with me."

18

A Chaplin Rehearsal Isn't All Fun

July 8, 1916

Charlie's third Mutual story, *The Vagabond*, is well on its way to completion. Although nothing more will be done on it for the next three days or so, because of circumstances I shall relate presently it is going to be a pippin when it finally sees New York.

After stalling around, and generally murdering his valuable time while Billy Poluski was in Los Angeles, Charlie suddenly got a work-jag on him, and started in to rattle off scenes as if the picture were due for shipment within the next two days, instead of the next two weeks. I imagine he was rather disgusted with himself for having devoted so much time to basking in the canyon air, or perhaps his old friend's visit had unconsciously put "pep" into him. Anyway, whatever the reason, he tore into *The Vagabond* on the day of Poluski's departure for San Diego without letting up for a moment.

Yet the picture did not suffer in quality because of his sudden and unaccustomed burst of energy. He had just as many "re-takes" as usual on every scene, and was just as hard to satisfy, too, so that our end of the making was quite a bit strenuous. There wasn't a fall that any of us made that didn't have to be taken over and over again before Charlie was pleased and assured that he had among the number at least one good "take" of it. That has always been his method—and presumably always will be.

The Vagabond is one of those little heart-interest stories that he promised us some weeks ago, you will remember. It deals, I understand, with a little waif who has been abducted by gipsies, whose chief hobby is to ill-treat her. But presently along comes a wandering minstrel (Charlie) playing plaintive melodies on his violin, and to him the girl relates her story. Afterwards, by a series of clever ruses and manoeuvres, such as only Chaplin knows how to conceive, all the gipsy tribe are "outed" one by one, and Charlie carries the girl away in their caravan, leaving her cruel captors all senseless by the roadside.

Upon this faction of the story we "fade out," and the next section shows the girl's return to her real high station in life. She is feted by everybody, painted by the peer of all painters, and the poor little vagabond who rescued her from her plight is left with nought to remember her by but the public view of her portrait which hangs in the gallery in the city. *[In the finished film the portrait is painted while Edna is still in the countryside with Charlie. When Edna's mother sees the portrait in a gallery she recognizes her daughter from a shamrock-shaped birthmark on her arm, precipitating the reunion.]*

My description of the backbone of the story is a lame one, I am aware. It takes a Chaplin to add the trimmings, and to shape the story with such technique as to make it worthy of his wonderful reputation as a director. But you can see for yourselves what possibilities such a theme holds for the great little star, with his quaintly, comically pathetic personality and his aptitude for the undoing of his aggressors, no matter what their number happens to be.

As is often the case in movie pictures, the last scenes of the gipsy section of the picture were taken first, and eight of us made up in various horrible disguises, and awaited the decisions of the "Great White Chief," as the American boys of the company jocularly call Charlie.

His decision was not long in coming. The chief thing in the faction was that we should all be "outed" as effectively as possible. And so that was the thing he started on first. It is not up to me to describe just how we accomplished this end, but never was a band of cutthroats so surely and speedily sent to grass as that gipsy gang in *The Vagabond*, under the deft mind of Charlie Chaplin.

No mishap occurred worth mentioning, excepting that we all managed somehow to fall on each other, and to elicit various grunts and gasps from the underdog. Being the last but one to be knocked out, I was on top of the pile, congratulating myself on the comfortable position; and, as we were supposed to be unconscious, I had my eyes closed, and couldn't see what was coming off.

I thought an earthquake had struck me presently, when Charlie, unable to properly carry Edna, tripped over the prostrate Lloyd Bacon, and sat bodily on my face! Charlie himself wouldn't have mattered so much, but with

Charlie showing the strain of carrying Edna in this production still from *The Vagabond*.

eleven-stone Edna in his arms I can assure you he was no marshmallow! *[Ac-cording to Goodwins, poor Edna has now ballooned from 138 to 154 pounds. Evidently her gipsy captors were feeding her well.]*

Then again, it would have been better if he had sat still once he had sub-sided, but my make-up must have been uncommonly greasy, for he promptly slid off my face and sat violently on the ground. The only thing I have to be thankful for was that my perfectly good nose wasn't completely removed in the course of his career to earth. It certainly hasn't been improved any.

When the camera had stopped clicking, Charlie got up laughing, and said he hadn't been able to support Edna, and that it would have to be a re-take. Then he suddenly saw me trying to ascertain what had happened to my physi-ognomy, and instantly he was all anxiety.

"What's the matter?" he enquired. "Did I hurt you?"

I grinned at his apprehension, and assured him that things might have been better, but that they could have been a whole lot worse. Whereat, finding I was in no danger of immediate death he whistled in a relieved way.

"Gee!" he exclaimed, "You startled me. I thought I'd broken your nose."

So on the retake, just to show there was no ill-feeling, he outed me with the club, and accidentally used the knotty side of it, with the result that there was speedily a most unphrenological bump on the top of my scantily-covered cranium.[1]

But this time he knew what he'd done and promptly fell out of the tree in which he had been hiding in order that he could examine the spot.

It was nothing by comparison with some of the injuries we fellows have received, however, so I laughed it off. But I think it was a cruel insinuation for Mr Manager Caulfield to say—"All right, Fred, people'll think it's intelligence."

I don't like that "think" part of it.

Charlie evidently felt he was under a ban that day, for if there is one thing he detests it is to injure a fellow-player, no matter how slightly, so he switched his attentions to the absorbing question of luncheon, which had been brought out from the city in individual boxes, rubbing shoulders in the friendliest way in the world with a huge urn of coffee.

The mountain air had sharpened up our town-spoilt appetites, and we made those lunches look like a bad penny, the way we tore loose on them. It was a most undignified party, for the canyon boasts no tables and chairs, needless to say, and we had to dispose ourselves in whatever position was least likely to result in upset lunches and rivulets of coffee.

Charlie, exerting a star's privilege, was given the only cup our "camp" boasted, and retired to his big touring car, where, muffled in a heavy ulster and a cap, he perched his lunchbox perilously on one knee, and began to satisfy the inner Charlie.

We gipsies, however, preferred the rurality of taking our tucker on the grass, on the fence, in the caravans—in fact, anywhere that was unconventional. We were beautifully dirty, and we knew it. Furthermore, we didn't care who else knew it. And if the ants made frequent raids on our boxes, why we only chased them off and continued to eat. When you're a gipsy an ant more or less cuts no ice.

Presently along came four ancient Ford motor cars, bearing about thirty school children out for a picnic. It is needless to add that they didn't get much further than that spot. The whole tribe of them, their excursion temporarily forgotten, tumbled out of those ancient products of the peace king,[2] and surrounded the big tourer which contained their favourite. There was no "may

I?" or "by your leave" about it. They just cut loose and came. For they knew their Charlie, and they knew that a rebuff from him was about as likely as a German victory.

Charlie knew what was coming the moment he heard the first auto-driver throw out his clutch and jamb on the brakes.

"Great Scott!" he muttered. "Now we're in for it!"

But nevertheless he had a kindly greeting for them all, and as usual manifested a complimentary interest in their scholastic careers that would have done credit to a County Council school inspector.

Stay, there's one gentleman that I have omitted to mention, and I must make good to make good right away, if I am to retain his good graces. I refer to "Billy Chaplin," the studio goat, and since he enlivened the proceedings on that memorable day by his studious devotion to our respective lunchboxes, it is up to me to relate something about him.

While Charlie was chatting to the scholars his goatship, having been driven away from the players' various repasts, took it into his head that he would fare better if he made a raid on the lunch of the star himself. So he surreptitiously stuck his head and paws into the car and was just about to make a violent onslaught, on a wedge of apple pie, when Charlie happened to catch sight of him. He didn't drive him out again. He just picked him up bodily and fed him on biscuits, what time the school girls looked on in glee.

It was oddly incongruous to see that group. There was Charlie, his unsavoury costume covered by a thick coat, and with a loudly-checked cap on his shaggy head, seated in an outrageously high-priced car, surrounded by school kiddies, and feeding a goat on cheap cookies.

Our simple lunch of sandwiches, salad, pie, coffee, and fruit was soon discussed [although Fred seems to mean that the food was dispatched (i.e., eaten), he uses the term in chapter 22 as well, so it may have been slang of the period], and as the light has a tendency to wane rather suddenly in these semi-tropical regions, we hastened to get along with the day's work.

We had already gained nearly two weeks on our time limit, because, as I have already recorded, of our projected Honolulu trip, and Charlie was more than a trifle pleased with himself and with us.

There were quite a number of chase scenes to be enacted, and some of them, for better effect, were photographed from the inside of the retreating caravan, with us gipsies following helter-skelter.

It is needless to say that several falls were expected of us, and we were praying for a nice, soft, sandy road. But there are other considerations beside actors' comfort in the picture game, you know, and the main difficulty that presented itself was the fact that the only soft-bedded roads in the vicinity were much frequented by automobiles and by pedestrians, who, by stopping in their course, and staring after the flying band, utterly spoiled the effect Charlie desired.

So it became necessary to drive us out to the nearest secluded spot, and, as luck would have it, it was made of the hardest macadam it has ever been my lot to encounter.

The camera was set up then, and the fun, if you can call it that, began.

I verily believe that was my unlucky day, but in a sense I had myself to blame, inasmuch as, in trying to save myself from the brunt of the big tumble, I had placed myself close behind the leading figure, that of the adipose Eric Campbell. With my usual foresight, I had utterly overlooked the fact that all the other six gipsies would naturally land on top of both Eric and myself.

And thus it was. Charlie wanted Eric to fall, and myself, in tripping over his body, to do what is known as a half-forward—that is, a half-somersault in mid air, landing in a sitting posture, the fall being broken by the hands.

Thanks to Charlie's training in earlier days, the fall itself presented no particular difficulty to me, and once I had landed I thought everything was O.K. But I had reckoned without mine host in the person of Albert Austin, who, not to be outdone, described a sky-high fall in the air and landed plumb on my journalistic head.

Let me not enlarge on the incident. But what my feelings were when I learned that the camera had gone wrong about three minutes earlier, and that we had been disporting ourselves for the benefit of the desert air, so to speak, requires a more experienced pen than mine to relate.

Altogether, that scene—which we have called the "macadam" faction of the story (because that is the part that most impressed us, in more senses than one)—was taken five times, and there wasn't a man jack of us that hadn't a minor casualty of some sort or other to report at the end of the day.

But the scene, which has been run at the studio for our benefit, registers beautifully, so that our labour was not in vain. That is some balm to our physical feelings.

A few more scenes were got before it became necessary for us to quit for the day, and, as they only concerned Charlie and a couple of others, the majority of us had a little leisure time to ourselves before the call came to pile into the motorcars and beat it home.

So, turning our backs on the question of work, we wandered about the camp, and presently I was attracted by a pair of saddled horses which had been ridden out by the two cowboys who guard our camp through the still watches of the night, lest someone should take a hunch to steal it in our absence.

Horses have always fascinated me, chiefly, I suppose, because I am what is vulgarly termed a rotten rider, and one of them, a beautiful chestnut colt, took my eye irresistibly, and I mounted him.

You've all seen broncho riders in your Western films, so you know what a broncho can do when he feels like it. And, believe me, Billy was the king of the whole broncho earth.

Before I had really touched the saddle I suddenly found myself a hundred yards up the canyon, while Billy took the bit between his teeth and made good. Half-accustomed as I had been to occasionally striding one of the old hacks they stick you on at the English riding schools, I never doubted for a moment that Billy had bolted and that I had written my last *Red Letter* article for you. I sat him all right, for the very good reason I hadn't a chance to do aught else, unless I wanted to risk an earlier death than I saw coming to me. But he did a greased lightning act such as I had never seen before. The gipsy camp lay a mile behind, and before me lay nothing but a stretch of Wild Western road, fringed by the foothills of the great mountain range, and I foresaw that I was going to gallop until I fell off, unless some means of stopping him came to my mind.

He answered not to the pull of the rein, but suddenly I remembered the way cowboys are wont to talk to their faithful steeds, and so, with a perfectly awful, and quite impossible American "cuss word," I yelled my mount to "Whoa!"

It is a good job that such a violent and uncomplimentary reference to one's parentage is not always so effective as it was just then, or this would be a bad sounding old world indeed. But it acted with Billy, for he pulled up so suddenly that I nearly repeated my "half-forward" performance of earlier in the day, though this time from an altitude.

I lost no time in dismounting, I can assure you, and, will you believe it, that incorrigible broncho turned round and thrust his soft muzzle into my hand for a complimentary caress. The dear old chap thought he had been giving me the time of my life. And as a matter of fact so he had.

I mounted him again to return to the camp, and just at that moment another rider came flying round the corner. It was one of the cowboys, and when he saw me he grinned.

"Gee, kid," he remarked, "you sure kin go some in that saddle. I thought Billy had bolted with you. Whar in heck did you learn to ride?"

Which, considering that I can't ride, and that I was scared blue, was probably gentle sarcasm, though I'd hate to think so.

Charlie kidded me unmercifully when we got back, and when I told him I hadn't been in the saddle for six years he laughed, and said—

"Well, you've got nerve all right. I wouldn't ride either of those gee-gee's on a bet."

I noticed while he was speaking that he shivered slightly, and on closer inspection found he was soaked with water from the waist down.

I asked him what he'd been up to, and he said he'd been falling into a tub of water for a comedy effect, and had retaken the scene four times.

I feared that he might catch cold, for the evening was drawing in on us by this time, but presently he wrapped himself in his ulster and got into the car, so I said nothing, and we bowled away to the studio.

Next day the inevitable had happened. Charlie turned up on the stage with a perfectly wonderful specimen of the genus cold in the head, and told me he had been spending the night at the Turkish bath in company with young Jack Pickford, who had left for New York that morning.

He insisted on working, however, and again allowed himself to be immersed in wetness and that finished him. Next morning our quiet little card game was allowed to proceed until nearly noon, and still there was no sign of the great white chief.

At precisely twelve o'clock the word came forth from the managerial head.

"Go home, boys, if you want to. Charlie's sick in bed, and won't work to-day."

By which you see that even the great—the greatest of the great—cannot play monkey tricks with old Mother Nature.

Everything is pretty good with him now, however, and next week I propose to tell you something about the rest of the story, and also about the way the public received the showing of *Police*, which is being released in Western America for the first time next Monday.

19

Billy Helps to Entertain the Ladies

July 15, 1916

Charlie's sickness wasn't a serious one. His hardy British constitution has been accustomed to frequent taxes in the matter of wettings, and but for the fact that the hot, dry air of Southern California has thinned his blood he would in all probability never have caught cold at all. At any rate, he was up and doing at the studio by the early afternoon of the day following the close of my last instalment, and, if appearances are to be believed, was none the worse for his twenty-four hours in bed.

The first intimation we had that he was on the premises was his irrepressible laugh which came from the projecting room as he watched the "run" of the scenes he had made two days before. So we slipped in through the rear door of the miniature theatre, and watched the rest of the run.

I don't think even Charlie himself had realised how hard a day's work he had put in on the afternoon in question. Altogether there were nearly three reels—about an hour's run[1]—of stuff that had been photographed in the canyon, and I counted that he had taken his wetting scene no less than eight times; so that when one takes into consideration the fact that he probably spent ten to fifteen minutes in rehearsing before each retake, and that he was soaked in water a way up to the middle of his back the whole time, it is not a very wonderful thing that he did catch cold. *[Chaplin actually takes four dunkings in the film. In the first, he plays his violin for Edna with such enthusiasm that he falls backward into the tub. After playing a second piece he bows to her as though to a cheering crowd of thousands, and once again backs himself into the tub. When gipsy chief Eric arrives, Charlie innocently holds out his hat for a tip, and Eric promptly knocks him in a third time. Finally, when Charlie knocks out all the gipsies and tries to rescue Edna, Eric plunges his head in the water to drown him. The repeat dunkings, far from becoming monotonous, illustrate Chaplin's growing ability to build elaborate comic routines from the simplest of props, and stage them with choreographic panache. The tub business comes to a satisfying conclusion when Edna saves Charlie by beaning Eric, who ends up in the tub himself. It was worth catching that cold!]*

Yet this scene was not a record for the day. There was another that had been enacted before the camera as many as eleven times before Charlie had properly "felt" the situation, and decided that it had been done in the best possible way. This, in film-cost, especially considering how expensive is Charlie's own time, means quite a little cash, but it makes for good pictures—witness the perfect technique of Charlie's past work—so nobody has any cause to criticise. *[Chaplin's shooting ratios became legendary in Hollywood, going as high as fifty to one.[2]]*

Speaking of this continual retaking of scenes carries me back to the days when we were making *Charlie Shanghaied*. There was a scene there in which the captain of the ship thumps the table, and so sends a plate spinning into the hands of Charlie, who fills it with soup right away. All this looked very wonderful on the screen, yet it required innumerable rehearsals, and was photographed fourteen times before Charlie succeeded in catching the plate. Perhaps I am letting the cat out of the bag rather in telling you this, but it goes to show the amount of pains and perseverance that is necessary in order to get that perfect, quick-fire action that is such a feature of the Chaplin productions.

It is an odd thing to sit through a "rough run," as we call it, of a day's work. The scenes, as I have pointed out before, are not taken in the order in which they appear on the screen; most people know that, I imagine; and as Charlie has so many takes of each scene one consequently sees the same thing happen in quick succession from three to eleven times before another situation flashes on the screen! In a case where a man rushes on and is knocked out immediately, it looks absurdly grotesque to see him coming up for more, so to speak.

Poor old Charlie didn't feel like much work that day. Of course, he made a brave effort to fix his mind on the situations he wanted to direct, but his day on the sick-list, if it had not impaired his health, had certainly blunted his quick conception of points, and after making a few scenes with a German band outside a public-house—especially built in the studio, by the way—he finally gave up until the morrow.

That night there was a huge Empire Day celebration at the Shrine Auditorium here, and although he had refused to appear in his public capacity I had persuaded him to be there as one of the audience. *[Empire Day had been introduced in the UK and its colonies in 1904 as a public commemoration of the might of the British Empire. It was declared an official holiday in 1916, and was celebrated on May 24, Queen Victoria's birthday.]*

Right down in his heart Charlie Chaplin is a Briton and a patriot; his pulse quickens just as yours and mine would when, away out there under the Stars and Stripes, he comes into contact with his fellow-countrymen or sees the old red, white and blue in all its glory. That is why, I suppose, he did not hesitate long about going to the celebration when I assured him he would not be pestered by a lot of busy-bodies!

To my discredit, be it said, I had feared the affair was going to be but a sparsely-attended one—charities usually are in this part of the world—but what a sight met our gaze when, after checking our hats, we passed on into the big concert hall! It was packed from floor to ceiling, and only a few seats remained from which to choose, while the walls were literally covered with flags of the Allied cause, and every man, woman, and child in that assembly of 5,500 souls wore a miniature silk flag upon his or her breast.

I noticed how Charlie's eyes widened when he took in the scene, and I could see in a flash that the true import of it all had dawned upon him, as it had upon me—the realisation of that great and wonderful patriotism, the like of which exists nowhere else in the world, which binds together the sons and daughters of the British Empire by a tie that not all the Teuton militarism in the world can shatter.

Suddenly he realised that we were standing there like a couple of idiots, and that he was going to attract a lot of attention to himself if he did not slip into a seat pretty soon, so he nudged me, and commissioned me to hunt out a quiet seat where he would not be seen by too many people.

During the evening a lot of cables and letters from the big men of our Empire were read out from the stage by Tyrone Power, a prominent American actor whose work on the film is not unknown to some of you, and here, if nowhere else, was borne upon us the wonderful blood-union which has made that Empire possible. *[Although he built his reputation in America Tyrone Power was actually British. His namesake son, then two years old, would become a major Hollywood star of the 1930s and 1940s.]*

These included communications from Sir Arthur Conan Doyle, Mr Asquith, Mr Balfour, Admiral Jellicoe, Lord Kitchener, Sir John French, "Jacky" Fisher, the French President, The Mikado of Japan, and the Prime Ministers and Viceroys of every British possession and colony under the sun. If it had been Charlie's true intention to remain incognito he certainly forgot all about preserving his obscurity during the reading of those letters.

He had his round of hearty applause for each one, but when Admiral Jellicoe's stirring note was read he dropped his programme and whistled and clapped alternately until he could almost have been heard above all the others.

It was a side of the wonderful little man that not even I had ever seen before. He was simply carried away with patriotic excitement. It did my heart good to see it.

The evening closed with a dance, prior to which three huge flags were carried round the auditorium, bearing each the respective crosses of St George, St Andrew and St Patrick, and into them were thrown coins and bills of all values from the humble nickel (representing 2½d) to the five-dollar gold piece (approximately one guinea). As we stood by the entrance ready to leave the flags passed by us, and I saw Charlie draw his hand from his pocket and throw two coins into the foremost one. I don't know what they were, but they gleamed suspiciously red in the light of the electroliers.[3]

It was a wonderful night, as Charlie said, and all the way home he kept taking out his miniature Union Jack and looking at it.

"I wonder how much money they got out of that to-night?" he said presently.

I made a rough and rapid calculation, and set the figure at five hundred pounds minimum net profit.

He whistled softly.

"That's quite useful, in England," he commented. "It's for a charity, isn't it?"

"For the soldiers blinded in the war," I told him. "It was organised by the Caledonian Club of Southern California."

He thought a while, then.

"Good for Caledonia!" he said approvingly.

And good for Caledonia it is, and California as well.

Next day Charlie seemed to be back into his regular form, for he attacked work with right good-will, and before the afternoon was properly on its way had disposed of the German band scene completely.

This particular scene, which opens the picture (despite the fact that it has been photographed three weeks after the main plot of the story!) deals with a German band which sets up outside a drinking saloon, and, after playing for half-an-hour or more, suddenly finds that Charlie has been inside and made a little collection all by himself. The complications that follow are absurdly funny, but the funniest thing to me is the German band itself. It consists of three Irish men and two English men! *[Since the presence of a German band in the film would have raised hackles in England at this time, Goodwins assures his readers that Chaplin was not really consorting with the enemy.]*

Speaking of this reminds me that I counted altogether eleven Britishers working on the studio floor this week. Who questions Charlie's devotion to his own land after that? Needless to say, he doesn't engage people just because they happen to belong to the Union Jack, but if they're "there with the goods" as well, why, the fact of their being British gives the scale a handy little tilt in their favour—which is as it should be.

Work proceeded but slowly during the ensuing days. This picture, like *The Floorwalker*, appears to have Charlie "guessing," and although it is due to be shipped to New York within the next four days there is still fully half of it to be completed. So there looks like being some tall hustling to be done before the end of the week.

Monday came, and still Charlie appeared to be stuck in the mire of uncertainty—a state from which he emerged by telling us to take off our make-ups and accompany him down town, where, as I told you last week, his last Essanay picture *Police* is showing for the first time.

Charlie doesn't always take the notion to transport the entire company to Los Angeles proper for the mere sake of seeing a picture run at a cinema, but I suspect he had a method in his action on this occasion; he probably wanted to see whether we all considered his past work better than his present. Charlie, like every really big man of the world, is not too big to be guided in some measure by the opinions of his brethren.

The lady of the cinema must have thought an earthquake had come when that bunch of players, fully twenty strong, thronged at her little window, and as quickly departed in the direction of the entrance, headed by Manager Caulfield with two dollars' worth of tickets in his hand. How was she to know, poor damsel, that we were the guests of our great white chief?

I suppose all men are apt to regard their past work with something of amusement, believing, either rightly or wrongly, that they have made progress that leaves that past work far in their wake. And Charlie, being but a man, pretty surely felt just that way as he entered the moving picture show.

He seemed, judging from his manner, to think he was going to show us something that was quite a joke, although at the time it was in the making it was a very, very real and serious thing to him.

Police, however (ill as it becomes me in my capacity of press manager to the Chaplin-Mutual Company to say so), is not a joke. It is to my sentimental mind the best picture in its own way that Charlie has ever turned out. It doesn't bring the roof down with laughter from beginning to end; neither does it bring tears to the spectators' eyes throughout its length. But it has its laughter, it has its tears, and also has some of the prettiest pieces of legitimate acting that Charlie Chaplin has ever presented during his picture career.

It is precisely eighteen weeks since I first set down for the benefit of the readers of the *Red Letter* the early stages of work upon *Police*, and all that time the picture has been withheld from the market. So there is little wonder that a lot of the situations had been forgotten by us, parts of the picture coming as something of the nature of a surprise even to Charlie, whose own conception it had been.

Just how truly and sincerely he feels his work was evidenced that day, for he laughed as heartily as the youngest child there at the comedy scenes, while the intense dramatic action had him gripping the sides of his fauteuil for all the world as if he had never seen the picture in his life before. *[A fauteuil is the French term for a sideless, upholstered armchair—in other words, a typical theatre seat.]*

Whatever view he may have harboured before he went in, that visit to the Alhambra undoubtedly removed from his mind any thought of disloyalty to his four-month-old-work, for as we came out I noticed he was smiling in a very satisfied way, and on the way back to the studio he said, "Not so bad, boys, eh? Your uncle Charlie isn't such a punk dramatic actor after all."

Which, if it was a bit of self-glorification, was also perfectly permissible— for the very good reason that it was perfectly true.

When we got back to the studio Charlie was still full of enthusiasm; so full, in fact, that he made us all put on our grease-paint again and work till the sun went back on us!

Yet still the picture was a hard nut to crack, and during the next two days, his work with the majority of us being done, Charlie got back to into his old trick of having the entire section of the stage in which he was working boxed in by pieces of scenery so that nobody but those immediately concerned could either gain access to him or see what was afoot—a circumstance that did not unduly bother the many, who promptly went out and to the adjoining field and practised baseball! *[Goodwins is the only commentator to reveal that Chaplin occasionally worked on closed sets this early on. At Essanay and Mutual he simply wanted privacy from the non-essential cast members; in later years closing his sets would become a necessity to protect his ideas from being stolen by other studios.]*

But privacy is not for the famous, apparently, for Charlie had not been working more than two hours on the second day when he was disturbed by the sudden entrance of a troupe of classical musicians who are playing in Los Angeles this week. Since they are never likely to see this article—and wouldn't know I was talking about them if they did—I haven't a scruple in saying that they bored Charlie to distraction. Temperamental as he is himself, his temperament is diluted, so to speak, by that brand of solidity [*sic*—stolidity] and rationality peculiar to the Briton, and the effeminate flutterings of those birds of Orpheus got on his nerves so badly that he couldn't work for an hour after they had gone.

"They must be awfully clever," he remarked, as we went to lunch at noon.

"Why?" I asked.

"Well, surely they must be gifted if they're so utterly impossible in every other way!" he answered.

That must have been a sort of visitors' day in Hollywood, I think, for the afternoon brought a limousine full of ladies, accompanied by one gentleman, who had motored up from San Diego especially to see Charlie.

Had they any acquaintance with Mr Chaplin? Oh, no, but they would love to meet him. This was Mrs Davidson, wife of the President of the San Diego

National Exhibition;[4] this was Mrs So-and-So, &c., none of which conveyed anything at all to me, but they were all so extremely nice—and so refreshingly human, after those Hungarian fiddlers—that I took my life in my hands and went to ask Charlie if he would care to see them.

I painted such an ornate picture, I suppose, that he gave in out of sheer deference to my power of description, and a few seconds later he was entertaining them on the grass-plot inside the studio walls, while Billy the goat made violent onslaughts upon his legs.

Finally, to cut it short, it appeared that their mission was to get Charlie to consent to visit the Exposition as guest of honour, and bring with him the entire company. The event (if it ever comes off) is to be called "Chaplin Day," and we are to have a royal time of it. (I am only wondering if it ever will come off; I know Charlie so well).

Of course, he promised. That is perhaps Charlie's greatest failing. He cannot say no to anybody, irrespective of whether he intends to seek shelter afterwards. But I'm hoping for once he'll make good, for if San Diego isn't much of a city, an American's idea of a royal time is going some—and we of the company like to "go some," especially when it's by invitation.[5]

After the visitors had gone Charlie mopped his brow, and did a mock stagger into his dressing-room, thereby indicating that he had passed through an ordeal.

But they hadn't conquered his taste for work, before he went home that night he sent word to the company to be ready by nine next morning, for we had to re-take that fight with gipsies in the canyon.

Once again I swooned!

20

"Do I Look Worried?"

July 22, 1916

By the time this article is speeding somewhere across the frontier of the State of California, *The Vagabond* will be finished, the last few scenes being due for completion in the early forenoon tomorrow.

It has been rather an uneventful week—at least so far as I am concerned—for Charlie, in one of those sudden changes of mind that characterise him, took it into his head at the commencement of the week that the main body of the story should consist of action between Edna, Lloyd Bacon, and himself. In order to do so he set to work, and skilfully invented little scenes which take the remainder of the characters gently but firmly out of the story.

The Vagabond, which starts with such a burst of humanity, resolves itself finally into a series of duologues and triologues, if these terms be permissible in speaking of the "silent drama."

Charlie is an odd character. The longer I know him the more convinced of this I become; indeed, I sometimes think I have never understood him thoroughly, although few know him or his modes better than I.

I say this largely on account of his actions during the taking of this, his third Mutual production, for while it has been in the making he has switched from idea to idea, wasted literally thousands of dollars, authorised the hiring of countless "extra" people, and then, as I say, finally decided to make the story around the three characters—himself, as the vagabond musician; Edna, as the waif; and Lloyd Bacon, as the Academician who, in painting her portrait, is finally instrumental in bringing about her restoration to her former station in life, from which she ultimately flees back to Charlie.

Artistically, this sudden action of his put the rest of the company into a rather disconsolate mood; on the other hand, it has given them a sudden and unexpected holiday. The fact that none of us have made a particle of good use of our temporary emancipation is rather to our discredit, however.

One day Charlie realised of a sudden that we were all having the time of our lives, and promptly swooped down on us, just as we were in the middle of some trivial game or other, and held forth—

"Hello!" he exclaimed. "What's this—a half-holiday?"

"A week's holiday, rather," someone ventured to correct him—and that, in the vernacular of the London streets, "fairly done it."

Ten minutes later we found ourselves being thrust into automobiles and taken down town to a local clothier's store, not a word having being vouchsafed to us as to what we were going there for.

"Scotty," wardrobe master, head property man, and general factotum-in-chief to THE chief, turned a deaf ear to our requests for enlightenment, but we finally arrived at the costume shop, and the secret was revealed.

For some reason—we found out afterwards what it was—Charlie wanted us all fitted out in dress suits.

Of course we protested that it was utterly unnecessary, that we all had perfectly wonderful dress suits of our own, and that we didn't care to be seen in "slop shop" attire. But it was of no use whatever. The relentless "Scotty" wouldn't let one of us out of his sight until we had all been measured, hung, drawn, and quartered by the unctuous gentleman who kept the store.

When we got back to the studio, with a pile of dress-suit boxes obtruding itself in our midst, the day's work was done, and Charlie and the others were cleaning up to go home.

With consummate nerve I ventured into his sanctum, totally ignoring the tense but unmistakeable notice on the door, which read—"Keep Out," and asked his majesty what we were expected to do with the dress suits which had been thrust upon us.

He looked at me absently for a moment, and then rubbed his chin.

"Well, now, let me see," he murmured. "You might use them for doormats, or you might change them for a pot of geraniums, or—."

I besought him to cease "kidding" and tell me, as spokesman for his hench-men, what he had in store for us and the evening clothes.

"Or you might put 'em on," he continued, "and make up as human beings at eight o'clock to-morrow morning."

So that was it. After a week's baseball practice (and other less innocent forms of amusement) we were to resume our occupations on the morrow in the conventional garb which Fate has decreed to be correct for the evening wear of waiters and gentlemen.

But the time pleased me not, and I ventured some more.

"Nine o'clock, then?" I said casually.

"Eight," was the laconic reply—and I retired, beaten. Dreamer though he be, there's no "putting one over" on Charlie.

The news was received in glum silence by my brother-supporters, who, although they are none of them lie-abeds, would much rather spend the hour after breakfast in digesting the awful truth-perversions that pose as news in the American dailies than hustle off to the studio an hour earlier than usual. But the word of the King of our castle is law, and at eight, or thereabouts, seven lusty men and true were strutting about the stage in full evening dress, each confident that he wore his—shapeless though they all were—better than his fellow-men. (That bit about shape refers to the suits—not to the actors, by the way.)

Nine o'clock would have chimed from the belfry of the little church behind our studio if the former had a clock. So would ten and ten-thirty; but, at any rate, our watches registered the latter hour before the big black touring car with red wheels, which transports Charlie around the angel city, finally drew into the lot, and the comedian jumped out.

"Hello!" he grinned. (Charlie always grins when he isn't in his sentimental moods.) "Look at all the waiters."

Before we could think of suitable repartee he had darted into his dressing-room, so we retired to a corner of the stage and started a quiet little game of cards until such time as he should send for us. A big tarpaulin was partly hung over the scene and under its shelter we were able to proceed with our game undisturbed by intruders.

Lunch-time came, and still no call came from headquarters. We had heard motor cars coming and going, but that is the general order of things all the time, so we had paid no attention to it.

But when we emerged from our hiding we discovered the place was practically deserted. Investigations followed, and then the horrible truth dawned upon us; the whole bunch had departed in the cars to some exterior location or other, leaving us beneath our canopy until we chose to emerge.

We couldn't quite figure it all out. There was the big dining-hall set, in which we were to enact the final scenes of the story. It was decorated with an array of glasses and epergnes *[ornamental centerpieces]*; was, in fact, all ready to work upon. But Charlie and his retinue of carpenters and property men had departed, taking with them Lloyd Bacon and Edna, and we of the full dress suits were alone.

We lunched and returned and still there was no sign of the great white chief.

At four o'clock, however, the cortege of autos blew into the studio; Charlie, peeling off his moustache, headed the procession. He spied us as the car came to a standstill and sent up a whoop of delight.

"Great Scot!" he cried. "Have you fellows been here all day?"

We assured him with much dignity that we certainly had; whereupon he only laughed the more.

"Gee whiz! And I'd forgotten all about that scene," was all the satisfaction he offered us.

We retired to our dressing-chambers and cleaned off our futile make-ups.

When I asked Charlie later what time we were to make up on the morrow, and suggested with scathing sarcasm 5.30 a.m., he went off into the most remarkable expressions of glee.

"You fellows are the easiest to 'kid' I ever saw," he chuckled. "You don't have to make up to-morrow at all."

"Do you mean we're not going to be used in that set?" I asked.

"No," he replied with redoubled amusement, "I'm only going to use Edna and her 'mother' in that scene."

"Then why—" I began.

"Why did I have to get those dress suits?" he took the words out of my mouth. "Because you were making too much noise playing baseball, and I wanted to get you out of the way so's I could think! I knew you couldn't play baseball in evening dress clothes, so I—Well, that's why."

Nice way to treat us, wasn't it?

I mention this little scheme of Charlie's chiefly to show you the erratic things he is prone to do when his mind is bent on his worst. Just to get us out of the way and stop us distracting his attention by our shouting he pulled the fifty-dollar gag of hiring dress suits for us!

His mind wasn't really on frivolous things that day, however, as a later conversation showed.

He was through with his work for the day, and as the mental tension slowly relaxed he grew into a talkative mood, what time he was getting into civilised clothing.

"This picture is going to be a 'crackerjack,' unless I am very much mistaken," he predicted. "You haven't seen all of it taken, have you?" (He knew perfectly well I hadn't.) "Well, I tell you, the dramatic faction of the story is going to make people sit up and take notice. I have never in my whole career constructed a more beautiful story than this one. Indeed, the theme has been such a romantic one, and has opened up such splendid possibilities for legitimate appeal that I have eliminated a lot of my laughs in order to give the heart-interest side of the story a free rein."

"Do you think the public prefer that kind of a picture?" I inquired. "They regard you as a comedian, you know, Charlie, and as such you have made your name ring through the world."

He mused for a while, then—"I've given the matter proper thought from every angle, and I have come to the conclusion that unadulterated comedy is more liable to surfeit people than the kind of work that is relieved by touches of nature."

"In a word, then," I queried, "you consider it likely to prolong your reign, this dramatic relief business?"

He looked at me quizzically.

"I'll sit you in the wash basin if you say that," he threatened. "I don't say it'll affect my career in that way, but I do think the public will value the comedy end if it is not handed to them in chunks. The framework of the story, being dramatic or sentimental, must inevitably bring home the bits of side play with far more strength than would otherwise be the case."

And that being evidently his ultimatum, I pursued the discussion no farther.

[In his Autobiography *Chaplin called the Mutual period the happiest time of his career, but he also made it clear how much agonizing went into creating the films. Goodwins provides his readers with a good front-row seat in this installment, describing Chaplin's unorthodox and costly method for getting rid of his cast for a day "so I can think." In the conversation that*

*concludes this article Chaplin is frank about the creative and legal challenges
that he was facing.*

*He had so far dealt with his creative challenges in the best way possible, by
turning out two action-filled comedies in a row, the first of which was already
proving to be a hit and the second of which was in the can. Unwilling to rest on
his laurels, he now felt emboldened to return to the territory he'd begun explor-
ing in* The Tramp *and* The Bank—*how to deepen his comedy by combining
it with serious romantic content. In all three films Charlie suffers the pangs of
unrequited love for Edna, but the romantic scenes in* The Vagabond—*the ones
Chaplin felt the need to develop in relative isolation—cut much deeper, and represent a significant artistic leap. The rustic breakfast scene with Charlie, Edna,
and the handsome artist, Lloyd Bacon, is particularly notable. As Charlie looks
on helplessly Bacon effortlessly entrances Edna, leading Charlie to express his
growing annoyance and frustration with a series of gross but very funny comic
bits involving crushed flies, even as his heart quite believably breaks. The charming and beautifully wrought romantic scenes in* The Vagabond *introduced a
new level of realism to Chaplin's work, and set the template for the unique fusion
of comedy, romance and drama that would become his trademark.]*

• • •

The balance of my story this week I am writing upon the day which witnessed
the taking of the final scenes of "The Vagabond," which, after puzzling Charlie to distraction, and demanding retake after retake, is finally ready for assembling and despatching to New York. *[Mutual's publicity magazine,* Reel
Life, *described a different ending than the one Chaplin ended up using. In the
magazine's account, after Edna is driven away in a chauffeured limousine
with the tuxedo-clad artist and her newly found wealthy mother, a despair-
ing Charlie tries to commit suicide by jumping into a river. He is rescued by
Phyllis Allen, a stout woman who played a battle-axe in a number of his films.
But one look at Allen and he jumps back into the river.[1] Evidently realizing
that the film's realistic tone didn't support a farcical suicide ending, Chaplin
instead contrived a happy one in which Edna has a sudden change of heart and
demands that the limousine turn around to retrieve her rescuer. But this ending is too facile, dodging the question of what sort of life the scruffy vagabond
could possibly have with Edna's new family, not to mention how the artist fits
into the picture. The scenes of the lovelorn Tramp vainly courting the besotted*

Edna had become the heart of the film, and they are simply too powerful to be resolved in such a perfunctory fashion. No wonder Chaplin was puzzled "to distraction." A similarly unsatisfying happy ending mars his otherwise brilliant and emotionally wrenching masterwork The Kid.]

If it is indeed to be what he terms a "crackerjack," why he certainly has that satisfaction due to him, for the picture, during the four and a half weeks it has taken to produce, has come nearer to making Charlie "impossible" than anything I have known.

This last day, however, has restored him to his old good humour, and has been just such a day as we were wont to have before his hand placed the name of Charles Chaplin at the foot of his 670,000 dollars contract.

For weeks past (and I would not be surprised if it has shown in my writings) Charlie had seemed to us all an entirely different man. His attitude towards us all had been no less democratic, neither had he altered in the essential things, but after his return from old New York he seemed more aloof and less of a "mixer" than he had previously been.

I don't need to be reminded that I myself was the very one that advocated—and still advocate—the exercise of a lot more reserve than Charlie was wont to practice—a sentiment in which I was heartily joined by many people--but I had never deemed it possible that Charlie Chaplin of Essanay days and Charlie Chaplin of the Mutual days could be so dissimilar. As the days went by he seemed to grow more and more within himself, while his irritability was more often in evidence than it had ever been in bygone days and we of his company (particularly those that had worked with him for any length of time) grew to wondering what had come over him.

But to-day opened our eyes more than anything has ever done to the true meaning of his position. He has not altered in himself; he has been just obsessed with worry and mental anxiety, and rather than bother others with his affairs he chose to keep himself to himself and let them rest upon his own shoulders.

The subject came up while he was sitting on the grass thinking out the final scene of the picture, and it was one of the boys that opened the ball. He asked Charlie what made him so terribly worried-looking nowadays?

"Worried?" echoed Charlie. "Do I look worried?"

"You've been looking like Hamlet for the past few weeks," Lloyd Bacon assured him.

Charlie laughed; then grew serious.

"Do you fellows realise how much I've got on my shoulders?" he said. "Just take a few of the principal things. I've got to keep my popularity up to pitch until next spring by turning out pictures, each of which must be better than the last. To do this I've got to consider dozens of problems, think out thousands of gags, write my stories, direct the company and myself, maintain neutrality in my themes, so that the pictures won't offend hyphenated Americans, and then, when each picture is finished, sit up all night with the boys and cut and assemble the film ready for shipment to New York. *[It would be interesting to know which "hyphenated Americans" Chaplin was worried about offending, because there are certainly plenty to choose from in* The Vagabond. *The film begins with him competing with a German band for the tips of saloon patrons. Inside the saloon, he sees an Orthodox Jew sneaking bits of ham from the buffet table and helpfully switches the "ham" and "beef" signs. Then there are the thuggish gipsies, who have kidnapped and enslaved a white woman. Such characterizations were too commonplace in American entertainment at the time to raise many eyebrows, although Leo White's portrayal of the sneaky Jew violating his dietary laws makes some modern audiences uneasy.]*

"At the same time I have to be thinking out in my spare time what my next picture is going to be, and who is to play what. Add to this the fact that I am in litigation and counter-action with a certain firm, many thousands of dollars being involved, and you have a pretty good idea what kind of beanfeast my life has been during the past month or so!"

[On March 11, on his way back to Los Angeles from New York, Chaplin had stopped in Chicago to view the completed versions of Carmen *and* Police. *He was shocked to find* Carmen *padded to twice its original length, and even its title padded to the clunky* Charlie Chaplin's Burlesque on Carmen. *This, he later reported, "prostrated me and sent me to bed for two days."[2] Despite the threat of a lawsuit, Essanay released the film on April 22. The following day Chaplin's lawyer sought an injunction to prevent distribution. When this was dismissed Chaplin appealed the case to the New York Supreme Court, adding a claim for $100,000 in damages. Essanay countersued, claiming damages of half a million dollars for Chaplin's breach of a supposed verbal contract to make four more films for the company. On June 24 the court ruled against Chaplin's suit; Essanay's dragged on until 1922. The company continued releasing "new" Chaplin films that Chaplin, having lost one lawsuit, had no stomach to contest.*

June 24, 1916

Reel Life

" The Mutual Film Magazine "

Price 5 Cents

© 1916

Charles Chaplin in The Vagabond

Mutual's promotional magazine featured busker Charlie passing the hat to an unmoved Leo White in *The Vagabond*.

*However, a flood of pirated and bogus Chaplin films and Chaplin imperson-
ators now began appearing onscreen, and they would keep his lawyers busy for
years to come.]*

Here was food for reflection, indeed, and most of us were pretty silent
for a minute or so. It had never occurred to us in that light, you see, and we
felt rather guilty for having supposed Charlie to have altered in his attitude
towards us.

Yet putting this worry proposition outside the question, it would hardly
be surprising if one day he did take it into his head to "act the star," as the
saying is over here. The philosophy he loves to dabble in teaches him that
there is nothing in the world like reserve to keep a man at his best in life, and
I suppose my long absence from Britain, where this system of "equality" does
not prevail, has caused me to regard as a matter of course that Charlie should
intermingle and lark around with his "boys."

True, his want of reserve has never, so far as the company is concerned,
placed him in a humiliating position, but be it in sober, civilised Britain or the
wild and woolly West of America, the fact remains that "the boss is the boss,"
and has the right to assert himself as such.

So if, as I say, Charlie Chaplin should ever find it expedient to exercise his
prerogative to stand at the head and not in the midst of his company of players, he is but doing as ninety-nine out of every hundred stars have done since
show-business was first invented.

Incidentally, he would be "getting wise to himself." It doesn't always pay
to be too free and easy.

21

Playing the Part of Half a Cow!

July 29, 1916

Some days ago a learned young American bluestocking was looking through the back instalments of these articles, and criticising them in the frankest possible way.

Put briefly, her opinion was that they were quite good, very interesting, and dealt with Fred Goodwins—"and occasionally Charlie Chaplin." This set me thinking whether I have not dwelt rather heavily on the personal note in setting before you the happenings in this studio of ours, and consequently makes me rather apologetic in having to start my story this week with mention of myself.

Yet I can't avoid it, for Charlie himself is to blame, and this is how it all came about.

The Knight Templars, a big fraternity organisation in the U.S.A., suddenly took a notion to get up a benefit performance for themselves, using the good services of the members of various studios in Los, and, of course, ours was the very first one that came into their heads.

So Charlie, as head of the family, had to undertake the schooling of the crowd in the item chosen by us for performance on the occasion in question.

He therefore called us together one morning and read to us the script of the sketch, which was written by his adipose lieutenant, Eric Campbell, and is a burlesque melodrama, entitled "The Peril of Primrose."

It was full of nonsense and hokum, utterly inconsistent and crazy, and since it combined all these qualities, eminently suitable for the delectation of a charity audience.

As Charlie pointed out "People who go to see a benefit show don't want to go, don't want their money's worth and are therefore disappointed if you give them something that's as good as they would get at a regular entertainment. Shove 'em a lot of hokum and they'll laugh their fool heads off."

So far so good—the script is eminently satisfactory. But then came the question of the allotment of parts, and here is where I must break the tidings concerning myself that have been causing me such dismay during the past few days.

The cast is as follows:—Pretty Primrose, the village damsel (Eric Campbell); Niffit, a French Count, the naughty villain (Leo White); Dippy, the dope fiend (Lloyd Bacon); Percy, the photo-faker (Albert Austin); Mick Arson, the fire chief (James T. Kelly); Percival, his assistant (Frank Coleman); Phillip, his assistant (Larry Bowes); and, whisper it low, friends of mine, for it is an awful professional tumble:—Cutey, the cow (John Rand and Fred Goodwins).

There, it's out. I am not even a whole animal. I am half a cow—and the rear half at that. Small wonder that I sometimes think my day in this cruel profession is done. I have played many parts, as Shakespeare says we all must. I have migrated from plays like "The Girl from the Jam Factory" to the Broadway runs of big New York successes. But never, until Charlie decided that I was fit for naught else, have I been thrust into the rear end of a cow skin, even behind so talented a jester as Johnnie Rand.

It's an awful slide, believe me.

Seriously, though, this hocum show of ours looks like being quite a "go," and for the first time in his career Charlie Chaplin is producing a spoken play and incidentally giving us an idea of what kind of a stage producer he will be when he realises his life ambition and puts on a regular legitimate show with himself as author and producer.

He is just as easy to grasp when he is conveying his idea of a certain speech as he is when he is directing a scene for a picture, and I imagine when he gets into his stride again, once the stage reclaims him, he will add to his already weighty laurels by turning out to be a stage producer of considerable note and ability.

This striking reissue poster captures the onscreen relationship between Charlie and Eric, making it even more incongruous that the big man played "Pretty Primrose."

He will not take part in the thing himself, because he has so much to do at the moment in framing up his new story. My readers will still have fresh in their memory his statement, made at the termination of *The Fireman*, that no sooner has he finished one picture than he has to start worrying about the next. *[Regrettably, Goodwins says nothing more about "The Peril of Primrose," and there is no known record of how the performance was received—although one can imagine that Eric Campbell was quite a sight as "Pretty Primrose." During his time at Essanay, Chaplin developed a close friendship with G. M. Anderson, who staged many such charitable fund-raisers with his crew members, and it appears that some of the cowboy star's community spirit rubbed off on him.]*

The Vagabond was, you'll remember, completed last week, and despatched to the headquarters of the Mutual Film Company, and we all fully expected that Charlie would go flying away to the mountains for a vacation. But on the day following he showed up at the studio, looking very tired and fagged, and began to wander around the stage, which, stripped of every particle of scenery and effects, looked like a big skating rink elevated two feet from the ground.

I chanced upon him while he was strolling up and down the bare boards, and he came out of his brown study and greeted me.

"Hello," he said. "Lucky beggar, you don't have to worry your head about the next story, do you?"

"Why, no," I agreed. "Are you worrying about it?"

He laughed oddly.

"I always worry," he said. And that is one of the truest words Charlie Chaplin ever spoke.

I have never in all my career come across a man who allows his mind to become obsessed so utterly by his responsibilities as he does. Be it the problem of a big picture or a mere trifling detail of his private life, Charlie invariably makes a mountain out of every molehill that besets him.

"You're going to have a peach of a breakdown one of these days," I warned him. "Why do you worry so much, Charlie?"

"Can't help it," he said, snapping his fingers nervously. "Couldn't do my work if I didn't worry. I wish to heaven I could ease up once in a while. But even my vacations are a torment to me. I'm always itching to get back to the job, even when I know I'm not ready in one single detail."

I couldn't help comparing the almost carefree existence of us fellows with the perpetual nervous tension under which Chaplin lives, and reflecting on what he once said about his huge remuneration—"the man who says I don't earn my 670,000 dollars a year is crazy in the head. I lose that much fun out of my life."

Dare I, a mere unit of his scheme of things venture to question the absolute necessity of that eternal strain and mental wear and tear of his? Time and again I have seen him, under a relaxed spell, go before the camera without a rehearsal, and frolic about in a scene more for his own amusement and ours than from any idea of keeping the result of his work as part of the picture. Yet time and again he has achieved such great results from this spontaneous fooling that all the rehearsals in the world could never duplicate or better them. And he has just as often kept them in the picture.

While, on the other hand, I have known him, as he did in *The Floorwalker*, to sit for hours and think in solitude and silence until he has evolved a gag that scarcely brought a titter from the audience when it came to be shown on the screen.

I don't say that all this goes to prove any set rule in regard to the making of motion picture comedy. Indeed, it does rather the opposite, inasmuch as many of his best situations have been the result of countless rehearsals. But what I am trying to point out is that to my mind Charlie might, in justice to himself and with better success, "relax" occasionally, and allow his own personality to carry him away. It would take away some of those deepening lines in his countenance and quite a few of those sleepless nights. *[Indeed, Chaplin began suffering from insomnia at this time. To avoid losing any precious ideas that might occur to him during the night hours he began keeping a Dictaphone beside his bed, a practice he continued for years to come.[1]]*

All the while we were walking the stage that afternoon he was alternately snapping his fingers and tapping his forehead, struggling and striving after the theme of his fourth Mutual picture. I didn't speak again until he spoke to me, and then it was too excuse himself and rush away to his dressing-room.

"I'll come back with an idea; see if I don't," he said, and the old twinkly smile broke through the clouds again. I saw nothing of him for fully half an hour, and then I happened to look out towards the trees that fringe the studio wall.

At first I could hardly believe my eyes, knowing as we all did that there wasn't a possibility of his starting on the picture for another week at least. But there was no mistake about it. He had put on his make-up and suit and a straw hat, and was sitting beside one of the cameras, which he had had stuck up on its tripod for no reason in the world that I could see.

Then it dawned on me what had been in his mind. Unable to think out anything to his liking, he had made-up in order to get the spirit of the thing, and had the camera placed beside him, so he could feel the atmosphere of a busy day.

I left him to it.

But all his wiles and hard thinking availed him nothing apparently, for the next thing I heard from him was that he had decided to "chuck it" and build his picture as he went along.

He accordingly ordered a big ballroom set to be erected on the stage within the next few days, and insisted that the floor be given a high polish.

"I ought to be able to get some fun out of a slippery floor," he said half to himself. "Perhaps it'll help to frame up a good story."

There is a possibility about it. *Charlie by the Sea* was, as you know, built around a chance puff of wind which entangled the guards of his and Billy Armstrong's hats. Who shall say that a slippery floor and a chance fall of Charlie's may not develop into a "scream," as the trade posters are wont to say?

Here again is something of a contradiction. *Charlie at the Show* originally had a strong dramatic plot, involving not a few thrills and a quick-action fight. Yet when it finally shook down, so to speak, in the comedians imagination it turned out to be a mere set-out of pie-slinging and streams of water.

Yes, a small beginning, so far as Chaplin is concerned, may mean quite a big finish when it comes to the show-down.

For the present, then, in the face of his absolute indecision I can't tell you a thing about the forthcoming production, but one thing he has said which may interest my readers. He is going to play his part on the lines that first brought him into prominence when he made his debut into the picture game—the lines of an apologetic, blundering gentleman sadly under the influence of his cups.

On the evening in question a party of us boys went downtown on a bachelor party, and happened across a fellow-countryman, one Jim Cassey, keeper of a big licensed house in town. Cassey has often told me, when we have been discussing Charlie and his work, of how he had put the boy up on his return to Los Angeles to start on his picture career.

"He was so nervous about it that the missis and I used to hear him wandering up and down his bedroom—he was staying with us at the time—and muttering to himself until four in the morning. Then we'd ask him at breakfast time how he'd slept, and he used to put on a cheerful front and say—"pretty good, Jim. Could have been better, but I had a lot to think about." Poor old Charlie, he was just the same then as he is now. His face showed everything he was thinking. He couldn't deceive us for a moment.

"I used to think he'd forgotten us," continued Charlie's old friend. "But one day a couple of weeks ago he slipped into the bar and grabbed me by the hand. I guess the sight of me brought back a lot of memories of his early picture days, for he had a lump in his throat when he tried to speak. 'Haven't forgotten, Jim,' he said. 'Those were good old days.'

"I took him home to supper, and he just fell all over the wife. She gave him a real English feed of roast beef and Yorkshire, and he walked into it like a two-year-old. He was just the same Charlie of two and a half years ago.

"After a while he asked the missis to take a good look at him, and tell him how he looked.

"'You've not seen me for two years, Mrs Cassey,' he said. 'You'll tell me the truth, won't you?'

"'Well, if you want the truth, Charlie,' the missis told him. 'You look your two years older—and then some.'

"Charlie shook his head and said—

"'I worry too much. I've got to cut it out.'

"He gave me a fine new picture of himself that night, sent his secretary to fetch it from the athletic club, and signed it 'To old Jim, my friend in need. From Charlie.'

"And before he left he promised on his oath that he wouldn't stay away from us anymore."

"You found him no different, then, Jim?" I asked him. "He seems to me to have changed, even in the year I have worked with him."

"Yes, he's changed in some things," confessed Jim. "But in the main he's just what he always was—dear old Charlie."

And when Jim said that "he said a mouthful of truth."

22

Twelve O'Clock—Charlie's One-Man Show

August 5, 1916

Friends—Scotsmen, Englishmen—lend me your ears. I have some news for you which will make you prick them up and wonder if there is any limitation to the possibilities of our friend Charles.

For nearly a week and a half after the termination of the *Vagabond* production the Lone Star Studio presented a quiet and desolate air. The boys were wont to arrive somewhere about 10 a.m., and depart before the noon-day whistles sounded from the distant manufactories on the outskirts of Los Angeles.

Of Charlie we saw but little. He was invariably either down town on business or pleasure, and by the time he arrived—generally somewhere around 2 p.m.—we of the supporting company were over the hills and far away.

We knew there was nothing doing until such time as the great white chief had his next story mapped out, and felt, therefore, that we were safe in skipping off to our trivial pleasures. Golf and exceeding the speed-limit have always been my own chief hobbies, whereas the majority of the Chaplin boys do not feel the day has been well spent unless they have witnessed a baseball game at the big professional "park" which stands in the heart of Los, right next door to the Horsley studios.

But to get back to my point. For a long time past I have realised that my diminutive car was hopelessly inadequate to cope with the half-dozen or so of boys that invariably demanded to ride down town whenever I was getting ready to go. So I took unto myself a new five-passenger touring car.

Within the next two or three days I was glad I had done so, for one morning Charlie issued a call that we were to report at the studio at 10 a.m. the next day and hear what he had to say.

There was quite a lot of conjecture as to what the news was going to be, some of us declaring that he proposed to make his next picture in Honolulu, while others said we were all going to get fired. Pessimists!

However, we arrived at the plant well on time the next day, and at about noon Charlie showed up.

Then it was that we heard our fate.

"Boys," he said, "you can all go away for a four weeks' holiday. I shan't need you until the next picture but one."

We could hardly credit our ears. Were our services so unsatisfactory that he had elected to hire a new set of actors and actorines? Or was he going to make a picture entirely by himself?

The latter was the case. After three pictures, in which he had used at least a dozen supporters, Charlie had decided to try an experiment and make a solo picture, using nobody but Charlie Chaplin!

It is novel, and it is daring, and if he can carry it through to a successful issue it is a stroke of genius, for it is to be two reels in length, and all turns upon one theme, as I understand.

The picture, he tells me, is to be called *Twelve O'Clock*, and deals with his adventures after leaving the club in a rather hilarious condition, and with his pathetic efforts to get indoors and to bed without awakening the house.

It is not a new theme—indeed, even the idea of a one-man picture is not entirely new, as I shall show presently, but never has a comedy with a cast of one been put on the screen, and since nobody is more capable of handling so difficult a task than Charlie Chaplin, it would seem that that remarkable young man is going to create yet another precedent in motion-pictures.

Of course, we all wished him the best of success with his new idea, and if our wishes were not altogether disinterested—in view of the fact that this picture affords us a long spell of leisure—they were none the less genuinely meant, for Charlie's success, be it either individual or shared in part by us boys, is something of a religion at the Lone Star Studio.

If there is any cause for regret at all, it is to be on the part of readers of the *Red Letter*, for the making of *Twelve O'Clock* is being conducted in camera, as they say in the law reports, and it has been utterly impossible for me to take any current snapshots. Big signs commanding "everybody" to "Keep off this set, and don't come near it," have appeared on all hands, and vast screens have been erected around the portion of the stage on which Charlie is working. Thus Charlie, Vincent Bryan, and the working staff have kind of segregated themselves into a little kingdom of their own, from which everybody else connected with the works is strictly barred.

There has been no particular motive in this screening off other than to keep Charlie's mind upon the ticklish job he has undertaken. Certainly it is not that he is afraid we are going to steal his ideas. The emancipation from work is no end welcome to us chaps, although goodness knows that, except for the time we were making *The Floorwalker*, we really haven't known the meaning of overwork, and most of us have taken the fullest advantage of it.

During the week, Eric Campbell moved from his home in Hollywood to Santa Monica, a beach town some twenty miles from Los Angeles, and Albert Austin, Lloyd Bacon, and myself accompanied him down for the specific purpose of expressing our admiration of his new quarters.

He is an admirable host, full of that hearty British spirit of hospitality that has ever characterised the Midland man, and he entertained us royally until the following day. One odd thing I notice about Campbell is his love of things that are small and "'cute." He stands some six feet two[1] in his stockinged feet, and weighs something over twenty stone, yet he drives the smallest automobile known, has for a pet a diminutive dog that could easily stand on one of his hands, and has rented a cottage which looks more like a doll's-house than a regular habitation. *[By all accounts a gentle and cheerful man, Chaplin's most memorable onscreen adversary was about to become world famous because of his outstanding performances in eleven of the twelve Mutual films. However, as the series drew to a close Campbell suffered a string of catastrophes. On July 9, 1917, his wife died from a heart attack. A few days later his sixteen-year-old daughter was seriously injured when she was struck by a car. A couple of months after that, Campbell impulsively married a woman he met at a party, who left him within weeks and sued for divorce. Finally, on December 20, following a night of drunken revelry at a Christmas party, Campbell, reportedly driving sixty miles an hour, crossed to the wrong side of the road and collided with another car. Campbell's passengers and the other driver survived, but the thirty-seven-year-old actor was killed instantly.[2]]*

I don't know whether this mania for opposite things is a human characteristic or not, but it reminds me forcibly of Charlie's fondness for things that are big and stupendous.

There was a big carnival at the beach that evening, and nothing would do but that we all pile into his diminutive roadster, leaving my own roomy vehicle in his garage, and go down to join in the revels.

We must have presented a funny spectacle. The little Saxon is built to contain two ordinary-sized humans, so you can imagine how comfortable we all were in that trip along the promenade. I was squeezed in beside Campbell. Albert and Lloyd, perched on each of the running-boards, clung to the sides for dear life, while Eric made thirty miles an hour in typical defiance of all the rules and regulations of the street ordinance.

The carnival was nothing to write home to mother about. They hold them so frequently in the three rival beach towns hereabouts that they resolve themselves into more of an institution than the exceptional treat they pretend to be, and just as we were getting to feel a trifle blasé, who should happen along but Charlie!

He was dreaming all by himself as usual, but he soon came out of it when he spotted us.

"Hello, boys!" he grinned. "What are you doing down here? Seeing the carnival?"

Eric hastened to assure him that we were there delivering a load of bricks, and Charlie laughed.

"Yes, I suppose that was a foolish question," he agreed. "Let's go and eat a little supper, shall we?"

An extra passenger, even of such importance as our own Charlie, being utterly out of the question so far as the little Saxon was concerned we sought out Charlie's big touring car and drove down the coast to Venice, the locale of *Charlie by the Sea*, you will remember, where Charlie knew of a nice, quiet little restaurant that would shield him from the gaze of the too inquisitive tourist.

We found a secluded corner, sheltered by a lot of natural palms and discussed [*sic*—dispatched] an excellent meal, the courses whereof were chosen by our host, and when we reached the cigar stage conversation drifted to the inevitable topic, *Twelve O'Clock*.

"I hope you boys don't feel I'm pulling temperamental stuff," said Charlie suddenly—"I mean by having the stage screened. But, you know, the least noise detracts from my train of thought when I am handling a knotty situation, and I thought prevention was better than cure. That's why I did it."

We assured him that such a thought had never entered our heads, and he was satisfied.

"I've bitten off a beautiful mouthful, though," he continued, "in essaying this solo thing of mine. I got the idea from something a flattering young scribe wrote about me in a magazine the other day. He said, 'If you stuck Charlie Chaplin in an empty room with nothing but his make-up and a table and chair, he'd still be able to turn out a one-reeler that would have it over every other comedy on the market.' At first I was inclined to laugh such a piece of obvious flattery to scorn, but when I came to turn it over in my mind I saw possibilities in it, and wondered just how many legitimate situations I could make without using any factors but myself and some furniture and 'props.' It necessitated an awful lot of thinking, as you may imagine, and I guess that is why I went about 'looking like Hamlet,' as Bacon called it." (He meant Lloyd Bacon—not Francis!) "Anyway, I finally got the thing down to a regular basis, and decided that, if it didn't do me any particular good, it certainly couldn't do much harm. So that's how I started it. I've got enough gags to make a four-reeler if necessary, so I'm pretty optimistic about the result."

"Well, it gives us a nice little vacation," murmured Lloyd, blowing a wreath of fragrant Havana up to the ceiling. "That's one thing to be grateful for."

"Sure," agreed Charlie, making a minute examination of his coffee-spoon. "But I'm liable to make you sit up and work all the harder on the next picture. You lot of loafers."

"Work!" murmured Austin. "What is it—a herb?"

The subtlety of which remark was not lost upon Chaplin, who grinned in his twinkly way.

Practically every restaurant and café in America has what it calls a "cabaret" entertainment, consisting of anything from one to twenty performers, whose mission is, so Charlie once said, "to upset people's digestions and appetites, and make table conversation an utter impossibility." I say it has what it calls a cabaret, because it is in most cases such a hopeless travesty on the real French institution after which it is named.

In this particular restaurant the management had thoughtfully provided us with three singers and a ventriloquist, mercifully sparing us the necessity of being yelled at by a chorus of raucous-voiced females, for which consideration we were duly grateful.

From time to time our conversation was interrupted by the contributions of these performers, and presently one of them, the ventriloquial gentleman, came to our table and began, all unbidden, to give us an example of his talent. This is another imposition which is permitted over here, and one which is pretty generally resented even by the Americans themselves. The entertainers are allowed to butt in on any party they think is likely to unburden itself of some shekels and start an exclusive "turn" *[idiomatic British term for a performance; a music hall turn vs. a vaudeville act]*. I personally have had many a pleasant little tête-à-tête rudely interrupted by this method, and I like it not. Neither, I imagine, did Charlie, but he was very tolerant towards the voice-thrower, and gave him an easily-earned dollar for his pains.

Suddenly an idea seemed to strike him, and he called the man back to the table.

"Lend me your figure for a minute, will you?" he asked, and the ventriloquist, who, of course, knew his man, complied.

Charlie turned the grinning dummy over in his hand, examining the mechanism which operated its cavernous mouth. He was for all the world like a kid with a new plaything, and conversation on the business topic was suspended indefinitely while he mastered the pulling of the strings. Then he started a ventriloquial show all by himself.

To give him his due, however, I don't think he intended it to be taken seriously, for he soon handed the figure back to its owner, and fell to talking about the ventriloquists of his native land.

"Do you remember them?" he asked. "They were always a source of amusement to me when I was a kid, and I used to wonder how it was all done. I'll never forget what a disappointment it was when I found that the figure contained no wonderful engine capable of transmitting the human voice in answer to any question that was asked. It took away all my illusion for ever after. The first ventriloquist I remember seeing was Fred Russell, and I used to hang around stage doors when he was working, on the chance of seeing him walk out leading his little coster figure by the hand." *[Considered "the father of modern ventriloquism," Russell was the first ventriloquist to sit a dummy on his knee. Costers or costermongers were street hawkers of fruits, vegetables, and other food from rolling carts or stalls, and they appear in many Chaplin films, including* Easy Street, A Dog's Life, *and* Pay Day.*]*

Presently conversation drifted back to the one-man picture theme, and I asked him if he knew of any such a picture having been attempted before.

"In comedy, so far as I can find out," he said, "never, but I recollect having seen G. M. Anderson in a one-man dramatic picture of one reel a few years ago,[3] and I believe King Baggot put one on with the Imp people somewhat more recently. Those, however, were both dramas. I think it has been left to me to try the experiment with comedy. It is, as I say, a big lump to bite off, but I think I'm going to be able to digest it nicely." *[We have already noted how Chaplin was reluctant to credit some of his mentors and creative collaborators, minimizing Fred Karno's influence and having Goodwins issue a retraction when he referred to Vincent Bryan as a contributing writer and co-director. In fact, Bryan was hired by Mutual as "scenario writer," and credited as such in official publicity materials for the first three films in the series. This practice would cease with the fourth and current film, which was eventually released as* One A.M.—*even though, as Goodwins mentions above, Bryan was one of the few crew members allowed on the closed set.*

Chaplin's reluctance to credit others stands in sharp contrast to the generosity of Keaton, Lloyd, and Fairbanks, all of whom freely acknowledged the contributions of their creative teams, even giving writing and directing credits to others when they could have claimed them for themselves. Nevertheless, there are numerous testimonials to the easy give and take at the Chaplin studio, with everybody pitching in with suggestions. Chaplin's habit of using virtually everyone around him as a sounding board is also well documented; in a couple of instances reporters came for interviews and ended up staying for days, as Chaplin drew them into his creative process.[4] There is a fascinating bit of behind-the-scenes footage in Unknown Chaplin *that catches him pacing on the set of* The Adventurer, *deep in discussion with Albert Austin and Henry Bergman.*

However, Chaplin's reluctance to credit others, or in some instances pay them for their contributions, occasionally got him into trouble. It almost happened with One A.M. *He declares above that he got the idea of doing a solo film from a flattering magazine article. But another and more direct source of inspiration was likely the vaudeville sketch* Too Full for Words; or, A Lesson *in Temperance, performed by Billie Reeves. Reeves, another Karno alum, also made a film called* The Club Man, *released on May 22, 1915, which has the same plot as the sketch. The film no longer exists, and it is not known whether Chaplin saw it. But he is believed to have seen Reeves perform the stage act in October 1912.[5] Reviews of both the film and sketch reveal a number of striking similarities with* One A.M.; *Reeves certainly thought so, because when* One A.M. *was released he told* Variety *that he intended to sue.[6] Luckily for Chaplin he did not follow through, possibly because of Chaplin's close relationship with Billie's brother Alf.[7]]*

We arose from the table shortly after that, and Eric insisted that we should all go to his bungalow for a "nightcap" before Charlie drove back to Los Angeles, and Charlie, after a little persuasion, gave in, and the two cars, literally the long and the short of it, sped down the Santa Monica driveway just as the church clock chimed the first hour of morning.

For the dreamy individual he is, Charlie has a remarkable faculty for picking up interesting things in life. The smallest things will suggest to him something from which he can evolve a piece of originality, and thus I was not surprised, when he put on the gramophone at Campbell's house, to find him experimenting with the needle.

Suddenly he yelled like a kid on a holiday, and we all went over to see what he was up to.

"Listen," was all he said, and I noticed that he was holding a visiting card in his hand. He held it carefully over the revolving disc, and touched the surface ever so lightly with the corner of the card.

The result was weird in the extreme. As if from some distant band came the far-away air of "King Chanticleer," Nat Ayer's popular rag.[8] It was the oddest thing I have ever heard, for it sounded so far, far out on the wind, that it might have been the strains of a launch party away out on Santa Monica bay. The card was acting in precisely the same way as a metallic needle, except that, being softer, it conducted the melody in more muffled tones.

For fully fifteen minutes Charlie amused himself in this way, putting on one record after another, and then a new idea seized him, and, putting down the visiting card, he applied his finger-nail to the record. He fairly jumped for joy when he found that the air was just as clearly audible by this means as it had been when he used the card. And another ten minutes went to the deuce!

The hour was getting late, however, and pretty soon the party disbanded, or, rather, Charlie and the chauffeur took their leave, and we retired to our respective cots.

As we heard the big Mitchell car humming away into the silence of the night, Eric turned to us and smiled.

"A wonderful chap," was all he said, but he "said a mouthful" just the same.

23

"Speak Out Your Parts," Says Charlie

August 12, 1916

Charlie's one-man picture is still in course of making, and the signs of warning ranged like stern sentinels around his sacred domain. From behind the screens occasional sounds of grinding mechanism come out on the breeze, so to speak, but beyond that there is nothing in the world to show that a world's super-comedy is in the making.

It seems odd to us of the company to go out on the "lot," as they call the huge piece of land upon which the offices and stage of the Lone Star Studio are erected, and not hear sounds of altercation, interlarded by an occasional bump of heavy bodies meeting the earth, or rather the stage. The making of a Chaplin comedy has always been rather a noisy affair, for Charlie is a staunch believer in the policy that strength of utterance begets strength of action, and that is why he insists on all speeches being delivered as loudly as if the actor were on the legitimate stage.

I imagine it must seem strange to the general public that so much energy should be wasted on the desert air, but it is Charlie's policy, as I say, and—well, it's been pretty successful so far.

In the days gone by, when motion-pictures were an institution to which an actor had to be dragged by the hair, in order to persuade him to appear in them at all, nobody had thought of the idea of using actual words in playing a part, and still less had they thought of the effectiveness of putting any acting emotion behind those words. It used to be the way to just move the lips in a meaningless way while making gestures before the camera, but one day— (and I got this history of "screen-words" from Charlie, who seems to have all the data of motion-pictures at his fingers' ends)—one day the Vitagraph Company was making an American Revolution picture, and in the great tribunal scene one of the actors started to his feet, shook his fist at the picture of King George, and cried—"You Royal rascal! This means war!"

The result of this unprecedented action was so wonderfully effective on the screen that thereafter the Vitagraph Directors insisted on every scene being played with properly-spaced words, just as if the actor were playing a part on the stage.

One company after another adopted this plan, until it became such an institution that many of them even go so far nowadays as to give their actors properly typewritten "parts," which they have to learn—words, inflections, and business—before they even start on the rehearsals of the big subjects. This, to my mind, is carrying the thing a bit too far, for it makes the pictures very talky, whereas all that is required is just enough speechifying to make the actor feel what he is doing.

In the case of Charlie's productions, of course, such a plan would not only be farcical, but utterly impossible, for he has never in his life kept to his original idea of any story he has turned out. Occasionally the change has not been an improvement on his original plot, but it has invariably been made just the same.

No, with a Chaplin comedy, one just goes right in, made up according to instructions, and does and says whatever one is told. In nine cases out of ten it is altered until the original instructions are completely lost sight of, but that is what Charlie calls his boiling-down system—a newspaper expression he has probably picked up during his remarkably varied globe-trottings.

"It's the best way," he declared, in speaking of this the other day. "I don't care what anyone says. The only way to get the best out of your subject is to see how it plays in the rough, and then cut out all the unnecessary bits of business, prune it like a tree, and boil it down like tallow until you get the 'meat' out of it all. That's the making of good motion-pictures. It's no earthly use to get a set idea of a scene and stick to it just because it originally came to you in that light. Second thoughts are always best."

Shortly afterwards he spoke of this aim for realism, which makes him insist on the use of speeches in his pictures.

"Surely it's right," he said emphatically. "If you're playing a German in a picture, what kind of inspiration are you to your fellow-actors if you talk with an English dialect? No, you have to talk with a German accent if it is going to "get over" on the screen that you are portraying a German. In just the same way"—he turned to Leo White, who was standing by—"I always make White use his French accent in playing that Frenchman of his. It makes me think I'm dealing with a Frenchman, and so I get realism."

"But about that idea of using your voice to its natural strength," I said. "Do you feel that, because a man is supposed to be shouting on the screen, it is absolutely essential for him to be actually straining his voice?"

"Certainly I do," Charlie retorted. "I was in at the Garrick only the other night looking at *The Fireman*, and I noticed how wonderfully effective was the scene in which White rushed into the fire station shouting 'Fire! Fire!' at the top of his voice. Whether he had shouted it or not, the public would have seen from the movement of his lips what he was saying, but what I contend is that it wouldn't have been nearly so effective because the temperamental power would have been missing from behind it. I talked it over with White, and told him my idea on the point, and by following my instructions he got the thing over like the Briton he is."

White laughed.

"And a peach of a hoarse voice into the bargain," he added reminiscently.

"Even so," repeated Charlie. "You got the result."

To leave this incident and return to what I was saying at the start, however, the stage is comparatively silent these days, for Charlie, strongly as he advocates the use of the voice by all his supporting characters, hardly speaks a word himself in any of his scenes, and, as he is alone in this picture of his, nothing but the sound of his actions and the bits of mechanism he is using to enhance his effects can be heard throughout the day.

Speaking of this, have you ever watched Charlie's lips on the screen, and noticed how seldom he frames even a couple of words with his mouth? He gets everything over by sheer personality and the peerless artistry of his pantomime.

It hardly seems like a motion-picture studio out here now. During the making of both *The Floorwalker* (which ought to be with you in Great Britain very soon, by the way) and *The Fireman*, the stage was literally thronged with people who were being used in the production. There were forty or fifty girls and men used in the first-named, and they were wont to gather in little knots and hold conversations in odd corners of the stage so that it presented more the appearance of a conversazione than of a busy "comedy manufactory."[1]

But nowadays the stock people seldom even show up at the studio. They have for the most part taken themselves away on fishing trips and mountain parties, while not a few have availed themselves of the manager's generous permission to go and work in other studios until such time as they are needed again, coming only on Saturday to receive their salary cheques, which, to use an Americanism, is "pretty darned decent."

For my part, of course, a vacation has been rather knocked on the head by my official position as press manager to the great white chief, which forces me to line up at the office not later than 2 p.m., and leave not earlier than 2.30. But, none the less, it ties me to Los Angeles, and I can only sit over my pipe of Craven and wonder how those lucky "vacaters" are getting along with their holidays.

Occasionally I have been able to sneak out to the stage and watch out of the corner of my eye, so to speak, the progress of this all-Chaplin comedy, but there is nothing very brainy in flouting rules and regulations, and I have never stayed more than a minute or so.

Charlie's reason for excluding us all from his working ground is a perfectly logical one, and there is no reason in the world why he should make an exception even in my case.

Indeed, I even think he holds me in a kind of awe since the Mutual people elevated me to the position of pressman. He hardly ever talks to me nowadays without saying at least once during the conversation, "By the way, Nat, don't publish that."

Yet he awaits with just as much eagerness as the rest of the boys and girls the arrival of *Red Letters* that are sent to me by your good, kind editor, and seldom lets anything go by him that I have written in these notes since I put them before you for the first time just twenty-three weeks ago.

He is but human after all when it comes to those little things that give gratification to the average man.

While I was watching him thus surreptitiously one day this week, he was enacting a portion of his business, wherein he tries to come downstairs with a bowl of goldfish in his hand, finishing up with a terrible fall at the bottom, but without spilling even one drop of the water the bowl contains.

Everything went swimmingly—no, I'm not referring to the goldfish!— while he was rehearsing, and five times he enacted the whole gag effectively and without mishap. But by the cussedness of things inanimate when it came to the actual taking of the scene, the stair carpet must needs slip and upset his balance beyond recovery. I nearly let out a yell of alarm, and so betrayed my presence, as he fell the whole length of the stairs, goldfish and all, ripping his evening dress coat "from soup to dessert" as they say in America and smash-ing the bowl to a thousand pieces.

Even from where I was I could see that he had cut himself in some way, for a spurt of blood from somewhere had stained his dress shirt front, but the first thing he said as he rose to his feet was:—

"Quick! The goldfish! Pick 'em up. Are they hurt?" And his voice was full of genuine concern.

The ever-attentive "Scotty," who had sped to the rescue almost before the big bump had come, picked up the frightened fish, gasping in their unaccus-tomed element, and dropped them at Charlie's bidding into a near-by pail of water.

The hurt to Charlie's hand was but trifling, it appeared, and after a hasty treatment with collodion and the replacement of his torn dinner jacket with a new one, he went ahead, and enacted the whole gag to a successful conclu-sion. *[Chaplin's fall with the goldfish bowl doesn't make it into the film, but he does manage to step into the bowl several times while climbing in and out of his front window.]*

There's only one kind of injury that will make Charlie abandon a situation upon which he has set his mind. And that is an injury to another actor.

I remember, while we were making *Charlie at the Bank* over a year ago, one of the actors—an Englishman, too—who played a bank robber, made an awkward fall after Charlie had hit him with a bag of "money," and struck his head on the corner of the desk before he finally lit on the ground.

Of course, we heard the bump, but the actor didn't make any sign of hav-ing been hurt, and the camera continued to turn, while Charlie finished the scene sitting on the gunman's face, and telephoning for the police.

But when the camera man had ceased to "grind" and Holland, the actor, got to his feet, the place looked like a shambles, for the fall had inflicted a deep scalp wound.

It was typical of the Britisher's spirit that Holland had made no sound or indicated in any way that he had received an injury, but had allowed the scene to run its full course before he rose to his feet. But when Charlie saw that mess—!

I don't think I have ever seen a man in such a state of mind as he was then. He ran around the studio like one demented. His eyes filled with tears of anguish, and he sank into at least half-a-dozen chairs in turn before we finally succeeded in assuring him that he was a good deal more concerned about the accident than Holland himself had been. But even then he could do nothing until the latter had been despatched in our speediest car to the California hospital, and had received proper surgical attention. The gag was kept in, too, but only because the particular "take" in which the accident had happened was a satisfactory one. Had a retake been necessary, it is highly probable that the scene would have been eliminated from the picture altogether. Rough as Charlie's films may seem to the average picture-goer, he takes no chances on human beings. *[Adding insult to Holland's injury, he is not currently credited in any published or online filmography for his roles in either* The Bank *or* Shanghaied, *although his appearances are mentioned in several 1915 trade magazines. Harold Holland (1885–1974) is the full name of this stalwart performer.]*

As a matter of fact, while I am on the subject, there is really nothing particularly rough about these modern Chaplin productions when one gets down

RED LETTER PHOTOCARD.

(*Charles Chaplin.*)   " Charlie is Shanghaied."   (*Shanghaied.*)

Charlie is *Shanghaied* by Laurence Bowes and Harold Holland.

to the truth of it. So many tricks are possible with a motion-picture camera that a fall which registers on the screen like an attempt at suicide is in reality a well-timed, slowly-performed piece of acrobatics. It is only the fact of checking the speed of the camera that makes every fall look so violent. *[As discussed earlier, silent comedies were shot at a slower speed than they were projected so that the action would be seen speeded up. The industry term for this practice was* undercranking.*]*

For the rest of the production Charlie exercised a good deal more care with himself, I noticed. I suppose he realised that it wasn't altogether necessary for him to put himself on the sick list in order to amuse his public.

Yet nevertheless he has introduced some hair-raising things into *Twelve O'Clock*, and I, along with several other sceptics, am beginning to wonder if, after all, he is not going to add to his laurels with it. Truth to tell, the majority of people who have heard about it have expressed the belief that it can't be done. What a feather it will be in his cap if he does finally turn out a screamingly funny, entertaining picture!

It has cost him hours of thought and several sleepless nights, and he has encountered more than a few disappointments in the course of the making of those two reels, but official news from the front assures me that *Twelve O'Clock* is going to be a crackerjack of a picture, and nobody will be more pleased than we boys if it is.

The only thing we do hope is that it won't be the forerunner of several more of its kind, for a holiday is a holiday, but a life made up entirely of holidays is the very dickens, and there is not one of us, I dare swear, that is not longing for the feel of the old grease-paint stick on his comely visage.

There's nothing like work, and plenty of it, after all!

24

Charlie's Doings Up to Date

August 19, 1916

Our unsought spell of idleness is soon to come to an abrupt end, friends o' mine, for Charlie's solitary feature is finished, shown in premiere, and is now travelling by Wells-Fargo express to the big City.

I don't think any of us had realised how utterly necessary to true contentment of mind is genuine, honest, hard work, for the enforced idleness which the making of *Twelve O'Clock* has visited on us has bored us all to distraction, and there is not a man-jack among us who does not welcome the prospect of once more doing something for his living.

But, if it has been a tiresome proposition to us, it has been a positive nightmare to Charlie, and this is how I know.

I was sitting in my office pounding out fables for the delectation of the American public, when I heard someone calling my name, and, putting my head out of the window, beheld Charlie, in evening dress, but minus his collar, coat, and waistcoat, walking about the plant and peering into odd corners, presumably in search of yours truly.

Presently he spotted me, and came over.

"Have you got your car here, Fred?" he asked.

"Sure," I replied, wondering what on earth was afoot now.

"Would you like to take me over to the shave-shop right away?" he inquired. "I got up late this morning, and I've got a beard on me like Lord Salisbury."

I left the office, and led the way out to my Buick, and within a few seconds was transporting the most famous personality in the world toward the little village barber shop.

"I wouldn't ask you to run me over," he said apologetically, "only someone's swiped my car and chauffeur and gone down town, and yours is the only one left on the lot."

I begged him not to mention it, and pulled up outside the saloon.

"How long will you be?" I asked him. "I'll come back and fetch you."

"Won't you come in and wait for me?" he pleaded.

So I did.

While the tonsorial gentleman was covering his famous visage in a morass of creamy lather, he got to talking about *Twelve O'Clock*.

"Never again," he said fervently. "This is the last time I do the one-man act as long as I live. I started it with the idea of making a novelty, and there isn't a doubt that it's going to be that alright, but it's nearly driven me off my head thinking out new stuff to do without repeating myself. You fellows have had a jubilee, haven't you?"

I pointed out to him the "laying off" is far less of a jubilee than working, and after a moment's thought he agreed.

"I suppose it is," he said. "I know how unsettled I am when I'm not busy, and I suppose it affects you chaps in about the same way. But that doesn't alter the matter at all. *Twelve O'Clock* has got me more times and in more ways than anything I've ever attempted since I first stuck my face before the lens."

"Got you," I repeated. "In what way?"

"Oh, it just got me stuck and puzzled and apprehensive, and I don't know what all. To tell the truth, I was funky at times that the thing wasn't going to get over."

"And do you think it will get over?" I inquired. "When you get it finished?" I mean.

"One night next week I'm going to have it taken downtown in its completed form and shown at one of the local houses, just to see how the public is going to take it. Then I'll answer."

Conversation was suspended for the next few moments by the fact that Charlie's face was completely swathed in hot, steaming towels—a stage of American barbering which tends to soften the chin and impart a clean, refreshed sensation to the skin.

Presently he started grunting from among his pile of face covering, and the barber whipped off the towels and inquired what seemed to be the matter.

"Not hot enough," said Charlie. "Get 'em as hot as—as the deuce. You can't hurt my skin any."

So the barber made them as hot as Charlie said and there he lay, steaming like Dante's Inferno, while the hairdresser stropped his razor, preparatory to fitting the comedian's face for the grease-paint.

"I don't believe in making too many good pictures in succession," said Charlie, as the barber negotiated delicate portions of his chin. "If you make them so mighty good at the start, you have your work cut out to make the next ones better. I'm saving a lot of my best stuff for the later pictures. It's the only way."

"When do you figure on finishing up?" I asked.

"Oh, not before the middle of next week," said Charlie. "I've very little more to do, but every little scene is so ticklish in this thing that I can't gauge to a day how long it's going to take me."

Whereupon he arose from his chair, and we returned to the studio.

As it afterwards turned out, however, Charlie's estimate was over-generous, for by two o'clock the following Sunday afternoon he discovered only four more scenes to make in order to say finis.

"All right, Charlie," said Vince Bryan. "There's only the bathroom stuff to do. Let's cry off until to-morrow."

Whereupon, with one accord, and as one man, the entire staff raised their voices in a mighty "No!"

Charlie looked at them and laughed.

"Right you are," he cried. "I'm on."

So they went at it tooth and nail, and before the sun went down that day, the last scene had been photographed, and *Twelve O'Clock* was all over bar the shouting.

The shouting was provided by the staff, too. As the camera ceased to grind upon the final scene, they gave vent to a big cheer, expressive of both jubilation and relief, for the picture has, strangely enough, taxed the resources of the studio to the utmost.

Carpenters and property men alike have worked in double shifts, many of them doing twenty-hour stretches on successive days, and it is small wonder that they welcomed the coming week's rest that invariably follows the completion of each Chaplin production.

"Boys," said Charlie, "we must celebrate this. To-night we will all go down-town and forget that motion-pictures ever existed. I'm going to be a bad lad for once in my life, and I'm going to lead you all from the path of rectitude as well."

From which the boys gathered that they were in for a "party," with Charlie as chairman.

But the Fates intervened, and postponed that function until a later day, for twenty minutes later a big, cream-coloured car, upholstered in ornate tapestry cloth, pulled up at the door of the studio, and from it alighted no less a per-sonage than Sir Herbert Beerbohm Tree!

He was accompanied by his daughter Iris, and both of them had just ar-rived in town from New York where the actor-knight has been running a Shakespeare Tercentenary Repertoire, at the termination of which he had left poste-haste for California, here to resume his motion-picture contract with D. W. Griffith.

Tree thinks very highly indeed of both Charlie himself and all that the name of Chaplin conveys, a friendliness which Charlie warmly reciprocates, so it is needless to say that the coming of Sir Herbert put the "kybosh" on that projected downtown party with the boys so far as last Sunday was concerned.

It is odd how one can get to know a man's ways, and to learn to read from his moods just what is happening or has happened with him—at least, so it seems to me. It may be vanity my supposing this, or it may have been mere coincidence, but this is what causes me to make that statement:—

I had spent all day Sunday running about town in my car with a lady friend, and at about 4.30 the idea suddenly seized me to drive out to Santa Monica Beach and call on Eric Campbell.

The Chaplin studio, as you may remember, lies just off Santa Monica Boulevard, the main thoroughfare from Los Angeles to the town in question, and as we bowled along toward the coast I espied a gaudy-looking automo-bile coming from the opposite direction. I was at this time all unconscious of the happenings at the studio, so it was something of a surprise to me to see Charlie, hatless, and with his hair blowing about his forehead, seated in the tonneau of an unfamiliar car with Iris Tree, while Sir Herbert was ensconced in the seat beside the driver.

"That was Charlie," I exclaimed. "I'll bet he's finished the picture to-day."

"What makes you think that?" asked my friend.

"I can tell by the expression of his face. I'd bet ten dollars I'm right."

And, sure enough, when I arrived at the studio the next morning, the boys told me of the circumstances that had attended the finishing-up of Charlie's first and last solo picture.

Some odd form of mental telepathy had told me in that momentary flash, both of us making thirty miles an hour in opposite directions, that it was so.

A happy little incident of his sudden departure with Sir Herbert was the fact that even in such entertaining and illustrious society he did not forget the boys who had stood up beside him so staunchly on the making of that strenuous picture.

It seems he was at the Hotel Alexandria—the "Ritz" of Los Angeles"—and was just about to dine with Sir Herbert, when he recalled his temporarily-forgotten promise to the boys. Immediately he excused himself, and rushed to the telephone. Of course, the boys had left for their homes by this time, and only one of the office staff remained at the plant, but Charlie delivered him his message, which was repeated to the staff the next day.

"Tell 'em I am sorry to have rushed away like that," he instructed, "and say I haven't forgotten my promise. Tell 'em they've stood up like Trojans and that their Uncle Charles is mighty proud of them."

At which the boys all agreed that, even if the party is never destined to materialise, such praise is payment enough in itself.

We saw little enough of Charlie during the next few days, for he and Tree—different as the proverbial chalk and cheese—are almost inseparable whenever the former is in the Angel City. Charlie and he have dined and wined and celebrated almost every evening, and after the picture was assembled and shipped East he did not show up at the studio at all, and has not done so up to the time of writing.[1]

I met him one evening in the restaurant, however, and had a chat with him about things both personal and business, what time we sipped a cordial.

"I'm just about all in," he declared. "I always feel more fatigued after I have finished a tough production than I do while I am making it, and this one has hit me amidships for fair."

"Well, if it's going to 'knock them off their seats' I suppose you don't care about that do you?"

"I don't care about anything, so far as my own person is concerned, so long as the stuff gets over in great style. We're showing it to-night down at the Woodley Theatre. Like to run over and see it?"

I accepted his invitation with gusto, but before the time came to leave he suddenly espied a lady who had just entered the car.

"Great Scot!" he exclaimed. "That's Grace La Rue, or I'm wrong. Excuse me a tick."

The next moment he was down by the door wringing the great American soubrette's hands violently, and dragging her and her escort down to the table. It was perfectly unconventional, of course, but Miss La Rue was just as delighted to see Charlie as he was to see her, and she just made herself at home. Thereafter everyone else faded out of the picture for several minutes, for the way those two chatted about England, Scotland, Ireland, and Wales, and Palaces and Hippodromes and Empires and the whole gamut of "shop" talk, as we understand it in England would have done your heart good.

Miss La Rue will be remembered by thousands of my readers as one of the biggest hits America ever sent across the water to play in British Vaudeville. Her style was of the kind that tickled the palates of the British audiences to a nicety, and forthwith, as several Columbian artistes have done, she rose to the headlines within less than a month of setting foot on the soil of the United Kingdom.

Presently they condescended to remember the presence of us others, and became apologetic right away.

"You see," Miss La Rue told me, "Charlie played on several bills with me when I was in dear old Britain, and I always told him he was going to make a hit someday."—(Charlie nodded and grinned)—"And, like the Briton he is, he's gone and justified my prophecy right away."

"But in those days you were the big star, and I was only playing the lead in a sketch," Charlie reminded her.[2]

"Surely. Things are a bit different now aren't they?"

"A bit," Charlie agreed. "I don't struggle for my bread and dripping like I used to. But I'm going to tell you something, Miss La Rue. Whatever talent I may have now, I had just as much then. I wasn't such a bad comedian, was I?"

Grace La Rue screwed up her mouth, and admitted with a show of grudgingness that she didn't feel, that "Charlie knew how to walk the stage all right in them there days."

"I guess you're not so punk as you might be even now," she added, still kidding him. "Anyway, whenever you lose your job and have to look around, come to Gracie. I don't mind recommending you as a capable and reliable comedian."

After a little more conversation we arose, and made our way to the theatre, where *Twelve O'Clock* was being shown at eleven o'clock.

The fact that it was to follow the last "run" of the regular programme had been heralded from the screen earlier in the evening, and the majority of the audience had waited over for it, so there was, as Charlie put it, "a goodly crowd at the Woodley."

It was a riot. That is the only way to describe it. That audience simply jumped up and down in their seats and yelled themselves sick at the antics Charlie has introduced into the picture. I have never seen him make such terrible falls. Indeed, he has not made many falls himself, when you come to remember, in any of his pictures. *Twelve O'Clock* is just one situation after another, and, if it has cost him a world of worry and mental strain, it justifies every moment of it.

I would never have dreamed it possible that one man could have got so much fun out of a mere roomful of "props," but Charlie, using nothing but inanimate objects, which by mechanical means have a happy knack of making the result of his intoxication worse than it is, has succeeded beyond his wildest dreams in turning out a picture which is one laugh on top of another.

Furthermore, he has put in some of the funniest sub-titles I have ever read—a little trick of the trade which characterises most of his present productions, and which means a good deal more than the average picture-goer realises.

We left the Woodley that day feeling that we had been granted one of the joys of living.

And we certainly had.

25

Charlie in a Gay Mood

September 2, 1916

Well, friends, here we are again, as I remember the clown in the harlequinade was wont to observe in my juvenile days.

Up to the time of writing I can't tell whether or not our kindly Editor told you what happened to me last week, but, if he didn't, I will. It was nothing romantic. No tragic happening beneath the California sun, with Charlie Chaplin and myself as the chief actors. It was just a common—disgustingly common—attack of what the Briton is pleased to call "flue."! Americans, in the same spirit that prompts them to call a motor car an "automobile" in common parlance, refer to influenza as "La Grippe"; but you can have it which way you like—I don't want it any more.

You see, friends, when you're sprawling on your back for about ten days wondering why you were put on earth you're scarcely in the mood to call for your typewriter—either her or it—and begin to panegyrize someone else.[1]

Besides, during that siege of sickness I hadn't enough thoughts left in me to fill a single, solitary page, let alone ten, so for one week only, as the theatrical posters have it, Charlie and his doings went by the board.

Now, however, we are in that perplexing condition known as "convalescent"—a state which means you are well enough to get out and do something, but that you haven't, in case, &c.

However, since I'm well enough—and an American flat is the next best thing to a cell in Wormwood Scrubbs[2]—I took a chance and my automobile and went out to the studio to assure the world at large that Richard was himself again.[3]

The boys were glad to see me in quite a flattering way, and so was Manager Caulfield, but he had a severe eye to business, and nothing would please him but that I take another four or five days off.

"Am I to be so easily dispensed with as that?" I asked.

He laughed, and clouted me on the back.

"'Tisn't that," he said, "but I can't afford to have Charlie laid up with tonsillitis as well, and I think if you'll stick at home for a day or so more we can get along without you, and it'll be safer. If Charlie sees you, he's bound to start buzzing around you, and asking you a lot of questions about your condition; and he's pretty sure to catch a packet himself. You know what he is."

Unfortunately, I had to agree, and so the Lone Star plant saw me no more until the day on which I am writing these first few pages of my notes.

Figuratively speaking, Charlie mopped his brow and offered up a prayer of relief when his one-man picture was shipped to New York, and, like Poe's raven, he quoth "Never more."

Just as we had expected, it was several days before he started to give any instructions about the scenes for his next picture, but at last the workmen began to show signs of activity and weird two-walled rooms sprang up in odd corners of the stage. In one a garret with a sloping ceiling rose from the ashes of what in the previous picture had been a bathroom; in another a splendidly-equipped kitchen, a regular housekeeper's dream in white enamel, reared itself, while in another corner a fashionable drawing-room began to grow.

For several days Charlie made no effort to get to work. Doubtless he was thinking it out, but a casual observer would have declared that he was simply idling, for he spent hours of each day in playing golf-pool on the dilapidated billiard table which had been brought in for one of the sets.

The fact that he is no particularly brilliant player didn't seem to upset him in the least, for he played steadily on with whoever happened to feel like a game, while Manager Caulfield made occasional tentative excursions from the office, as if to urge him on. But if the latter was Caulfield's intention, he changed his mind apparently, and always returned disconsolately to the office—and Charlie continued to play. [*Chaplin was all too aware of the pressure to produce: "The mere sight of the management or the actors gaping at me was embarrassing, especially as Mutual was paying the cost of production. . . . Some-*

times the solution came at the end of the day when I was in a state of despair,
having thought of everything and discarded it; then the solution would suddenly
reveal itself, as if a layer of dust had been swept off a marble floor—there it was,
the beautiful mosaic I had been looking for. Tension was gone, the studio was set
in motion, and how Mr. Caulfield would laugh."[4]*]*

But he soon grew tired of stalling around, and one day, with a sudden burst of energy, he threw off his coat and darted for his dressing-room, where he proceeded to make up with considerable care.

When he got on to the stage again, however, his enthusiasm evaporated, and he was sad and looked at first one set and then another. This went on for an hour or so, and then he got up and retreated to his dressing-room again, whence he did not emerge for the rest of the day.

When we arrived next morning, however, all the sets had been "struck," and a series of elaborate and costly rooms were springing up in their place.

There's no accounting for what Charlie will do. He arrived full of pep and ginger that day, and started to make up right away, first giving instructions for everyone who happened to be around to make up in evening dress.

When I wandered out onto the stage, I met the rest of the boys, who all inquired very solicitously after my health. I assured them that I wasn't in any danger of expiring at the moment, and they told me the happenings of the past few days, which I have recounted above.

Eric Campbell, I found, had assumed the horrible and much-bewhiskered disguise he used in *The Floorwalker*, only in the current picture, it seems, he is playing some sort of "diplomatic dodger," as he calls it.

Indeed, everyone seems to be playing some sort of "diplomatic dodger" or other; I never saw so many whiskers in my life. If my friend Frank Richardson, that whiskatorial expert of the Old County, could have been there what wonderful material he would have found upon which to discourse![5]

There was John Rand, resplendent in a long, pointed blonde beard of the soup-gathering variety, while Leo White favoured one that looked like that of one of the ancient Pharaohs run to seed. Lloyd Bacon, more conservative, had contented himself with one of those mystic creations that have always awed and inspired me when on the Continent—I refer to the kind that are comparatively close, but are parted in the middle.

What a distinguished, mysterious air of diplomacy such a beard is wont to give its wearer! If at any time it becomes my fate to have to grow hirsute appendages, I declare the first one I shall try will be upon those lines, though Charlie declares they look like a field of hay after a fat man has walked through it!

He was in no end of a gay mood that day. He kidded everyone unmercifully, and generally put an air of joviality on the proceedings. Only, unfortunately, he was so gay that there were no proceedings—he didn't do a single thing except sit around and talk.

And here I have to relate something about Charlie which will make you want to shake a reproving finger at him, for he has been rather a naughty boy.

You will remember many weeks ago I told you how I taught Edna to speak in the Cockney rhyming-slang vernacular, and how Charlie, when he found it out, made a great show of being indignant with me, chiefly because she was now able to understand him when he kidded her in that peculiar jargon.

But when I went on to the stage that day what was my horror to hear Edna, our divine Edna, turn around and greet me with a number of perfectly horrible London intensives which would have curdled the blood of anyone but a professional!

Of course, I hushed her, and asked her where in the name of goodness she had learnt such ghastly language, and she assured me in wide-eyed innocence that she had had no idea they weren't perfectly proper names to call anybody, and that Charlie had taught them to her! And all the time that mischievous young gentleman was hugging himself in silent glee at the expression on my face. But I ask you—wasn't it a low trick to play on a young and trusting American girl?

Sometimes it seems to me that I know Charlie Chaplin like a book, and then at others he seems to be the biggest enigma in the world. I suppose it all turns on that one all-embracing word—temperament; but, whatever it is that makes him so, Charlie is a fellow of moods that change as rapidly as the designs of a kaleidoscope and are just as varied.

Ever since he started on this picture, whatever it is, he has been in that perplexing mood of inactivity that makes one wonder how he ever succeeded in making any pictures at all. He seems to have favoured anything that would waste time; has allowed the most trivial of things to detract his attention from the business of motion pictures, and then, at the finish, has invariably sauntered off to his dressing-room, leaving the throng of actors and actresses in full make-up to while away their time as best they may.

The stock actors find it excessively boring, but the "extra talent" are having the time of their lives. Every day that they make up, irrespective of whether they actually appear before the camera or not, they receive their full remuneration of one guinea per diem, so to use a popular Americanism, "they should worry!"[6]

If Charlie told the truth, he would admit that he hasn't the vaguest kind of notion what the picture is about. He has adopted a plan that has often been successful before—that of having various sets put up, and then sitting and looking at them until they give him an inspiration for a story.

For my part, I'm having a field day.

I arrived, thanks to my "flue," several days too late to be given a part in the picture, and so I have been the only gentleman of leisure on the lot.

"Lucky dog!" the other boys say, when I make an early departure, leaving them to perspire in their make-ups beneath the diffused heat on the stage until such time as Charlie decides to go home. "If we were working we wouldn't mind, but it's this perpetual sitting around that gets us."

"I'm open to bet," said Leo White, with the air of one who has known his man for years, "that Charlie will never get far enough ahead of himself to make that trip to Honolulu possible. I'll bet that when the last and twelfth picture is made Chaplin'll be hurrying himself to death to get it through in time."

He was shouted down for being a pessimist—for we're all a bit keen on that trip out to Honolulu—but there's more than a shred of possibility that he spoke the truth, for Charlie simply cannot do battle with time unless his ideas are flowing freely of their own accord.

What the remainder of the week will bring forth I, of course, cannot say, but the report for the current half of it is just simply, "Nothing doing."

And at that we've just got to leave it!

How Charlie Works His Gags

September 9, 1916

I have often referred while I have been writing these notes to the facility with which Charlie Chaplin overcomes his difficulties once he gets his mind fastened down to his task, so it will be no particular surprise to you to learn that his period of "stalling" took a sudden turn, as the doctors say.

Thanks to the fact of my absence from the studio (during the casting of the picture on which we are working, I had been spared the necessity of getting to the plant early, for all I had to do was my publicity writing. I think I spoke of that fact last week.

But one day I wandered out to the stage (just to see that everything was running as smoothly as could be expected, in view of the fact that I was not about), when Charlie caught sight of me. He was seated at a huge circular dining-table, which was figuratively groaning beneath the viands that were spread upon it. On one side of him was Edna, and on the other Eric Campbell.

When I walked over to the set Charlie was busily mesmerising a piece of macaroni which hung from Eric's mouth, the idea being apparently that the aforesaid delicacy was to disappear into the aforesaid mouth upon a given signal, the motive power being, of course, suction! Thus Eric was compelled to inhale, so to speak, pipe after pipe of macaroni, until Charlie was satisfied that they had mastered the trick of the situation.

Poor old Eric! He told me later that day that the call of lunch left him quite apathetic nowadays, for he had spent four weary days cramming himself with various articles of diet, each of which was to furnish a gag for Charlie.

"First it was soup," he said, reflectively picking up a can of consommé. "Charlie made me drink soup for about five hours yesterday, until I was ashamed to look a soup can in the face." Then in a doleful voice, which made me want to laugh outright, he said, pointing to the label on the soup can, "Look at that! They even put my name on the tins!" The can was printed with the inscription, "Campbell's Soups—Consommé."

However, to get back to my point. Charlie spotted me while he was in the middle of the scene, and called out to me to come over.

I went, never suspecting what was in store for me, and right away he started to inquire pleasantly after my health, and what kind of a time I'd had. His interest was so suspiciously marked that I presently got wise to him, and realised that he was gently kidding me.

"And what's the big idea of all this solicitude," I asked when he had got through with his inquiries.

"Oh, nothing," he said. "Only I wondered if you wouldn't like to be here to-morrow, and take part in our little picture?"

"But you didn't give me a part," I told him.

"You don't have to have a part, old dear," he said. "Come and dance in our ball-room scene among the throng."

Which is precisely what I did, when the morrow came. I guess Charlie thought seven weeks' holiday had been quite enough for the time being.

The rapidity with which Charlie changes his mind is an odd side of his character that has always puzzled me rather. He is liable to get an excellent idea into his head and starts to build a picture on it, and then, when he has gotten about a quarter of the way through it, often having spent hundreds of dollars for the services of extra actors, &c, he will switch the whole story into another channel, retaking nearly everything that has already been "shot."

Thus it has been with this picture, for which he has found no title so far. He started off with weird visions of diplomatic plots, spies, government officials, and what not. Then of a sudden he flopped into a chair and stuck his feet against the wall.

"This is a lot of bosh!" he said. "I'm going to twist it around into something else."

So the bewhiskered potentates faded into the background, and so far as I can see, the picture is now pure comedy from beginning to end.

He has taxed the resources of the property-room to the utmost in this picture, and I am wondering where he would have been had he not been blessed with one of the most capable and conscientious property-masters in the world. I refer to "Scotty," as we call him, though he has always gone under the stage-name of George Cleethorpe, and was born to the name of O'Neill.

I imagine Charlie would as soon lose any of us as lose Scotty, and the reason for my thinking this is Charlie's own statement, made to me when we were at lunch one day.

He had been in one of those pensive moods of his for the past half-hour, and presently I asked him what seemed to be engaging his attention so deeply. I could tell from the expression on his face that it wasn't the question of motion pictures—not the production of them, at any rate.

"I've been thinking," he said, "of the hundreds of details that go to the making of a motion-picture—the details of which the public know nothing. They simply see the picture in its finished state—just what we want them to see, in fact; but they hardly give a thought to the men who do the real hard work, the executive end of a production.

"Look at *The Floorwalker*," he continued. "People went to see it and laughed at the moving stairway and the fun we got out of it; but what they didn't see or know about was the days and nights at a stretch that Ed. Brewer (the head carpenter) and his men spent in making it. We tried to get one ready-made, but they wanted two thousand dollars for it, so it fell to Ed. to make it as best he could. Including the hiring of the electric motor we used to drive it, the whole thing was turned out for about a tenth of what the stairway-makers had asked. Then, again, there are the men who stand by at every trick and turn I make—the men who have to watch everything and always be on the job—not you lazy actors, who only have to work when I call on you, but the property boys, the camera men, and the others behind the gun.

"It has always been a principle of mine to appreciate the manual worker as much as I do the big supporter, for without the former and his technical skill we'd all be nowhere. Where'd I be without a man like Scotty, for example? That beggar stands by me, listens to what I'm saying when I'm sketching out a scene, and makes mental notes of the props I'm likely to require—let alone those I ask for. Then, on top of that, he has the job of engaging all the extra people, and he manages to discharge it tactfully and well, in spite of his other calls, keeping the goodwill of everybody and sticking to his job like the Briton he is. Yes, sir, I appreciate good service, and I'm not backward in admitting it."

All this may not be as interesting to the man who reads as would be the doings of someone or other of the actors, but it shows Charlie's realisation of the true value of things. How many great or near-great beings give credit to the under-dog in a way like that?

It's typical of Charlie.[1]

While we were taking the ballroom scenes the Chaplin studio came nearer to being what most people picture a comedy studio than it ever was before, for Charlie was in one of those odd moods of frivolity that used to characterise him in the old Essanay days.

With the idea, I suppose, of giving his mind a contrast from his one-man picture, he has had the company engage about fifty supernumeraries and extra people for this present production, and the stage presents rather the aspect it had when we were making *The Floorwalker*. On all hands beautiful—and near beautiful—women have sat around for about fourteen days, accompanied by dashing cavaliers attired in dress suits that would have shamed the pre-war German waiter.

These people have had the time of their lives on this picture, for when Charlie has not been thinking out points or directing scenes he has devoted his energies to amusing them, for all the world as if they were, relatively, audience and entertainer, instead of supporters and star.

A complete string band has been engaged for the scenes in question, and Charlie has certainly kept the musicians busy, for when a scene was completed he would have them start all over again and play an Irish jig, to which he would execute some of the most brilliantly conceived dancing steps imaginable.

It sounds like "laying it on thick" to keep telling of the number of things at which Charlie Chaplin is an adept, but, as Albert Austin once said, "there hardly seems to be a thing the little beggar can't do." So I'm going to state unblushingly that Charlie Chaplin hasn't a rival in the world when it comes to genuine, clever, eccentric dancing.

While the musicians were playing him that jig there was never a position he found himself in that didn't suggest to him some new eccentric step. He slipped from one movement to another, sometimes making the final "break" of the dance with his feet, and sometimes, in the most opportune way in the world, finishing it with some odd trick with his hat or his cane.

It had nothing whatever to do with the picture—at least, not then; but he just did it to keep his people amused, and incidentally, no doubt, to amuse Charlie Chaplin himself.

Meanwhile the extras sat around and enjoyed the performance more than if they had been at a circus, and when he finished each dance they gave him an unrestrained hand, whereupon he promptly gave them an encore!

The slippery floor of the ballroom, which had been specially surfaced with an electrical machine at no little cost, seemed to help his dancing rather than hinder it, and at one spot, right upon a slur in the melody, he let his feet slip apart until he was almost doing "the splits." Before we had time to really wonder how he proposed to come up to his normal position, without using his hands on the floor, however, he just slid back to the upright as easily as if it were no effort in the world; and then we noticed that before he had made his slip he had artfully hooked his cane in a huge electrolier which hung above his head!

The trick brought forth shouts of laughter, it was done in such an absurdly grotesque way, and Charlie, apparently tickled with the idea, decided to keep it in the picture.

When it came to the matter of photographing the scene, however, the electrolier protested feebly, and then proceeded to tie itself into an intricate knot.

"Too bad!" was all the comment Charlie made as he surveyed the wreckage that hung above his head. "Did it cost much?"

"One hundred and ninety dollars," the manager told him, and Charlie sat down on the floor as if someone had hit him.

The hot weather has been with us fairly during these past few days, and the business of dancing in heavy evening clothes hasn't been a pleasing one to the actors. Poor Eric Campbell has been walking around with his make-up mingling with his heavy beard in little pink rivulets, while even the slimmer members of the company have felt the ferocity of old Sol as he beat down on their heads.

With kindly foresight however, the firm had provided huge glass bowls of iced lemonade which helped to save the players from dying of thirst, and I can assure you that lemonade was very much in demand throughout the day.

The unfortunate part about this sudden heat-wave is the fact that Charlie is rather late with his picture. It has to be finished and despatched by to-day week, and he still has quite a lot to do on it, so there is going to be some strenuous work before the date in question.

Between takes one day I had a short conversation with him about technique, and our views seemed to differ at the start, though in the end, as was inevitable, he convinced me that he was right.

"Technique," he said, "taking the word in its accepted meaning, can't be applied to motion-picture directing at all. Technique means, as I take it, the perfection of a system of doing things; it's a splendid thing in business, all right, but you can't possibly systematise anything that requires individuality as its chief factor of success."

"But you've got to have a method of doing things, Charlie," I protested, harping upon a favourite string of mine. "You can't jump right into a thing, knowing nothing about it, and make good right off the bat, can you?"

"Not a chance," he agreed, "but if you try to systematise in a game like this you're going to be dead out of luck. You may jump in, as you say, and be awkward and unaccustomed at first, but it isn't system that makes you a successful man in the movie game. It's simply the bringing out of what's good in your personality, and the elimination of things that tend to mar your work. That's not system—it's just the adaption of yourself and your individuality to the necessities of the art."

I thought it over, and had to admit to him he was right, as usual.

"There's an odd thing I've noticed about you, Charlie," I told him presently, "and that's the singular luck that attends you at times in your scenes."

"Such as what?" he queried.

"Such as that scene in *Police*, for example," I said. "The scene where you fall on your back in the hall, and the washing basket falls off your head. Nobody but you would have had the luck to have that basket fall sideways, right onto your feet, so that you could spin it with your soles."

"I remember that," he laughed. "That was a bit of luck."

"Then again," I told him, "not ten minutes ago, in that scene where you're following the girl in the harem dress, she slipped a bit on the polished floor as she went round the corner, and you, although you didn't know just how she had shaped up when she did it, came right on after and skidded in precisely the same attitude."

"Did I?" he said, grinning. "Yes, I guess that was luck too. But if I depended on luck to get things over I'd be nowhere, would I?"

Presently he grew serious.

"I'm going to be out of luck next week, though, unless I'm much mistaken," he said, staring thoughtfully in the direction of the cameras.

"Why?" I asked. "What's the trouble?"

"Billy Foster," he said. (Foster is the head camera-man.) "He's leaving me flat on Saturday, to take on a better job with the Fox people."

This was news to me, and no end of a surprise, for Billy had become quite a fixture at the Lone Star plant and is an uncommonly popular chap as well.

"Well, cheer up," I said. "You'll get another good camera expert, I guess."

"Sure," he agreed, without enthusiasm. "But I hate to have a breach in the family. It takes time for a newcomer to fall into the ways of a concern, and when I get used to people I get attached to them, to a certain extent. It's a pity."

"It is," I said.

"But, anyway," added Charlie, rising to his feet, "keep yourself open for Saturday night, we're going to give Billy a farewell party—strictly 'stag'*—at the Bohemian Cafe. At least, that's where it's going to start. I refuse to try and say where it'll end."

"I'm on," I promised. "You're going to preside?"

"You bet you!" he exclaimed. Then he leant over and whispered in my ear. "And I'm going to bring two spare chauffeurs along—in case!"

I foresee terrible doings on Saturday next!

---

*Stag—American slang for "men only."

27

The Chaplin Boys' Beano[1]

September 16, 1916

The farewell celebration given to Billy Foster by the boys of the Chaplin studio was certainly "some"[2] party. I may safely say that one such entertainment would be enough to last the average man several years.

Unfortunately, I was prevented by the sickness of someone (who means something in my young life) from going to the supper party itself, but I freed myself at about nine p.m., and drove down in search of the Bohemian Café, wherein the supper was given.

When I arrived, however, after a difficult search for the place, it was to find the boys had left over an hour earlier—destination unknown. I accordingly retired to the tonneau for a few moments' reflection. I had to find those boys somehow, if I was to keep their goodwill for the rest of my connection with them; but the point was, how, in a city of half-a-million, was I to discover a mere dozen and a half?

Finally I resigned myself to the fact that, come what would, I would be able, at any rate, to see them at one a.m. at the Garrick Theatre, for the enterprising manager of that cosy little cinema was giving a "One a.m. Matinee" of Charlie's one-man picture. (The picture, by the way, has been re-titled *One A.M.*, hence the matinee.)

I accordingly drove up and down Broadway with the idea of killing time until the appointed hour, but boredom (and the exorbitant price of petrol) sent me back to the theatre at 12.30. Outside I met an old friend in the person of Crane Wilbur, star of the Horsley Company, with whom I chatted a while. We talked of the days when I played beside him in serious drama, and I told him that the first of his Horsley pictures, *Vengeance Is Mine*, in which I had played the defending counsel, was due for release in Great Britain at about this time. *[Wilbur was not only a successful actor, but also a prolific director and screenwriter; he wrote* Vengeance Is Mine*, and later penned such 1950s horror classics as* House of Wax *and* The Bat.*]*

He was very interested, for the correspondence he was wont to receive in the days when he played the male lead in *The Perils of Pauline* had given him a pleasant opinion of the British people, and since it has been so long since the serial in question was shown over there, his British mailbag has not been so bulky as in days of yore.

Perhaps I am digressing somewhat, however; I merely wanted to lead up to the Big Arrival.

It came at about 12.45 a.m., and, oh! wasn't it some arrival! Altogether there were seven automobiles, in which were distributed eighteen bad men and true—a batch of them, like the Mad Hatter's tea party, being crammed chock-a-block into one of the cars, leaving some of the other cars with no-body inside but the driver.

The boys were very angry with your Uncle Fred for "quitting" on the sup-per party, until they had my assurance as to the reason, when they waxed apologetic, and, having obtained my vow that I was "with 'em now, anyway" proceeded to bundle me into the theatre.

It seems that after leaving the Bohemian they had gone out to a popular resort just outside the city—a spot known as the Vernon Country Club, where a select few of the public are admitted, and where the goddess of dancing holds sway. Here, it seems, they had danced and reveled until the time came for their return to Los Angeles.

"Where's Scotty, though?" I asked presently, noticing the absence of our worthy head property-master.

A blank look came into the eyes of my vis-a-vis, and he gave the crowd the quick "once-over."

"Jiminy!" he gasped. "We've left Scotty out at Vernon!"

Scotty, it afterwards appeared, however, made the best of a bad job, and accepting the invitation of a party, had motored back to his home, where he philosophically went to sleep, and slept until the sun shone again.

The Garrick wasn't as full as it might have been, for everybody hadn't the energy—or disregard for slumber—that is necessary in order to attend a picture show at one in the morning; but there was a goodly crowd there all the same.

The picture, as I told you before, is a brilliantly clever piece of work technically, for there are difficulties in the making of such a production which would be hard to explain in detail to any but a motion-picture man. The chief of these—and I will try to make it plain to you—was the fact that the camera must necessarily be on Charlie himself throughout the whole 2,000 feet, and as the camera could not run continuously without a pause for that length of time, it was necessary to break in after every scene with a sub-title or a close-up of Charlie's face, returning them to the long scene itself.

The reason continuous camera action is impossible is, of course, the fact that every section of this picture (like any other), had to be rehearsed separately, in short lengths, at the end of which, as I say, a sub-title or close-up had to be interposed. I hope that isn't Greek to you, although I know it is rather technical. *[Indeed, there are more subtitles and close-ups to cover cuts on action in* One A.M. *than most of Chaplin's other films.]*

The picture went with a yell from beginning to end, and the house has been packed to capacity almost every hour since that first trial run. *[By Goodwins's own account Chaplin had already previewed the film at the Woodley Theatre, and there was a third preview at the Garrick, which occurred at 9 p.m. on July 11.[3] Another member of the studio's British contingent, Chester Courtney, was present at one of the Garrick screenings, and at the end of the film he asked Chaplin what he thought of it: "'One more film like that,' he answered, 'and it will be* Good-bye Charles!'"[4] *Chaplin's remark proved prescient, for* One A.M. *proved to be the least popular of the Mutuals.[5]]*

It has its faults, the chief of which is the repetition that seems to have been necessary. For example, Charlie spends nearly half the picture in trying to get upstairs; but his adventures when he finally does get there fully justify the amount of time and trouble he took to do it.

It is rather a pity the American firms make England wait so long before they send over their pictures, particularly as Great Britain and the British Empire are virtually their best market. If they released their subjects in England within a reasonable time after their completion, my readers would be better able to follow the doings it has been my privilege to describe to you and compare them with the various scenes in the pictures.

Original release poster for *One A.M.*

It cannot be long now, however, before they will be releasing his first production, *The Floorwalker*, on the home side, and, if I may offer a suggestion, I would advocate those of my readers who are in the habit of saving their back issues of the *Red Letter* to re-read the articles dealing with each picture when that particular picture comes their way. They will find a lot of additional interest in the film that way.

To return to that eventful summer morn, however. The party assembled outside the Garrick Theatre when the run was over, and Charlie came in for showers of congratulations before he betook his tired body to the Athletic Club and slumber.

"Good night, boys," he called as the car drove away. "Don't forget, eight-thirty to-morrow morning."

As a matter of fact, he meant this morning, but there was much to do before the matter of grease paint and film could be given consideration. The fun had not yet begun.

"Where now?" inquired Eric Campbell, depositing his huge frame inside his tiny automobile. "If anybody wants to go home to bed, he's got to reckon with me first."

Fortunately, however, nobody wanted to go home to bed—in fact, I don't think wild horses would have dragged any of us there—and after a short conference it was eventually decided to continue the celebration at another country club known at Watt's.

Five automobiles negotiated the five-mile journey at a speed that would have brought the entire Los Angeles police force about our ear had it been later in the day, but, fortunately, Main Street was deserted, for it was nearly two a.m., and our forty miles an hour mattered no more than five would have done.

Arriving at Watt's, we "parked" our cars side by side like a rank of soldiers, and entered the club. We were greeted hospitably by Albert Levy, the proprietor, a staunch Liverpudlian, by the way, and we knew that thereafter we were safe, whatever we chose to do. Al. has a belief that "whatever a Britisher does, goes," so it was like having a friend at Court.

Our main idea in going to Watt's had been to enjoy a final dance, only that final dance stretched into several before we decided that it was time to stop. Professionals are really disgracefully unconventional folk, and there's something in the air of Southern California that tends towards wildness.

Charlie and I discussed this climatic peculiarity a day or so later, but I'll save the discussion a while.

The hour was getting on when we finally unparked our machines and drove back over the crude, uneven road, but by now we had all grown so thoroughly awake that all the King's gee-gees couldn't have dragged us between the sheets right then. We felt the "evening" had been incomplete, and when we arrived back at Los Angeles, with no more serious happening to our account than one burst tyre and a few wonderful skidding exhibitions, caused by the fact that the morning toilers were watering the asphalt roads, we got into a conclave, which culminated in everyone driving from Los Angeles to Santa Monica, twenty-six miles way, for the express purpose of eating breakfast at the residence of Eric Campbell!

Eric's bungalow, as I have mentioned before, is about large enough to comfortably contain one quietly-disposed old maid, so you can imagine what a task we had when it came to about ten of us eating breakfast in a parlour barely the size of a stage box in an English theatre. But the breakfast was well cooked, the drive had made us peckish, and, besides, within two hours the whole outfit had to be back on the job making pictures, so there was no question of waiting for each other to finish.

Back to the studio we drove thereafter, arriving punctually at the appointed hour, 8.30 a.m.

Charlie worked like a Trojan for the next few days, inventing some of the weirdest situations imaginable, and then, just as the picture was nearing its finish, the camera man suddenly cried a halt.

"What's up?" inquired Charlie, stopping in the middle of a busy "scrap" when he found the camera had ceased to click. "Run out of film?"

"No," said the camera man, "but this set's been put up wrong. It shows you coming on from the right, whereas you left the other room in the preceding scenes from a right-hand door, which should bring you into the passage scene from the left."

Charlie pondered a second, then made a motion of placing the ballroom set beside the passage set in which so much work had already been done. Then he groaned.

I have never seen a man's face so fall as Charlie's did when he discovered that Rollie's discovery had been correct.[6] By some odd oversight the head carpenter had erected the hallway set in such a way that Charlie, leaving the ballroom scene by one door, would appear to come on from the other side when the two scenes came to be joined together in consecutive order.

It was a bitter blow to the poor chap, for many days had been spent in the latter scene, and it looked as if the whole scene would have to be changed around and everything retaken. The expense would have amounted to several hundreds of pounds.

But once again Charlie's clever brain came to the rescue, and instead of bawling out the mechanician whose mistake it had been—a man of whom Charlie thinks very highly—he spent a few moments in deep thought, and then smiled.

"I've got it!" he cried, leaping down the stairs. "We'll put up an 'angle passage' which is supposed to come between this scene and the next. It'll have doors at right angles, and that'll bring everything out right. All we've got to do is take short slashes of each character making his exit from one door and through another, and then insert the scenes in their right places between those we've taken." *[This is a bit difficult to visualize in print but works like a charm in the film.]*

Can you beat that for resourcefulness?

And here came a little touch of Chaplin spirit which made me want to chuck my hat up in the air and yell out "Bully for Charlie." One of the actors was sitting by, making rather ill-natured remarks about the carelessness of the man who had made the simple error which might have had bad results, when Charlie overheard him. His eyes flashed anger.

"Does it affect your salary any?" Charlie demanded sharply.

The actor gasped.

"No, Charlie," he answered meekly.

"And could you have put up that moving stairway in *The Floorwalker* or built that vault scene in *Charlie at the Bank*, or the rocking cabins in *Charlie Shanghaied*?" continued Charlie.

The actor was too abashed to answer, so Charlie closed the discussion with a few scathing sentences such as only a Briton can speak.

"Then confine your criticisms to yourself," he said. "I've made bigger bloomers than that myself, and I won't hear any remarks against —— after the kind of service I've had from him. If it displeases you, you know the options."

It has been said of Charlie that what he does is not always new, and more than one little gag and situation was familiar to us English fellows, but there stands the incontrovertible fact that Charlie has a way of doing something that's as old as the hills, and yet getting screams of laughter from the very people to whom it is oldest. It's that "way with him" that does it, people would say, and they'd be speaking better truth if they said it is his colossal genius.

Yet even in all that quick succession of comedy Charlie found sentiment, and it is hardly surprising when one comes down to cases.

The scene was over and the picture practically finished, and Charlie composed himself in a position that would have been horribly uncomfortable to anyone but him, and gave himself over to relaxation. But I noticed he had that far-away look that he invariably gets just before he's going to talk philosophy or lapse into his serious vein, and I scented that work for that day was done.

I was right. Two minutes later he began to talk, and what he said is worthy of record.

"It's a funny thing," he said, crossing his feet, and bringing his knee up under his chin. "Wherever I go, whatever I do, I never seem to get away from the memories of my early days. Hardly a day passes that doesn't bring me into contact with some object, some place, some phase of life that sends the thoughts of our early poverty rushing to my brain again."

He paused, and played with a reel of cotton, which had been put on to dress the scene.

"Oh, I don't mind it," he went on. "Only it's odd that even now, well off as I am, I can't lose those sordid memories."

"What I'm referring to now is this tailor's shop. After the old man died"— Charlie referred to his dad, the elder Charles Chaplin—"things went to pot completely with us. My mater wasn't strong, and we were only kids, Syd and I, but she stuck it like a Briton, and got some work to do with her needle. It was outrageous, sinful sweating, but it kept our bodies and souls together. Though she worked fourteen hours a day and we kids used to carry the finished goods from our home to the factory, all she ever had to show at the end of a week was fourteen bob, and on that we had to live.

"I never see a tailor's shop without thinking of those days," he finished, and unconsciously picked up a threaded needle from a near-by pincushion, and began to sew two bits of waste together.

Well, would you believe it, when Charlie had sewn those two scraps of cloth together I'd defy anyone to tell the job from the work of a practiced tailor's hand. After all those years he had never lost the trick his mother had taught him. *[In his* Autobiography *Chaplin vividly describes his mother try-ing to eke a living from her sewing skills, but this is the only mention that she passed those skills on to him. He would have found them handy as a traveling performer, and he made good use of them onscreen as well, as the Tramp is for-ever finding a handy pin on his person to hold up his pants, use as a toothpick, or pin up Edna's hair.]*

I interviewed Sir Herbert Tree about him a few months ago, and the actor-knight's words came to me forcibly on the day of which I write:—

"A wonderful man—a very wonderful man."

And Sir Herbert knew his subject.

28

An Accident in the Chaplin Studios

September 23, 1916

The powers that be have decided to title Charlie's fifth Mutual picture *The Count*, because he ultimately made up his mind to turn the plot into a mix-up between himself and a real Count, glorying in the romantic name of "Broko," a part played by Leo White.

There is no pretension toward sentiment or sentimentality in *The Count*; it is just a plain, Chaplinesque piece of farcical comedy, and as such will probably appeal to the few objectors (I wouldn't exactly call them conscientious ones) to dramatic touches in Chaplin comedies.

Among the eccentricities that prevail in the U.S.A. one may often see chirpy little notices stuck up in shops and cheap eating-houses, the chief of which seems to be, "You can't please everybody. If you don't believe it, start a restaurant."

That is exactly the way one has to look on motion pictures. There are many, many people in this extraordinary old world of ours who positively dislike, or have persuaded themselves that they dislike, Charlie Chaplin and his comedies. The only thing that upsets their apple-cart is the fact that they are vastly in the minority. Nevertheless, they exist, and their persistent knocking, both in private life and when they are sitting behind you in a cinema, is very irritating, all prejudice apart.

I know I, for my part, being gifted with a fine old-fashioned British temper, have often nearly gotten myself into a "clem" with someone or other of these audible "knockers," by telling them frankly "where they get off." Every man has a right to like or dislike anything he wants to, but, as I remember our old pal, Doc. Bodie, used to say, "he has not the right to voice that opinion in a public place of amusement." *["Doctor" Walford Bodie was an enormously popular stage attraction in England. He began as a magician and ventriloquist but caused a sensation when he came up with the idea of combining hypnotism, electricity, and "bloodless surgery"—manual manipulation—to heal the lame and infirm. When Chaplin was seventeen he had one of his greatest theatrical successes parodying Bodie in the* Casey's Circus *show.]*

The reason I am enlarging on this is chiefly my conviction that if ever a man in this world deserved everything he has attained, Charlie Chaplin has merited his, and it behoves nobody, least of all the nonentities who practice it most freely, to "pan" and criticise him and his work. There is no more romantic story in the annals of history than the story of the coming and of the meteoric rise of Charles Spencer Chaplin, and when it comes to be told, as Charlie himself intends some day to tell it, perhaps those busybodies will realise that it is the story of triumph in the face of awful odds—and hide their diminished heads.

Last week I opined that a few days would see the finishing-up of *The Count*, but as a matter of fact it was finished the day following the writing of my notes. Charlie suddenly realised that he was nearly a week late with the negative, and he put his back into the job and finished up everything just before the sun went to rest behind the top of old Mount Hollywood.

The story seems to have retained quite a little of the original idea Charlie had in mind when he started it, for it is full of weird conspiracies and dark doings between Charlie and Eric Campbell, who is at one stage of the story a repairing tailor, and later seems to be some sort of a diplomatic personage. Truth to tell, it was taken in such erratic form that few of us outside the "know" have been able to piece the plot together and get any idea of what it really means. However, it will be shown within the next few days, and I shall be able to describe the drift of it in better detail. As I have said earlier, however, it should please the captious critics who demand adherence to the old-time style of comedy, for in addition to the diplomatic mysteries, there's a lot of slop and pie-slinging in it, while ice cream figures in some of the scenes, with disastrous effect to sundry costumes.

A Chaplin comedy is not made in accordance with the rules usually followed by motion-picture directors, who, as a majority, work from a script
which has been previously written out in exact order of continuity by the
author or continuity-writer. Charlie, however, conceives his own stories—as
I have indicated on many occasions—and the consecutive number of each
scene is photographed before the scene is begun. When I say consecutive
number, I mean consecutive in the order of taking, not in the order in which
it appears on the screen. This number is thus indelibly placed at the commencement of each and every scene, and serves as a guide to the committee
which assembles the picture into its proper scenic order. (The portion with
the number is, of course, cut off and destroyed before the scene is joined to
the faction preceding it.)

This method takes more time and is more difficult than the customary
method, but it is unavoidable since Chaplin never uses a script with properly
numbered scenes.

Charlie never buys a scenario, and neither does he employ any outside aid
in writing his stories. He only holds frequent conferences with his assistant,
Vincent Bryan, and then begins to prepare a super-comedy of the kind that
has made him the world's highest-paid artiste. The only idea he has ever
bought from the outside was that which constituted the main body of *Charlie
Shanghaied*, but even that was added to and changed to such an extent that
only the mere thread of the original story remained.

I merely mention these details in order to give the man in the street the
basic idea of the way in which a Chaplin comedy is made.

After the finishing-up of *The Count*, Charlie fell into his customary trick of
stalling around for a week and more, what time we of his supporting company
had a leisurely time of it, devoting our days to various amusements and trivial
diversions.

But as the time grew near for him to think of the next picture, we got to
staying around the studio in case he should turn up unexpectedly and order
us all to make up, and these periods we turned into club meetings of a sort,
with glee-parties, serenading no one in particular.

One day, however, while the carpenters were busily at work upon the sets,
and we actors and actresses busily serenading the desert air with the strains
of "Soft and Low" and similar melodies of bygone days, there came a sudden
crash from the stage itself, followed by a dead silence. Never suspecting the

true import of the noise, we rushed with one accord to the place whence it had come, and found our mascot, Billy, whom you will remember as Charlie's pet goat, standing quietly beside a fallen piece of balustrade, with one of his hind legs dangling helplessly beside the other.

A brief examination showed that the poor little beggar had been indulging in a playful scrap with one of the studio dogs, and temporarily losing ground, had backed into the heavy piece of equipment, bringing it down on the fore-part of his hind leg, with the result that the latter had sustained a clean double break and was hors-de-combat.

Consternation reigned among us all, for Billy, as has often been stated to you, is Charlie's greatest pet, and an accident to him meant trouble from the great white chief.

However, the presence of mind of Lloyd Bacon, who had received in his earlier days a primary course of medical surgery, saved Billy from the necessity of extermination. Lloyd pushed his way to the forefront of the crowd which surrounded the goat, and lifted him bodily into the carpenter shop, where we laid him on a bench and strapped him down.

Lloyd, meanwhile, held the injured limb at tension, in order to save it from contracting, while one of the staff went and motored at top speed to the nearest veterinary surgeon for assistance. The vet., however, was out on a hurry call, and it was half-an-hour and more before he arrived, throughout which time Lloyd never relaxed his tension on the beast's limb, despite sundry vigorous convulsions of pain which racked Billy from stem to stern, so to speak.

When finally the surgeon arrived on the scene he lost no time in setting the broken member and placing it in both splint and plaster, and thereafter Billy was consigned to a comfortable cabin, especially furnished for his benefit, and given nothing but the best of eats, all of them of great bone-building value.

Charlie did not arrive until next morning, but when he heard of the accident he was just as grieved as he could be.

"Poor old Bill!" he said, as he examined the bandaged limb. "Is there any possibility of its not getting well?"

"It is possible that the bone won't mend," the vet. told him, "but in that case his life can be saved by amputating the limb at the middle joint."

Charlie shuddered.

"Why is that?" he questioned. "Is there any particular known reason why a goat's limb would not mend as easily as a human being's?"

"Simply that a goat is a herbivorous animal, living on nothing that would tend to build bone, whereas a meat-eating animal, such as a human being, or a dog or a cat, will mend rapidly, because of the bone-making properties of a meat diet. That is why horses have to be killed, as a general rule, when they break a limb. You see, the first thing that forms in curing a break is a callous, which grows around the broken place to bind it while the bone knits together, but with these vegetarian animals one generally finds, after a long period of splinting and bandaging, that the bone had not joined up; only the callous is there, and that can be broken with the fingers, leaving the break just as clean as when it was first made."

"Poor old Bill!" said Charlie again, patting the goats hard cranium. "He was always such an active old beggar too. Anyway, do whatever you can for his comfort, and don't spare the expense. In any case, he's not to be destroyed," he added anxiously.

The surgeon promised to do everything that lay in his power, and so Billy has been living in the lap of invalid luxury ever since.

It was many days before Charlie got to work on his next picture, despite the fact that he was away behind time. The head of the firm began to wander around the stage with a very worried expression, for his chief duty to the Mutual Corporation, under which the current Chaplin pictures are released, is to see that the negative of each picture arrives in New York upon the scheduled date.

In this case, however, Charlie has gone several points worse than his previous efforts in the way of delays, for he has but twelve days, instead of thirty in which to start and complete his next story.

We welcomed his sudden arrival when, one day about two weeks after the completion of *The Count*, he decided to start giving instructions about the sets that were needed for the story. The instructions soon came from headquarters, and the whole company was transported, as usual, to Los Angeles for the purpose of gathering up suitable costumes from the various gentry who specialise in the supplying of character clothing for the Thespians who grace the celluloid art.

When we learned what kind of clothing was being chosen for us, however, we became apprehensive about our future physical condition, for there wasn't a suit among the whole bunch that hadn't been made at least ten years previously; it portended rough-character stuff, you see, and that invariably means rough comedy.

Thus it proved to be when, two days still later, he ordered us all to make up as Irish-men and Jews, and to prepare ourselves for a perfectly good rough-and-tumble fight.

We discovered then that in the meantime the carpenters and property men had erected an entire street upon the vacant plot of land which skirts the studio itself. They had been working from seven in the morning 'til midnight for three days, and a more wonderful set from a point of realism I have never seen in all my association with the motion-picture industry. Edgar Brewer, the genius of technics to whom I have referred in my earlier instalments, has simply lifted the entire section of New York the spot is supposed to represent and transported it to Los Angeles. I hope by the next issue to be able to steal a snapshot of this remarkable piece of scenic art, and give you an idea of the scale upon which the Lone Star Mutual pictures are being made.

Charlie spoke during the day of the difficulties under which the motion-picture directors work in trying to secure suitable locations for their exterior scenes.

"Just think," he said, "of the thousands of dollars a corner of Whitechapel would be worth if it could only be set down in the Film City. A house of the type peculiar to London would be worth its weight in gold whereas it would probably be purchasable in London for a mere song. It's a fierce expense and trouble to have to build every extraordinary scene we need, but it just has to be done. I'm not going to put up with makeshifts that look like what they are—sections of Los Angeles."

So the street was sanded and prepared for the big fight, and to-morrow we are looking out for murder. What is worrying us most is the fact that while the fellows who are playing Jews are descendants of all kinds of nationalities, the Irish are all the genuine article.

Since I'm playing a Jew, I am devoutedly hoping the Irish won't be carried away by the realism of it and wade into us in real earnest. *[Given today's sensitivity to racial and religious stereotyping it seems necessary to point out again that such material was commonplace in the entertainment of the period, and that most of it was deemed inoffensive by the groups being caricatured.*

Chaplin was more sensitive to the issue of anti-Semitism than most. During his music hall days he had cobbled together an act as a Jewish comedian that got him hooted off the stage, a deeply humiliating experience that he relates in some detail in his Autobiography.[1] *In addition, his half-brother Sydney was purportedly half-Jewish, and Paulette Goddard, his co-star and domestic partner during the 1930s (it's uncertain whether they ever married), was born Pauline Levy. In 1940 Chaplin cast himself and Goddard as Jewish characters in* The Great Dictator, *putting both his career and his life on the line by attacking Hitler's virulent anti-Semitism in a film that broke Hollywood's silence about the Nazi menace.]*

29

Charlie Chaplin, Syd, and a Football

October 7, 1916

Once upon a time in my iniquitous career I got a romantic streak, and sat me down and wrote a love story, which was bought by a New York magazine. In that story I used the remark, "Heaven save us from our friends!" which was promptly deleted by a very scrupulous editor before the paper went to press.

Nevertheless, I honestly believe that we can get just as much harm out of excessive friendship as from studied enmity, and I should know, if anybody, for the too cordial attention of friends has been the greatest drawback to what might—or might not, as the case may be—have been a pretty successful career.

Whenever I have made up my mind to be an industrious young man, and spend several successive day in pounding out news for the specific purpose of raking in shekels, there has generally come a telephone call or a personal visitor and dragged me off my job, sometimes for an indefinite period. Such is the frailty of human nature! And thus do I reiterate—"Heaven save us from our friends!"

It was because of this that I decided to change my quarters to some building where I could hide myself in obscurity, and when the mood was on me sit on the safer side of locked doors and pound on my typewriter to my heart's content.

I accordingly folded my tent, Arab-like, and stole away in the night. (This is figurative, of course; I don't mean that I "shot the moon."[1]) My new habitat is a rather more pretentious one than the old building, and this, in my innocence, I imagined was going to afford me the greater security from the incursion of my friendly enemies.

I imagine I had in mind the old saying that a fugitive is safer in a vast city than he would be out on the open range. Anyway, I ensconced myself behind the aforesaid doors with not a soul knowing whence I had moved. That is how it seemed to me then, and for one blissful night I pounded the machine in solitude.

But the next morning, as I was leaving for the studio, I ran full tilt into the worst transgressor of all my disturbers, who, to my horror, informed me that he too had moved to the Golden Apartment Hotel that very day.

The same night I caught two more of them in the billiard-room of the place, and bolted for my room, whence I telephoned to the manager and asked him for a few names of the people who occupied flats there. Shades of my forefathers! I never knew the building could hold so many people who knew me. Gone were my good intentions. I knew that I was in a bigger dilemma than ever, and resigned myself to the inevitable.

Next day (and this is the reason I have mentioned the foregoing) Charlie told us that work was an unlikely proposition until the morning; the cause whereof was the return of Brother Sydney from the East to take up his position as co-director of the Chaplin comedies.

[The Count *was Chaplin's fifth film in as many months, and, as Goodwins's account makes plain, the pressure was wearing him down. On July 31, Charlie sent a desperate telegram to Syd, who was in New York, explaining the film's premise and asking him to "wire gags if possible." On August 2, Tom Harrington, who had become Chaplin's valet and secretary, took it upon himself to telegram Sydney as well, begging him to come to L.A. to work with Charlie, who, Harrington said, was in a depressed state. Finally, on August 7, Charlie wired Syd again:*

THE LAST TWO PICTURES HAVE GIVEN ME GREAT WORRY AND I NEED YOU HERE TO HELP ME DROP EVERYTHING AND ARRANGE TO BE IN LOS ANGELES BY SATURDAY AUGUST 12 TO HELP ME IN DIRECTING NEXT PICTURE WIRE ANSWER IMMEDIATELY

CHARLIE.[2]

Sydney wired back to say that he had been negotiating with Mutual for a salary of $2,500 a week for his services. It's not known what amount was eventually agreed upon, but within a few days Syd was on a train to L.A.]

We talked about his coming for a few minutes, and then I chanced to ask whether Syd intended to stay at the Athletic Club, where Charlie is quartered. I might have known better, for Syd is married, and therefore not likely to make an institution of that sort his permanent home. But I never expected the reply Charlie gave me.

"Syd?" he answered. "Why, I think he'll stay at the Golden Apartment Hotel," and I turned my eyes up to the skies and went home. There's no rest for the wicked.

Syd's arrival in town was something of a surprise to the majority, who had always understood that the star's brother was in retirement upon Riverside Drive, New York, and had no intention of returning to the picture business, but none of us dreamed for one moment that he was to take up his position in the Lone Star studio.

Charlie was a bit contrite about having to go downtown to meet Syd, for he had but a few days in which to finish the picture even then; but the call of the blood was strong, and he didn't do a stroke of work on the day of Syd's advent into town.

"It's a darned shame, though," he said half-guiltily. "After all the expense I've put the firm to in building this big set I oughtn't to waste time, but, at the same time, I wouldn't offend Syd by not going down. Make up by eight-thirty to-morrow, boys." And he hurried to his car, as if he feared his conscience would chase him.

But when Syd blew into the plant the next day the mere question of delay faded into the background before the radical change that began to be wrought, and this is how it all came about.

For several days Charlie had dallied with the big street scene, using dozens of people all made up in weird disguises, which seemed to afford him no little amusement whenever he set eyes on them. But after spending several hours every forenoon in surveying the set and the people he would suddenly get a burst of energy, and start rehearsing a scene just when everyone was thinking of the little restaurant across the street.

He employed about forty people a day altogether, in addition to the regular staff of actors and carpenters, which alone numbers over fifty men and women, and his opening scene was to consist of the entrance into the street of a limousine in which he was ensconced, and an argument with the chauffeur which, by a clever ruse, enabled him to bilk the latter out of his fare. Then came that memorable fight between the Irish and the Jewish—and then came Syd Chaplin, and the whole story was changed, the big set abandoned (either temporarily or permanently), and the story became a series of adventures in a pawnshop!

[In the factory town that Hollywood had already become, Chaplin's work habits were unorthodox, to say the least. The elaborate street set was already named "Easy Street," but the story that took place on it was still four films away, and it wouldn't feature a battle between Irishmen and Jews. The new film, however, would feature a Jewish pawnbroker locked in a pitched battle with his incorrigible assistant, played by Charlie.]

Sydney assumed the position of co-director with Charlie, and after the first little difficulty of co-operation in their views of comedy they finally evolved a succession of screamingly funny gags, which bid fair to develop into one of the funniest pictures Charlie has ever made.

I referred in a recent instalment to the extraordinary wealth of gags Chaplin garners from various sources and puts into his pictures, and this one, which has yet to be titled, has brought to light a flock of new ones, although Syd may have been responsible for a lot of them.

Syd is a capital director, and it was something of an education to observe the Keystone touches in his work and conceptions—little touches which have been outgrown by Charlie in his aim at the more legitimate end of motion-picture comedy. But the old saw which has it that two heads are better than one seems to be true where Charlie and his brother are concerned, for, in spite of their different viewpoints on the subject of humour, they are nevertheless an admirable team, and work with a smile throughout the day.

Sydney, who is a typical Londoner and does not resemble his younger brother in any way, has a cheerful disposition which is contagious and brings the best out of the players whose work he directs.

I suppose the majority of you have seen Syd's pictures of Keystone days, when he was presenting the character of an eccentric gentleman who gloried in the name of "Gussle"? If you have, and have an opportunity to see them over again, take particular notice of the multitude of odd little tricks and situations he used to introduce. One would hardly say that Sydney is within the same class as Charles as a comedian of the screen, but his aptitude for thinking out original gags and tricks of the business is quite remarkable and fits him splendidly for the work of producing comedies, which demand so many new laughs for each succeeding one.

[Unlike his earlier reticence about crediting Vincent Bryan, Goodwins makes no bones about the importance of Syd's creative contributions to the current film. As mentioned earlier, Syd cowrote several Karno sketches, and he was noted as an excellent gag man. Although it is impossible to determine who is responsible for which gags in The Pawnshop, *what is clear is that the film bursts with comic invention, maintains a breathtaking pace from start to finish, and represents another artistic leap for Chaplin. Surviving outtakes show Syd precisely choreographing the performances of several of the actors.]*

Everything was industry for the first few days of Syd's reign, but it wasn't long before the old order returned and Charlie got to spending whole mornings in trying out scenes that were never used, the cameras thus recording nothing at all until mid-afternoon.

In one of his gags he uses a metallic ball, which is supposed to be dropped on someone's head with dire effect, and as, of course, the real article could not possibly be used in the scene where the blow is delivered, lest manslaughter result, a soccer football painted to resemble the metal globe was substituted.

When the gag was over, however, that soccer football became the object of attention, and right on top of our luncheons we started in on a regular cup final, using the width of "Easy Street," the big set, as goals. It's a funny thing, and yet perhaps it is perfectly natural, that whenever a batch of Britishers get around a football all class prejudices and dignities fall off like so many mantles, and the bunch with one accord start in on a brisk bout of the national sport.

I remember it used to be so in my Territorial days.[3] The grim and fearsome colonel and majors and captains and subs who inspired such respect at the Westminster Headquarters would forget everything down at the camp on Salisbury Plain when some mere recruit would kick a football among his chums. It always struck me a singular example of the truth of the saying that one touch of Nature makes the whole world kin, and that is precisely how it was at the Lone Star studio that day.

Nobody seemed to know who'd won the game, for it was a regular scrimmage, and consisted mostly of artistic headwork exhibitions on the part of Syd and Charlie, both of whom seemed able to do as effective passing with their respective heads as we other boys could do with our feet.

"Suppose we get up an Association football team here?" suggested Charlie suddenly, and forthwith the matter of who would be best at half-back and centre-forward, etcetera, etcetera, was thrashed out. But then some genius suddenly remembered the fact that not one man in fifty thousand in the U.S.A. has the remotest idea of the rules of soccer, and, as this put the kybosh on the matter of finding opponents, the Chaplin-Mutual F.C. died an untimely death at the tender age of fifteen minutes.

I haven't an idea how long this picture is going to take before it is shipped to New York, signed, sealed, and delivered but it's a mile overdue already, and unless some tall hustling is done the New York office will be shooting frenzied wires across the continent to learn the why and wherefore.

Personally I shall be heartily glad when it's finished; not because it is an unpleasant picture to work in, but because the picture that is to follow it is likely to be a regular "beano."

After the finishing of *Charlie Shanghaied*, just twelve months ago this week, Charlie shook his fist at the good ship *Vaquero*, upon which that ill-starred picture was made, and said—"If I ever make another sea picture again I hope something awful happens to me." Whereby we gathered that he never intended to set foot on the deck of a steamer again; at least, not for the purpose of making a comedy. Yet the news came forth this week that we are to make our next picture around the sport beloved of Thomas Lipton,[4] i.e., yachting, the majority of the land scenes being staged upon a picturesque island called Catalina. Just how true the rumour may be I cannot say, but as things stand at present we are likely to be transported across the sound in a body and billeted at the Catalina Hotel for three weeks.

Possibly this is to be in place of the projected trip to Hawaii, which we think will have to be abandoned on account of the fact that Charlie hasn't got ahead on his work sufficiently to enable us to make the necessary four-day journey each way.

Charlie says he'll be tickled to death to get away from the Angel City, which, as I mentioned a couple of weeks ago, is from some climatic cause a hot bed of the things that wouldn't look well in print. I think I promised to quote his remarks for you, and, so far as I discreetly can, I will.

"I never realised that there could be such wildness in one moderate-sized city," he said. "Back home in England, and even through all my travels in the U.S.A., I was always a regular citizen, with sane inclinations and habits. But I hadn't been in Los Angeles a month before I got the weirdest ideas into my head of what constituted gaiety and the sweets of life. I never saw so much spreeing and alcoholism in my life, and unless one gets away from it every now and again one is going to lose sight of a lot of the beautiful things. It's odd that such a glorious-looking spot with such a wonderful climate should be so nasty in its ways. But there it is, and there's no gainsaying it."

He spoke in perfect good humour, as if the thing surprised him more than it revolted him, but it was, as he said, beyond denying, and that trip to Catalina, if only for the sake of the change of company and surroundings, will be balm in Gilead to more than a few of us.

New Chaplin Film a "Howling" Success

October 14, 1916

By dint of a lot of overtime and high pressure Charlie and Sydney managed to get the sixth Mutual picture off to New York within three days of its sched-uled time, and the poor, harassed manager of the Lone Star studio breathed freer when finally it was speeding by registered express towards the big city.

But a lot had to be done to it at the time I finished my last instalment, and although there was little of actual importance in the events that followed my last record—at least, so far as the picture is concerned—the cleaning-up of the story kept Charlie and Syd guessing and hustling from getting-up time till sunset.

The picture is to be entitled *The Pawnshop*, and once again, as in the case of *The Count*, Charlie has adhered to the old slapstick method, leaving out anything in the nature of dramatic plot or romance, although the picture does finally end (as usual) with his being given a comely bride in the person of Edna.

Speaking of *The Count* reminds me that that remarkable production was released and shown last Sunday, when the whole studio turned out en masse to see it. Sunday was a working day with the majority of the company, how-ever, and they postponed the official visit until the evening show, but as I am once more doing only a tiny bit in *The Pawnshop*, I didn't take the trouble to go to the studio that day, but grabbed the opportunity to slip downtown—un-accompanied—and see the three o'clock run. *[Goodwins's scene didn't make the final cut of* The Pawnshop.*]*

The place was packed to the doors, and were standing-room permissible in the U.S.A. it would have been packed still further, for there was a huge line of impatient Yanks ranged along the Broadway front of the block on which the Garrick Theatre stands.

About seven-eighths of the audience was composed of children of every age, and it was fine to see the kiddies indulging in the greatest joy in life—a view of the latest Chaplin comedy.

Maybe we are all creatures of the moment, or maybe our opinions lose their conviction even in our own minds, as they recede further back into history, but, be that as it may, I often wonder on seeing the latest Chaplin picture (whichever one it happens to be) how on earth I could ever have imagined the previous one to be the funniest on record. The current one always seems to me to be the best, and I am wondering if it is just because it happens to be the newest.

For once, however, I can speak with conviction and rely on myself not to change my mind thereafter, for I am backed up this time by the unanimous vote of the Los Angeles public and, incidentally, by the books of the Garrick Theatre.

Charlie Chaplin never has, and I doubt if he ever will, put on a comedy with so much continuous and unadulterated laughter as that which is brought forth from *The Count*.

From the little I saw of its making (for, you will remember, I was laid up at the start of the thing) I had rather gathered the impression that it was going to be a bit too much on the pie-and-panic order, whereas it is a succession of subtle situations and ideas, with which the pie-slinging fits in just at the right moment to keep the pot boiling.

If Chaplin is going to make a better picture than his sixth one *[The Count was actually the fifth Mutual]*, he's got to go some, that's all!

There's one little gag which has never been surpassed for subtlety since motion pictures were first invented as a comedy medium. I can't, for very good reasons, describe it in these columns, but, if you can manage to keep this paragraph in mind until the day you have a chance to see *The Count*, watch for it. It went right over the heads of most of the people here. *[Your annotator would love to share the gag with you, but it must have gone right over his head too; all the gags in* The Count *seem pretty self-evident.]*

Yet, successful as *The Count* was, Charlie met me next morning with a glum countenance, and I knew right away that some third party was responsible for it. I also knew that whatever the worry was it was groundless. He worries more over groundless things than he does over the big and ominous ones.

"How now?" I demanded. "More Hamlet looks, Charlie?"

He smiled cynically. "Oh, it's nothing," he said in a tone which indicated clearly that, although he knew perfectly well it was nothing, he couldn't get over it.

"Someone's sent me a cutting from a Chicago paper," he went on. "It's by some scare-headed staff writer, who finds it in him to occupy half a column with a statement that my popularity is on the wane, giving the reasons why.

He handed me the cutting, and I read, and as I read I got an insatiable desire to be walking along South State Street, "Chi.," where the offices of that paper are situated.

All the same, nobody with any gumption at all could read it without taking a grain of salt along with it, and had Charlie been less of a sensitive than he is he would probably have consigned it to the waste-paper basket without another thought.

The writer declared that Chaplin's day is all but done, for "although all the twenty six theatres in Chicago that show Chaplin-Mutual comedies are still taking the same leases on them" (and that is the prime bit of paradox in the whole write-up) "the public is getting tired of the little 'millionaire clown.'" Then, quoting in parenthesis one of my staff articles which the Mutual Corporation had evidently issued to the various trade papers, the scribbler used Chaplin's oft-repeated statement that he will never return to the stage as if that were a sign that Charlie realises that his day is done!

I turned the clipping over, and asked Charlie what he was worrying about it for. The people will have what they want, I reminded him, irrespective of what the yellow press of Windy City might say.

"Maybe," he half-agreed, "but I don't like to see those sort of articles in the papers of a big place like Chi."

I could see there was nothing for it but to take some step to cheer him up, so I suggested I should answer it with an article countering the charge.

"No," he said, and then wavered. "Do you think it'll do any good?" he asked.

"It won't hurt," I assured him, and beat it to my office desk before he had time to think.

Here is the argument I put up in defence of the world's favourite; I'm putting it before you so that you may judge for yourself if I am right or not.

While admitting that such a vogue as Charlie Chaplin has enjoyed, and still enjoys, cannot last for ever, because of the natural fickleness of humanity, I declare he is still without a successor, for the excellent reason that a successor (unless he follows on the demise of his predecessor) must be better than the man whose position he usurps, or the public is going to return to its old favourite. Nobody will stand for something worse in place of something that has always stood the acid test, and therefore until a better man comes along—one who can give them better amusement than Chaplin—he is safe on his pinnacle of fame.

Chaplin's appeal is in itself his greatest safeguard, for, while he tickles the palates of those who love deep and subtle comedy, his work is yet so full of artless humour that the tiniest infant can appreciate it along with his sophisticated dad. The basis of Chaplin's pictures is simple and designed for minds of every class, and it is a singular tribute to his natural genius that he can so intermix the deeper vein with the simpler.

Not since the days of Leno *[Dan Leno was a legendary music hall comedian noted for his pantomime "dame" roles]* (though I never had a chance to see that lamented artist, and was too young anyway to have appreciated his subtleties) has there been a comedian with that rare gift of combining the two forms of humour. Such an artist only happens once in a lifetime, as a general rule, and the successor to Chaplin, whoever and wherever he may be, has an awful long climb ahead of him if he's going to even come within an ace of Charlie's fame and cleverness.

It is probable that *The Pawnshop* would have been finished right on time but for one little circumstance, and it is such an odd characteristic of the actor that I mention it here.

Charlie conceived the idea of an old legitimate actor coming in to pawn his ring and acting a long farewell to it before he turned it over to the pawnbroker.

Now, any actor in the world will tell you that a brokendown actor ought to be the easiest thing in the world for an experienced stage player to "put over." Yet that one short scene took three days to get into shape, and it was not until three actors had been tried in the part that it was finally passed as near perfect and turned over to the laboratory man to be developed and printed. *[It's hard to chew the scenery convincingly, and outtakes show that Wesley Ruggles and Leo White weren't quite up to the task, despite being coached by Sydney. The*

third actor, however, nails it, making the scene one of the funniest and most
memorable in the film. Modern audiences usually miss what would have been
evident to audiences of 1916—that the actor is playing *an actor, the sort of*
old-fashioned ham we now associate with melodramas. This explains his florid
gestures and clothing, which is far too dressy for the shabby pawnshop. Regret-
tably, the identity of the fine actor playing this role is unknown.]

"It's a licker to me," said Charlie. "Yet I can't blame anyone. It's just one of
those irritating bits that crop up in almost every play and picture that's ever
put on, and there's no help for it. It's just the same in my own work too. Look
at the trouble I've had, time after time, with things that ought to have been
as easy as pie to me, whereas I've put over difficult things that ought to have
taken me hours of rehearsal without a bit of trouble. Seem to be the same in
everything, too; the tricks that look nothing on the stage have often cost jug-
glers and acrobats years of practice, and yet the public gives more applause
to the things that have come to them by pure accident. Life's one long irony."

Circumstances—not unconnected with a couple of expensive collisions,
and with the fact that a certain young lady refused to ride with me because of
my partiality for overtaking everything ahead of us—induced me to sell my
car, and so on the same night as the picture was brought to a finish I accepted
Charlie's offer to drive downtown with him.

Just as we were contemplating departure from the studio, however, who
should turn up but Bert Clark, of Clark and Hamilton, the English vaudeville duo, who is playing in Los Angeles this week. Bert recently invested in
a small automobile, which appears to have a nasty habit of putting on speed
whenever the traffic policeman doesn't seem to be around—at least, that's the
way he puts it—and he wanted to show us what an obstreperous little beast it
was. So he had brought it around to the studio, and insisted on driving beside
Charlie's touring car, until he saw an opportunity to scorch ahead of us.

We got out to a wide asphalt boulevard known as Vermont Avenue, and
then that roadster began to misbehave. The first thing it did was leave us far
in its wake; then it passed a big machine on the wrong side. The next thing
that happened concerns a khaki-clad figure on a motor cycle, which whizzed
past us at about forty miles an hour and didn't pause until it had overtaken
the miscreant vehicle and brought it to a standstill at the kerb.

Yes, you guessed rightly. It was a traffic "cop," and when Charlie saw what
had happened he yelled with glee.

"Poor old Bert," he grinned, and gave his chauffeur Fred instruction to pull into the sidewalk, whence we could watch the battle of wits between the minion of the law and the comedian.

Unfortunately, however, Bert seemed to be getting decidedly the worst of the battle, and as the officer began to fumble for his notebook Charlie grew serious.

"Turn back, Fred," he instructed. "Let's see what's going on."

So the chauffeur turned the car around and rolled up beside the wayward little roadster.

"What seems to be wrong?" Charlie inquired, putting out his head and looking the policeman in the eye. "Has my friend been a bad boy?"

The officer looked up, and presently a grin overspread his face.

"Howdy, Mr. Chaplin?" he observed, and the notebook stayed where it was. "Just a little difference of opinion between this gentleman and myself. But"—he proceeded to mount his cycle—"but I guess he was right after all. So-long!" and he disappeared in the direction of Hollywood.

Far be it from us to aver that Charlie or anyone else could deter a Los Angeles policeman from his duty; but as Clark afterwards remarked, it's kind of useful to have a friend like Chaplin around you.

[A few months earlier Bert Clark had talked Chaplin into going into partnership as the Charlie Chaplin Music Publishing Company, which published three of Chaplin's early compositions. "I think we sold three copies," Chaplin reported wryly in his Autobiography.[1] *The best thing to come out of the short-lived enterprise was that Chaplin hired Clark's dresser-handyman, Tom Harrington, as his own manservant, and Harrington proved to be as indispensable to Chaplin as Jeeves was to Bertie Wooster, even discreetly suggesting reading material. He can be seen as the stern-looking marriage license clerk at the end of* The Immigrant *and as himself in Chaplin's mockumentary* How to Make Movies.*]*

31
The Rough End of "Movie" Work

October 28, 1916

After what I've told you so often about Charlie Chaplin's changeable disposition, it is hardly necessary to report that the artist picture he started out to make never amounted to anything tangible.

For several days the whole staff laboured putting up studio scenes and art galleries, while the property department filled the property barns with paintings and curios aggregating two thousand pounds in value. Then one fine autumn day in walked Charlie, and surveyed the huge stack of chattels with the eye of a connoisseur in art.

At first we thought he was contemplating something with a beautiful theme concerning the old masters, for he handled the various objects as reverently as though they had been worth their weight in radium.

But our guess was a miss in baulk for once, for our worthy star suddenly came back to earth and called to the property man—

"Say, Scotty, I wish you'd clear all this junk off the stage and send it back to the owners. I'm not doing that Art thing after all. Just save me a few statues and art pots."

Scotty sighed, and placed a hand on his fevered brow.

"What's it to be, then, Charlie?" he queried.

Charlie beamed on him.

"I'm going to make a studio picture," he replied.

Scotty looked at him vaguely.

"Sure," he agreed. "But what kind of a studio picture?"

"A picture concerning life in a moving-picture studio." Charlie told him. "That's what I mean."

So that's what it's to be.

By the next morning every side of the big stage had given birth to a different kind of scene. Here was a kitchen, there a drawing-room, while in other corners stood throne-rooms, dungeons, dressing-rooms, bedrooms, Roman palaces, and low drinking saloons.

I gasped when I first set eyes on the lay-out, for it must have taken the whole army of workers at the plant several hours to erect so many scenes in so short a time. But they had certainly achieved the desired effect, for the place looked like a miniature edition of Universal City.

For a wonder, work really started on the following day, and the throngs of extra men and women who perpetually haunt the studio were hurriedly corralled and thrust into a variety of costumes and make-ups.

It has always struck me as an amusing thing here in movieland to see characters from various pictures which are in course of making standing around in knots and talking as if they were all costumed after the same period. Here one may see a man disguised as a Biblical character, while beside him, lighting a cigarette, is a knight errant in full armour. In the various restaurants one may find even greater incongruities, such as a low-comedy American policeman discussing soup alongside of an English butler, a medieval friar, and a modern Italian fruit seller!

That is the kind of aspect the Chaplin studio presented on the day in question, and for many days afterwards; yet underlying their motley costumes there was, for the most part, the same thought—"Thank goodness, we've got a few days' work!"

The office of a moving-pictures concern is no place for a sympathetic man to sit. Never were life's minor tragedies brought to light more strongly than there, where one has to do the best one can for every poor beggar that comes along. Most of these extra actors and actresses are willing, nay, thankful, to take the mere five dollars a day that is their reward for working in a scene. Oh, yes, I know five dollars is a guinea, and a guinea sounds handsome remuneration to the British reader, yet one can scarcely get along in America, even in the most modest way, on less than ten shillings a day, so you can see how far a couple of days' work in a picture would last.

Add to this the fact that those days of work are few and far between, and you have a pretty fair idea of how the life of the extra is spent. It's just one long drag from one studio to another, often meeting with cruel answers and oftener (which is worse) having the hope held out to them that a day's work may be possible before afternoon. In this latter case—one that doesn't often prevail at our plant, I am thankful to say—the poor fellow will stick around the doors until the failing light warns him that there is no hope, after all, for a five dollar note to slip into his pocket that day.

Yet most of them are typical soldiers and soldieresses of fortune, and, knowing this as well as I have cause to, I was none the less surprised to find that Charlie, who never went through the rough end of motion-picture work, knows the spirit of them as well as he does. We got to talking about them one day when work had got beyond him through too much hard concentration, and he surveyed the knots of minor actors that were ranged in different positions around the big stage.

"Poor beggars," he said thoughtfully. "They come around these studios, some of them young and full of ambition that precious few of them have talent enough to ever realise, others grasping on to the game because they're out of a job either on the stage or elsewhere; yet they're nearly all improvident as the deuce. They get around and beg for work, and sometimes they get it. At the end of the day they get a five-spot, and although they've been sitting around empty maybe throughout that day they turn up next day with a fat cigar in their faces and tell you they had a fine time the previous night down at some country club or other. It's presumed that they blued [sic—blew] every nickel of their five dollars.

"But there," he added, "it's the spirit of the profession the world over, and even the best and biggest of them in the Old Country do it. I was appalled when I read the other day a list of big English theatrical men who've gone broke to the wide earth since I left England. Oh, no, I don't mean the few who've lost on account of the war, but those who hadn't saved a nickel out of all the vast fortunes they've made. I don't know whether to blame 'em or not, for it's their free-hearted spirit of carelessness that makes them so—and, after all, it's that spirit that makes the theatrical game."

As he spoke he chanced to look towards the boardwalk that skirts the elevated stage on which the pictures are made. There stood an old, worn-looking woman, who, all unconscious that she was violating any rule or regulation, had wandered into the plant. Her face bore lines other than those of age, and the expression in her eyes seemed to tell of a life spent in battling against sorrow and adversity. Charlie looked at her for fully a half-minute, and then he turned away and seemed to shiver. He had a pained look on his face as he called Scotty to him.

"George," he said, "put that old lady to work. I can't bear to think of a woman of that age going in want."

"What part do you want to cast her for?" queried Scotty, as he turned to go. He was anxious enough to see the old lady fixed right for a five-dollar cheque, but he wanted to make sure what Charlie had in mind.

"Oh, anything," said Charlie. "I'll make a part for her."

So the old lady was shown to a dressing-room, and the part was specially put in. I thought I could see a touch of filial love in his action, and I'm pretty sure I was right.

That same afternoon there came to the studio a fellow quite unknown to any of us, but whose accent betrayed his Sussex birth. He had been a member of a prominent music-hall act over home, but had fallen on a rough streak and was looking for something to fill in the unpleasant gap, so he came to the Chaplin plant, knowing, perhaps, that it was pretty freely stocked with his fellow-countrymen, and I chanced to be the first to meet him. It didn't take long to introduce him to Scotty, whose Irish birth has given him an understandable preference for his brother Britishers, and so within an hour or so our new friend was making up as an executioner of the Elizabethan period!

This boy brought with him a highly-prized volume in the shape of an autograph album, in which he had gathered during the past ten years the contributions and signatures of practically every music-hall artiste and actor of note in the British Isles, many of whom have since passed away.

The book was of no little interest to the majority of us, and it was late the next day before it had passed through all hands and finally came back to mine. Charlie saw us looking at it presently, and came over to see what was so interesting. He is one of the most inquisitive men I have ever met—not in a mean way, you understand, but simply for the sake of gleaning knowledge that may help him on in his work—and when he learned what we were looking at he commandeered the book and sat him down.

For about half-an-hour pictures went by the board, while I stood beside him and helped to decipher some of the badly-written signatures.

How it brought back memories to him! He was so far up in the clouds that it would have taken a parachute to bring him down—at least, that's how Vincent Bryan put it—and he shook his head from time to time as each new name brought to mind some incident connected with his stage career in the Homeland.

It must have taken the owner of the book an awful lot of trouble to garner all those famous names into one book, and I dare swear that I was not by any means the only one to whom the sight of it brought back memories of happier surroundings. There is as much difference between the music halls of Britain and those of America as there is between the proverbial chalk and cheese, and some of us couldn't help making odious comparisons.

Charlie turned over the leaves one by one and each name brought some kind of exclamation from him. There were photographs and signatures of people whose names stood or still stand for much in the British profession; people like Arthur Roberts, Fanny Fields, Zena and Phyllis Dare, Olga Nethersole, Ellen Terry, Fred Earle, Dan Rolyat, Gertie Millar, Gabrielle Ray—but there, I might rattle on through the rest of my story simply telling names.

Presently Charlie turned his attention to the scene in which he interrupts the supposed execution of Lady Jane Grey by walking under the axe and having it just narrowly miss his skull. It was a clever bit of work, and when we saw it run on the screen the next day we gasped at the realism of it. There was the executioner one minute brandishing the great axe, and the next moment Charlie hurried on, the axe falling with such force that it buried itself into the stage fully three inches.

Yet it was nothing but a clever trick which I may not divulge; although the axe positively sweeps down Charlie's back so closely that it razes his coat tails and buries itself in the flooring right flush with his heels, he was just as safe as if he had been in his bed at home. There are more things in motion pictures in the way of tricks and deceptions than are dreamt of in our philosophy. *[Chaplin achieved this harrowing effect by working out the sequence in reverse. The axe is already buried in the floor; Chaplin walks backwards towards it, and just as he reaches it the executioner yanks it from the floor so that he can pass. When projected in reverse, Chaplin appears to be walking forward, and the illusion that the axe nearly bisects him as he passes is perfect. He spent a considerable amount of time developing this brilliant gag, and it is clear where it was intended to fit into the finished film. But for some reason he cut the sequence, and with it the performance by the unnamed music hall artist. Several variant takes may be seen in the documentary* Unknown Chaplin.[1]*]*

This incident brings us right up to the time of writing. As I pen these notes Charlie is out on the stage behind me showing the actor who is supposed to be the producer of the execution scene precisely the way he wants the part played. His idea is to have that temperamental, rip-roaring kind of a director—the kind that thinks he is D.W. Griffith, and that in order to resemble the peerless D.W. he must strain every nerve and fibre and curse and dance before the actors and call them sons of all the terrible things under the sun.

It is a type of producer that is common (disgustingly common sometimes) in this movieland of ours, the type that makes for the disagreeable element in the business, and causes legitimate actors to long for the courtesy of the footlight side of the game, yet withal the type that is a joke to every man who knows the difference between art and bunkum. Such men as the character Charlie has made this producer soon run to the end of their tether, thank goodness! But their reign is a discomfiting one to those under them, and they create a bad impression to the looker on, who cannot differentiate between the real artiste—the man of the Griffith or the De Mille or the Chaplin type—and the street-sweeping fraternity, who get in the game on a big bluff, and vent their temperamental ignorance on people who begin to know where they themselves leave off knowing.

It's a positive education to watch Charlie pulling that fake, temperamental stuff. He is running his fingers through his hair, twisting himself into knots—almost rolling on the stage—but it takes a man of the Chaplin temperament to assume a character to the life like that. Good as Johnny Rand is as a comedian and actor, he's got an awful long way to go to play that producer the way Charlie is showing him.

If he could he'd probably be where Chaplin is to-day.

● ● ●

A little girl reader of the *Red Letter* who lives in Essex has written the very nicest letter telling how she and all her friends love Charlie Chaplin on the pictures. She is quite deaf, poor child, but she can enjoy the pictures all the same. She loves Charlie best because he "makes her laugh." Will "Annie" please send her full name and address to Mr. Fred Goodwins, c/o "Red Letter" Office, 12 Fetter Lane, Fleet Street, London, E.C.

32

One Hundred Thousand Guineas for Chaplin Films

November 4, 1916

At last—and not before it is time—the negotiations have been completed for the sale of the rights of this year's Chaplin pictures made under the Mutual contract, which I have frequently mentioned in these pages.

J. D. Walker, a prominent man in motion picture circles on your side, has bought the British and Colonial rights to the Lone Star Company's productions for the fabulous sum of one hundred thousand guineas, and the first of our pictures, *The Floorwalker*, will be placed before the British public at the end of the month of October.

At last, then, as I say, you are to have a chance of seeing your old idol in something other than reissues and stale subjects, and perhaps you will, as I suggested a few weeks ago, derive some little pleasure from unearthing your back copies of the *Red Letter*, and once more going over with me the eventful happenings that attended the making of each of these super-comedies as soon as they come your way.

By the way, while I am on the subject, I have received one or two queries from various readers who want to know what parts I played in the different Mutual stories. Their interest is flattering, and I want to take this opportunity of easing their minds. I played very little in any of the pictures, for my time was too much taken up by my press duties. However, if you are anxious to pick me out in *The Floorwalker*, I played the manager of the shoe department, attired in all the glory of a loudly-checked golf coat.

Since I wrote my last few notes things have hardly progressed a particle so far as work is concerned. The same band of guinea-a-day extra actors and actresses thronged the stage, earning (?) their money by alternately sleeping, playing the pianos, and chattering, until Charlie was constrained to tell them to keep quiet, and during all this time Charlie paced the stage, concentrating his mind on the different situations that came to it.

He can't get away from his sense of burlesque, and it has shown itself in almost every situation he has thought out. He sees the absurd side of everything that is serious, and the pathetic side of everything that is absurd. He delights in showing how ridiculous creatures of great self-importance and pomposity can be made to look by a mere bit of eccentricity being applied to one's dealings with them, and that has formed the basis of the majority of his comedies—the undoing of high-and-mighties with whom he comes into contact.

"It's easy," I remember his having said once upon a time, "to get fun out of people who are too consequential and pompous. They have no sense of humour—otherwise they wouldn't be consequential—and nobody is funnier, or easier to get fun out of, than a person who is devoid of all sense of the funny. The greatest task I have in my work is preventing my supporters from trying to be humorous. In all my pictures I want my people to act as 'foils'—not as partners, and that is why I have generally chosen actors with a gift for looking frightfully important. It makes it so much more of a contrast when, as one writer put it, I 'dispose of them with one flourish of my foot, deftly placed in what is politely called their middle.' There is nothing more unfunny to me than the sight of two comedians each trying to be more humorous than the other. The audience is kept trying to sit on two stools, so to speak, and consequently the act (or picture, whichever it may be) falls, like the audience, directly to earth."

I recall how this viewpoint opened my eyes. I had even been disloyal enough to harbour the thought that Charlie tabooed all efforts at comedy upon purely selfish grounds. It just shows how a less adept mind may misjudge in forming conclusions on a matter of which it knows but little.

The particular little piece of business which led up to this train of thought on my part was this:—

Most of you are familiar with that type of classic in motion picture art which depicts a band of much-bewhiskered policemen, whose faces have a nasty habit of getting in the way of flying custard pies. I think they are referred to as slapstick comedies, and, although they really do possess a certain amount of ridiculous appeal, they are not, needless to say, any too full of subtle inspiration. Charlie, then, whose picture career actually commenced in the very thick of this type of comedy, has not missed the opportunity of making his little good-natured slam at them. To be precise, he has made one of the scenes erected on the Lone Star stage the "Comedy Company" scene, and I trow the sly dig that he has directed at certain comedy directors through the medium of that same Company will not be lost.

He'd been pacing the stage, as I say, for days, when suddenly he caught himself tapping his cheeks with his closed fists, and with a laugh came to himself.

"That was funny," he said. "I just caught myself doing what S— used to do when he was seeking inspiration for a comedy scene." (S— was the man who put C.C. into the business of moving pictures, and it is noted in the profession for the little peculiarity just described.) *[Any 1916 reader would know that the mystery man was Mack Sennett, whose Keystone Comedies launched Chaplin's film career two years earlier. Sennett continued to be a major creative player through the early 1930s, when he introduced both W. C. Fields and Bing Crosby in talkie shorts.]*

"How would it be," he continued, speaking to Syd, "if I made one of these scenes a burlesque on those pie-slinging comedy pictures? I wonder if the public would 'get it'?"

"Surely they would," exclaimed Syd, tickled at the thought of a sly dig at the old school of picture humour. "Let's do it."

Charlie, however, more cautious, pondered awhile on the subject.

"I don't want to seem ill-natured," he mused.

But finally the temptation proved too much for him, and he hurriedly changed Lloyd Bacon and myself from the guises of stage hands into those of director and French chef respectively, while two of the "extras" were transferred from cavalier costumes to the uniforms and make-ups of typical low-comedy policemen! He couldn't have achieved a more ludicrous piece of burlesque if he'd tried all night. The "cops" were refulgent with shining nose paint, and were decked out in whiskers such as no human being (outside of the comedies under notice) ever dared to wear, while Lloyd Bacon was made up in a long, straggly beard and moustache, horn-rimmed sun glasses, and a soulful, inspired mien.

I thought Charlie would never get through laughing. The thing appealed to him as irresistibly funny, for he has more than once in his picture career had to deal with men who treated those pie-hurling classics as if they were the salt of the motion picture art, and I think he pictured their feelings when they beheld themselves thus reproduced in burlesque.

The scene opened with a group composed of Bacon, as the inspired director, gazing into the distance and seeking for light to burst in on his classic brain, while the two cops and I were ranged beside him, temperamentally racking our brains for a wave of genius which should stagger the world. Then suddenly Bacon sees a juicy and copiously-filled custard pie which I am holding in my idle hand and cries, as Archimedes cried when he discovered the law of specific gravity, "Eureka! I have it!"

Then, accompanying his words by sufficient pantomime to convey it on the screen, he suggests that I take the pie, poise it carefully, and apply it gently, but surely to the face of the most bewhiskered officer of the law. Enraptured and spellbound by his genius, we exclaim "Wonderful, wonderful!" and gaze in awe at the mighty master-brain that could conceive such a stupendous situation.

Nonsense? Of course it is, and neither is it intended to be anything else; but there is a world of subtlety behind it, none the less, and I venture to predict that more than a few of the general public of both Continents will "get it" just as much as the people who come into contact day after day in this movie game of ours with men who truly think that every absurdly-prosaic thought that enters their heads is a veritable flash of genius. It's a clever slam, without a suggestion of proverbial sarcasm.

To show how utterly averse Chaplin is to hurting the feelings of anyone, either great or small, let me mention one little circumstance in connection with this incident before I leave it finally. Lloyd, quite by chance, had selected a beard which resembled in an absurdly grotesque way the hirsute appendages of the eminent George Bernard Shaw, and Charlie, the moment he noticed the odd resemblance, began to conjecture as to whether or not it would be policy[1] to alter the shape of the beard.

"I don't flatter myself that Shaw would attach any vital importance to it," he added, "but it doesn't hurt to be careful." However, the beard was allowed finally to pass muster, and the scene stands just as I have described it.

The next few days were devoted entirely to the scenes which start all the bother (and it is going to be some bother, too, the way Charlie has described it) which forms the body of the story. These particular scenes deal with the coming of a dowdy little-street girl of the type that delighted the heart of the late Phil May *[a popular cartoonist and illustrator, noted for his sympathetic drawings of the poor]*, who suddenly becomes a leading lady in the plant, an event that culminates in a strike of all the rest of the actors, their parts being played by the stage-hands.

The part of the waif is allotted to Miss Edna, and Charlie, as usual, is taking such pains with her characterisation that he has dropped into his old game of enclosing himself and his retinue inside high screens of white canvas. Everyone (not excluding myself) is consequently excluded and left to kill time until those trying "bits" are completed, when, presumably, the fun will start.

So I spent my odd moments in adjusting to my satisfaction another motor car I have bought—yes, the third one I have taken to my bosom within the past nine months, and so have scarcely noticed the flitting of the time taken up by those troublesome little duologues between Edna and Charles. Oddly enough, they are the things that tend more than aught else to set his nerves going, and one hears little petulant exclamations coming over the screens from time to time whenever he fails to get a point over to his complete satisfaction.

Only once during that session did he emerge from his enclosure on any business other than the call of the inner man, and this was to sign the receipt for a registered package of photographs which suddenly turned up at the office one afternoon.

"Hang those post office regulations!" he exclaimed. "Why can't someone else sign those receipts? All right, stick the photos in my dressing-room. I don't suppose they're anything much." And he returned to his job.

But it so happened that those photographs turned out to be of more than ordinary interest to him when finally he came to open them up.

They were only three in number, and had been collected by an old chum of his, back home in England. Two of them showed him in his *Casey's Court [sic—Casey's Circus]* days, when he played the part of the master of ceremonies at the street urchins' vaudeville entertainment, impersonating Fagin the Jew from *Oliver Twist*, Dick Turpin in his memorable ride to York, and others. The whole thing, which will be green in the memories of many of my readers even to this day, was a succession of skits and burlesques upon the salient points in the originals, and it was presumably here that Chaplin first developed his odd type of individual humour.

The two photographs showed respectively his impersonation of Fagin and a well-known figure on the variety stage.[2] They were remarkable effects in the actor's art, and I wondered yet again if there is anything under this old sun that Charlie Chaplin would have failed hopelessly to achieve. Certainly he has the right idea when it comes to what is professionally known as "character acting." I wonder if, when his great ambition comes to be realised, he will not turn out to be another Garrick, another Beerbohm Tree?

Knowing his versatility and the immense compass of his artistry, I feel I am voicing no foolish surmise. I am not blind to Charlie Chaplin's faults and shortcomings. We have known each other in numberless different phases of life since the first day we met as "Mr Chaplin" and "Mr Goodwins" and first shook each other by the hand; there have been times when we have not altogether agreed, but never yet, and I say it without a suspicion of hyperbole, have I found Charlie Chaplin lacking in anything pertaining to his art.

He is not only the world's foremost comedian—in a way I deplore that he should ever have made his first big stand on the ladder of fame as such, lest it prevent his peerless ability in other directions from being recognised—he is more than that; he is a genius of geniuses whose limitations are so far asunder that the lay mind, far greater than mine, can scarce realise them, let alone define just where they lie.

The mystery of mysteries to me is that it has taken nineteen years of professional life for someone to discover that that small body harbours a spark such as hardly a single other man has possessed in the history of the world.

There must be an awful bunch of men who don't know their business in this age-old profession of entertainment. Otherwise Charlie Chaplin would never have had to make his first big showing through the medium of a strip of celluloid.

33

Charlie's Great Pie-Slinging Scene

November 11, 1916

If you should chance, during these days of strife and warfare, to encounter a stray American on your side of the Atlantic—preferably one that hails from the south of California—and he happens to mention that rain is an unknown quantity in this part of the world, tell him from me that he is using the crown of his hat as a conversational medium.

Scarcely a dozen hours had elapsed after the despatch of my last jottings when several layers of thick vapour descended gently from the heavens, and burst asunder upon the respective peaks of the surrounding hills (called by courtesy mountains), sprinkling the lowlands with "soft refreshing rain." That is putting it poetically. Speaking in less flowery language, a beastly annoying rainstorm started in to pelt down on the linen-covered roof of the Lone Star studio, and put an end, for the time being, to all our industry.

It has been a good many years since the rain-god started his activity so early in the year, and he would have done well, for many reasons, to have postponed his attentions until his customary visiting day, for he caught many hundreds of folks totally unprepared, reduced the great Californian raisin crops to approximately one-half of their face value, and turned the multitude of motion-pictures studios into ugly morasses and piles of dripping canvas.

Another reason why his work might well have been set for a later day is the fact that orders have but lately been placed with a big Eastern firm for the building of a complete glass roof to cover the entire stage.

However, not even Charles the Greatest can control the elements, any more than His Majesty Canute can control the waves, so down came the deluge and swamped the great line-up of sets that adorned the stage.

The downpour only lasted a matter of twenty-four hours, though, and by ten o'clock on the following morning the stage-boys were busily swabbing up the mess with an array of mops and pails, while the sun poured down, exercising all its drying powers, and within the hour work was once more practicable.

The requirements of this story are so peculiar that it has been necessary for the majority of us stock members to switch from one make-up to another, playing stage-hands in one scene, Elizabethan courtiers in another, and such a variety of other roles that we are beginning to wonder whether we have any personality of our own left.

Part of the story deals with the vicissitudes and tribulations of Charlie who, as a property-man's assistant, does all the hard work, while his chief (Eric Campbell) dozes in a comfortable armchair and only awakes in time to receive the congratulations of the head producer. Charlie has meanwhile fallen into the vacant chair, utterly worn out from his arduous toils, and is subjected to a lot of violent treatment from his energetic (?) chief for his colossal laziness!

Thereafter he is the goat for all the rough end of the game, getting belaboured for nothing he has done, and in one faction he so enrages his chief that the latter runs wild with a huge stack of traditional pies of the "mush and marshmallow" order.

Here it was that the real fun of the picture began, for those who enjoy a well-aimed faceful of succulent pastry—and there was hardly a member of that great coronation scene who did not get badly soiled in the veritable cockshy [game of throwing objects at a target] that proceeded the moment the camera commenced to turn.

"Now, here's where Eric slings the pies at me, and they pass into this court-room set," said Charlie, in explaining the scene to the players. "First of all, he only throws one or two at odd intervals, but he afterwards cuts loose and slings them as fast as his hands can pick 'em up. What makes a good realistic pie?"

Syd suggested that you can't do better, for motion-picture purposes, than use a real pie, amply filled with chopped spinach.

"It looks like a lot of dark berries when it's shown on the screen," he said.

But Charlie had other ideas on the subject, so it ultimately fell to our lot to be immersed in honest dough, the tenacious whiteness of which appealed to Charlie better than the spinach idea.

"I'm the expert at mixing dough," he said. "Bring me a big bowl and a sack of flour. I'll show you how to make it."

"Be sure to get the right consistency," Syd warned him, and Charlie grinned.

"Consistency!" he repeated. The word tickled him, although he knew perfectly well what it meant. "Sure, I'll keep the—what's its name?—consistency, up to the right standard."

While he mixed the dough he began to chatter about the pie-slinging idea.

"I know it's a lot of old-fashioned stuff," he confessed, "but, after all, this is only a travesty of a motion-picture studio as it really is, and that's why I'm bringing this situation into it." He surveyed the ruffled and doubletted crowd that surrounded him and grinned again. "I honestly think these people are scared about getting these pies in their eye. You don't want to be scared of that," he told them. "I'd like a dollar for every one I've had slammed in my face. If it's the dough that scares you, I've had a fine dose of that, too. I remember, in *Dough and Dynamite*, what a mess of stickiness we went through. I made a lot of the dough used in that myself, and in the scene where I picked up a double armful of it and chucked it at Chester Conklin, I thought that fatal—what is it?—consistency had made a murderer out of me. I was standing at one side of the picture, you see, and Chet. was at the other, and I exerted all my strength, such as it is, and slung the whole thing right at him. It enveloped him like a shroud, and he went down and out. I heard him gasping before he passed into oblivion. 'Stop 'em, Charlie; I can't finish—I'm out!' and 'out' he certainly was. I'd knocked him stone senseless with it."

As he spoke he caught sight of the mixed expressions in the eyes of his supporters, and grinned again.

"Don't be afraid," he laughed. "I'm not going to make this lot the same—er—consistency as that lot was. This is for sticking purposes only—that was for 'outing' purposes.

The pies were soon made up—real, juicy confiserie *[French for confectionery]*—with a nice, thick layer of moist paste on the top, and Charlie stationed himself just outside the line of the picture and poised one of them in his left hand—he is, you will remember, hopelessly left handed—ready to launch in the direction of the face of the pseudo-king.

"What!" exclaimed his majesty. "Does anyone dare to question what I have decreed? I, the King of this vast empire—I who have declared that he shall die? To the Tower with him. I have spoken! He dies—and so much for Buckingham!"

At which juncture the succulent delicacy left Charlie's hand, soared through the air, and wrapped itself affectionately around the monarch's regal visage.

It was an appalling sight to behold. The king's hair, beard, and gold-laced costume were one mass of dough and fruit, and as he arose in anger to protest at the indignity which had been thrust upon him yet another one, of apricot contents this time, struck him squarely on the chin and added its flavour to that of the previous pie.

Here it was that the pies flew thick and fast from the outside of the scene. Charlie's left hand never faltered once in its aim, and the court looked more like a bad accident than anything else. The queen, the pages, the herald, and the bishop presented a sorry aspect, with pies and dough plastered on the faces and clothing, but what interested me most of all was the fact that I inadvertently stepped between the assailant and the assailed and intercepted the juiciest pie of the whole bunch. It hit me squarely in the physiognomy as if it had been projected by a gun, and so great was the impact that the contents of it overflowed across the top of my head and ended their career at the back of my neck.

Truth to tell, I was not to be blamed for getting in the way of that particular missile, for it was not one of those thrown by Charlie. The head scenic artist had taken an idea to do a little throwing on his own account, and it was this, his first effort that had such dire results. I told Roy afterwards, when the removal of the pastry had made conversation possible, that the Los Angeles baseball club was missing something by not grabbing him as its chief pitcher.

Taking it all round, that was "some" court. I never saw such a stuck-up lot in my life.

One thing, too, is certain—it will be many a day before any of us develop an appetite for fruit pastry. We are surfeited, with a vengeance.

Charlie let us rest on the pie section for the two days following, devoting his energies to the section of the story which shows the stage-hands eating their lunch, and what with the difficulty of evolving gags and situations, and the fact that the troublesome sun kept retiring bashfully behind the clouds we didn't accomplish an awful lot.

At last, however, the scenes were mapped out, and just as we made up our minds that they were to be disposed of for good and all, in blew Roscoe Arbuckle of Keystone fame, and put an end to work for several hours.

"Fatty," as Arbuckle is familiarly called, had just arrived from New York, where he had been making some special Keystone comedies, and his main idea in visiting us was to say how-de-do to the boys in general, and Charlie in particular, and to exhibit his latest pet in the shape of a brand-new 1917 model Rolls-Royce car.

America turns out some pretty good machines but they just fade out of the story when it comes to comparison with one of these beautiful pieces of British workmanship, and Charlie examined it from stem to stern with undisguised admiration.

"How much, Roscoe?" he asked.

"About 11,000 dollars in New York," said Arbuckle casually; then added, "But it cost me 870 dollars to ship it from New York to California. That is altogether"—he made a rapid calculation—"about £2374 in English money."

"Ye gods!" gasped Charlie. "It takes me a whole week to earn that much."

He spoke without any thought of having perpetrated a joke, and looked surprised when everyone laughed outright.

The light failed before we could return to the comestibles, and so Charlie called it off until the morrow—which, however, dawned upon a second edition of the great deluge!

It cleared up by noon, though, and we started in on that lunch business. I'd hate to think it was a deliberate "frame-up" on us, but why, oh, why did they have to make those lunches consist of pies, pies, pies? Was it not enough that we had all been liberally decorated on the exterior with pies of every description without being asked to take them internally as well? And what with the light, and what with the mistakes, each of us devoured at least a pie and a half before the mid-afternoon came—and with it permission to go to lunch.

Lunch, gentlemen! The business our little restaurant did that day wouldn't have paid for the cost of the fuel. No, sirs, we were in no mood for trencher-manship *[hearty eating]* just then.

But troubles of digestion, like all other things, must have an end, and the picture rapidly neared its finish before the closing of the week.

Thanks to the inclemency of the weather and the consequent indisposition of the great powers to buckle down to the work of trying to be funny, the picture is away late. It should have been shipped a week ago, yet there is still, at the time of writing, fully one third of it remaining to be doped out and filmed.

When it is completed it will, so Charlie says, be entitled *Behind the Screen*, but he is just as likely to change his mind.

Judging from past experience, I would say that it will be a very present-able specimen of the particular brand of humour that has made the name of Chaplin a household word.

But I doubt very much if it is going to be another *Count*. *The Count* still holds first place, in my humble opinion, as the funniest piece of work Charlie Chaplin has ever put before his world.

If he beats that, the picture's going to be a jolly good one—that's all!

34

Charlie Gets Busy with *Behind the Screen*

November 18, 1916

The weather has been kind to us ever since I finished my last story. The sun continued to shine down genially on the vast expanse of pasture lands that abound between here and the Rocky Mountains, and the palm trees seemed grateful for the soothing rain that has but lately bathed their parched leaves.

The sudden and untimely rain may have done considerable damage to the various crops, but it was infinitely more suited to the peculiar physical tastes of the Englishmen in the studio to feel a cool, damp breeze fanning their cheeks in place of the hot, dry winds that generally make California's southern part so intolerably monotonous. It was quite a change to be able to smell something in the air, and it reminded many of us, as only an odour or a certain strain of music can remind one, of things away back in our lives across the sea.

We grumble, back there, about our wet and murky climate, yet it is a godsend when you have been cooped up in a dry-aired, catarrh-infected land, to feel, once in a while, that you still retain your sense of smell.

Just as Charlie said but a few weeks ago, it's worth a lot to look forward to the smell of the old tar-block roads, the dust of the country lanes, even the reek of the London smoke, and when you can't get that because of the leagues that lie between, why, its balm in Gilead to get a little touch of wet weather, if only because it reminds you of the things that were.

Rain, however, is not a desirable element in the making of motion pictures— still less super-comedies—so perhaps I ought not to start writing thanks to it;

besides, if it gladdened the hearts of us Britishers it played havoc with the nerves of the powers that are held responsible for the prompt and punctual shipping of the negative to New York City. By hook or by crook, they are expected to see that each film arrives in the Big City upon a certain scheduled date, notwithstanding the elements or aught else, and so the air around the Lone Star Studio was not one of intense happiness while the heavens continued to pelt their torrents upon the earth.

With the coming of the sun came also an atmosphere of relief on the part of the authorities in question, and Charlie himself smiled when he walked on to the stage and found it drying up after the last rainstorm that has visited us.

"Now, perhaps we can get along with some honest toil," he quoth. "Hang my clothes out in the sun to dry while I make up my face."

So hung in the sun they were, and just as they neared the stage of "grateful warmth" I was seized with the stroke of genius that accompanies these notes. It struck me as ridiculously funny that the man's clothes should retain his character so completely even when he was not filling them out. The Chaplin clothes, even without Chaplin therein, are as characteristic of the man as if he had inoculated them with his personality before he had discarded them the previous day.

As I write, the picture, which, as I think I told you, is to be entitled *Behind the Screen*, is drawing to its close, and by the time this screed is in the United States mail-bag it will be off the fire, as the saying is, in movie-land.

But there has been no little cleaning up to do before we were able to say that the back of the work was finally broken and that a few days would see it off the shelf.

The great event to which we had all been looking forward was the descent of Eric Campbell into the depths of a pit in one of the scenes. Eric, because of his weight, had been a trifle scared of the drop, which had to be accomplished suddenly by means of pulling apart at great speed two folding trap-doors, and we had been kidding him incessantly for a week.

"Never mind, Eric," we would say, "camellias smell lovely on a freshly-watered grave. Have you made your will yet? I know an awfully jolly undertaker down town; shall I introduce you to him?" and so on. It was very heartless of us, but the mechanism of that trap-door, we well knew, was practically infallible, and the pit was rendered perfectly harmless by various means, so we had no compunction about coddling the life out of our ponderous friend.

But the laugh was on us when it came down to cases, for Eric accomplished the fall as naturally and artistically as could be imagined, while the kidders, most of whom are also required by the demands of the story to descend into the bowels of the earth, nearly all came to grief in some way or other.

Charlie was in rather a quandary at first as to how he was going to dispose of so many of the actors down the pit without repeating the method. The whole idea turns on the fact that a dramatic scene is in progress, and that a pistol shot is the cue for Charlie, as the property-man's assistant, to pull the lever, which lets open the trap in readiness for a body to be hurled down it. The pistol fails, however, at the crucial moment, and as the head "props" (Eric Campbell) is monkeying with it to see why it would not act, it suddenly goes off while the latter is standing on the trap, and Charlie, thinking his cue has come, pulls the lever!

This was all right for the disposal of one actor, but three more had to go down the trap in some way, and naturally the same gag could not be employed to dispose of them. It was an education to see the way Charlie brought his mind to bear on the problem, and finally succeeded in evolving four distinct "accidents" which would cause the trap to open at crucial moments.

In situations like those, which require judgement and thought, Charlie relies on his brain-power solely. It is no joke to sit down and think out four logical means of making people fall into a hole by a supposed accident, and have each means different from the last.

But sometimes, when it is merely a question of creating a comedy scene, he likes to go on to the stage and fool around before the camera until he has had about two hundred feet of film taken upon that one scene. Then he says:—

"All right. I guess I can get enough good stuff out of that lot to make a situation," and he will let it go at that.

Yet on other occasions I have seen him, as you know, worry and fret and try scenes this way and that, all of them apparently quite good enough to keep, yet he would discard them one after another, and finally play the scene several shades worse, to my mind, than his previous conceptions. It is just that he doesn't feel the spirit of the thing, and so keeps on at it until he does, regardless of the fact that it may possibly have looked better to the bystanders in its original form. He is right, of course. Unless he can feel the situation naturally it will not be worthy of the Chaplin trade-mark. That's the way he figures it, I imagine.

One little thing about Charlie's treatment of his supporters has always impressed me as typical of his nature. He never asks a player, either male or female, to perform what is popularly known as a "stunt" unless he is fully convinced that he or she is able to carry it through. Thus, in the trapdoor scenes previously referred to, he conceived the idea of having the villainess of the picture fall down into the pit, but then the fear took hold of him that Charlotte Mineau might injure herself in the fall, and after about half-an-hour's turning the matter over he finally instructed Albert Austin, who is about the same height as Charlotte, to make up as a woman and dress in her clothes.

Albert, who is an experienced tumbler, accomplished the fall in good form, and, if Charlie's little consideration did constitute a harmless deception of the public—the majority of whom will think that Miss Mineau actually made the fall—it also showed his thoughtfulness for others, particularly of the gentler sex.

The light throughout this production has varied, and come and gone with the passing of the winter clouds, so that the camera men have been at a constant tension to keep their attention on their work and the corner of each eye on the heavens. At times, too, the light was so badly obscured as to render photography practically an impossibility, and so the picture is just two weeks behind time!

It must be very worrying to the Executives, whose work begins when Charlie's leaves off, but the vagaries of the Californian autumn are more to blame for it than Charlie himself, and consequently there has been nothing for them to do but grin and bear it.

I had thought that the finishing up of the pie-slinging into the coronation scene was the finish also of the entire pie-faction of the story. I had reckoned without mine host. Charlie had other ideas than merely taking a scene of himself throwing those pies—the ones that are seen flying into the scene in question. He wanted something to be happening at the throwing end as well as at the receiving end, and, as luck would have it, it fell to my lot to be one of the chief participants in the former as well as in the latter.

The picture was so near completion on Wednesday last that I made bold to ask Charlie's permission to leave at midday and go to a matinee downtown.

"What!" he exclaimed, and bent an ominous glance on me.

I was somewhat abashed, but pursued my point—

"You won't be wanting me anymore in this picture, will you?"

He thought a while.

"No," he said. "Go down town and 'mat.' If I find I want you I'll postpone that particular scene until you're here."

So I went down town and 'matted.'

As a matter of fact, he didn't need me that particular day, but, oh, he made up for lost time on the Thursday! Everything went on quietly until lunch-time, and I was contemplating yet another excursion to the city—this time on private business—when down swooped Charlie, and killed all my hopes.

"We've got to finish up that pie stuff today," he informed me. "I think I'd better let you in on that end too, as you've been a good boy."

I turned my eye to the clouds.

"And do I get a pie in that faction, too?"

"I'll try and let you off," was the best answer he would vouchsafe.

It took him some time to figure out just the why and wherefore of those pies hurtling through the air, but after a lot of switching and changing of ideas and sundry cruel suggestions, which fortunately did not take effect, he eventually got the thing down to logic, and began to rehearse the scene.

"Now, you," meaning myself, "take this pie in each hand, and stand ready at this connecting door. Then the cop comes on in the other scene, and stands in the doorway with a pie in each hand too. He throws his pies at you, and you duck them; then you throw yours, and he gets them both in the face."

"Fine," thought I: but my hopes were short-lived, for somebody (I think it was Sydney) suddenly discovers that this would make the pies fly out in the wrong direction—that is, away from the direction in which the coronation scene lay.

"All right, then," said Charlie. "I've got it. We'll just reverse the whole ac-tion, so that Goodwins is the one that gets the pies in the face. That'll make the pies that miss the cop pass on into the coronation scene. Fine!"

Fine it was, from the point of view of the requirements of the picture, but it foreshadowed much washing of head and face with copious lather on the part of Goodwins. Not that I mind washing (once in a while), but if you've ever tried to wash dough out of your eyes and ears with nothing but a lot of soap and water you'll know what I mean. It dries into a nice, tenacious, mu-cilagenous paste before you can make any serious inroads into it, and in the end you come to the conclusion that it might have been better to have let it dry on and then brush it off.

However, I got the pies in the face all right, and that ended my connection with this particular production. Subsequent reports from the front assure me that they got over splendidly on the screen. I could have told them that myself.

Charlie is no shirker, it seems, for at the time of writing we are awaiting his coming to the plant after practically an all-night session in the projecting room which deprived him of sleep until the industrial classes were just on their way to their daily toil. Realising that the lateness of the picture presents a good deal of difficulty to those who have to turn it into hundreds of positive copies for distribution to the world at large, he returned to the studio on Thursday night at somewhere around the witching hour and sat through the entire run of nine reels. From these he selected the scenes he wanted for the requisite two reels, helped to sort them out, and retired to his couch just as the sun began to shine on Friday morning.

Some people are inclined to the belief that no man, not even Charles Spencer Chaplin, world's comedian-in-chief, is worth so stupendous a salary as 10,000 dollars a week. Possibly they're right.

But there are others who imagine that the earning of that sum is a "cinch"—an unmitigated sinecure. They're wrong.

Q.E.D.

35

A Hustle against Time in the Chaplin Studio

November 25, 1916

I had run rather ahead of myself when I stated last week that the negative of *Behind the Scenes* [*sic*] would be on its way East by the time those particular notes were in the mail to the homeland. Truth to tell, I had not dreamt that we were so far in arrears with it, or that so much remained to be taken in order to match it up in perfect continuity.

But none the less, at the time of writing—a week later—the film has been on its long journey a mere twenty-four hours. It was two weeks and two days after its schedule time, and in another twelve days the shipment of the next picture will be due. We haven't started on it yet.

But Charlie's excessive care and painstaking are not solely to blame for this unpunctuality. The weather has had a nice little bit to do with it, although now, when the Chaplin studio is clear and idly awaiting the starting of our next production, the sun is shining as cheerily as if it had never been obscured by a cloud or had its glory marred by a downpour of untimely rain. Thus the vagaries of Mother Nature.

The sorting out of the negative which had already been taken did not, as I had supposed, constitute the winding-up of our work for that particular production. Charlie had merely stayed up all night on that job so that the last stages—the cutting and assembling—would be easier for him and those whose duty it is to help him.

I was not alone, however, in my supposition that our work on this studio picture was done. Several others of the company had thought likewise, and there were consequently several stragglers on the morning following that all-night session of sorting. As luck would have it, and thanks to a friendly telephone call, I managed to get into the studio and made up just as Charlie called for me to take my specific part in the remaining scenes, so no harm was done in the shape of delaying the story's progress on my account.

Of course, he had changed his original idea all out of shape. Instead of making Edna blossom out into a leading-woman, he has had her slip into a suit of overalls and disguise herself as a stage-hand. She applies for a job after the regular stage gentry have gone on strike (because they were expected to work, forsooth!), and so becomes an assistant property-boy.

In that capacity she overhears a plot to blow up the studio, which is hatched between the strikers, and the story ends in a big fight between Charlie and the ringleaders, in the course of which he succeeds in knocking them, all unconsciously, into the very pit in which they have placed their own petard. All of which was very Chaplinesque and very funny.

But there were other things to do before this part of the production came in for notice, and if I had given more thought to what I was doing I might have known that it would take longer than a few hours. Those flying pies that entered the coronation set last week had to be accounted for. It's a cinch that pies can't come from nowhere.

He started right in on the cook's set, which was, you will recall, the comedy faction, wherein Lloyd Bacon is shown directing two policemen and myself (as the cook) to throw pies at each other.

Here, then, was the beginning of that fusillade which wrought such dire destruction in his majesty's domain. First of all, it seemed, I was to fondle two rich and succulent custard pies in my cook shop while the policeman in the other room balances two more tentatively on each palm. Then, at a given signal, I let fly, missing the cop, while his two pies are to hit me squarely in what Americans commonly term the "mush"—in colloquial English, the "chivvy."

But our official friend is hard of aim, and while mine, as they were supposed to do, miss him completely, his, which were supposed to do the mush-smearing, spread themselves on the wall. For which little slip the comedy director incontinently fires him, his place being taken by the head-property-man (Eric Campbell).

Eric's aim is a little too certain, however, and I get both those pies in a way that reminds me of the kick of my old Lee-Enfield down at Bisley.[1]

Angered, I walk off, and the comedy director is left cookless, but again the property department comes to the rescue, and Charlie, playing the assistant property-man, is stuck into my place.

From here the real fun begins. Instead of missing Eric and getting the pies himself, Charlie invents a more comfortable routine. He himself ducks the pies thrown by Eric, and by his quickness succeeds in hitting the latter with every pie within reach.

You can imagine for yourself the kind of uproar that follows. Both sides are equally well armed with ammunition, and many were the retakes—for Charlie loves to throw pies!—so that at the finish of the day the place looked as if a volcano had burst into eruption shedding, not lava, but pastry on the Lone Star Film Corporation's premises.

Altogether those scenes took us four days, and every pie that had been ordered was thrown by someone or other. In all three hundred and twenty pies flew through the air, and at least fifty per centum of them found a billet on the anatomy of some hapless soul or other.

Eric Campbell got sixteen in the face and two on the back of the neck, and by the time Charlie called off for the day he looked as if he had been sleeping in a baker's trough and had afterwards gotten himself into a bloodthirsty combat.

But there is never a grumble or a grouse be heard in the Lone Star plant, and the only comment Eric had to offer was when his day of playing target to Charlie was over was—"Ye gods, what a smell of Christmas!"

Thereafter he and I betook ourselves to the hot and cold shower with which the Lone Star studio is fitted, and fifteen minutes apiece of copious lathering and manipulation of taps removed from our offended persons all traces of the making of that strenuous comedy.

Charlie laughed when he saw us coming out of the shower, wet-haired and wrapped in dressing-gowns and towels.

"Some comedy!" he grinned. "This'll put the kybosh on pie-slinging for ever; any motion-picture comedy company that dares to put on a pie comedy after this will be shunned by the public for good and all."

And that was no wild statement, let me say. If any misguided soul of a director does conceive the aged and time-worn notion of constructing a "pastry classic," he'll probably go into the bankruptcy court—after the public has set eyes on *Behind the Screen. [Actually, Laurel and Hardy would have the last word on pie fighting a decade later, when over three thousand pies were thrown in* The Battle of the Century *(1927). The logic of the escalating battle is so impeccable, the variations on the hoary idea so ingenious, and the action so perfectly paced that the scene is not only monumental in scale but devastating in its effect on audiences, which are left quite literally gasping with laughter.]*

The last day of the production was a fight against time. There were, as usual, a dozen or more odd scenes, all in different locales, needed to make the picture complete, and the last hour or so grew into a battle—pictures versus the daylight.

In rapid succession the cameras were rushed from set to set, cleaning up those final scenes. Here they caught a flash of Charlie kicking Johnny Rand (as one of the strike leaders) out of the scene. In the next set they caught him staggering backwards and falling headlong into the pit of explosives. Then they were rushed to the carpenter shop—the real, genuine carpenter shop of the Lone Star studio, too—outside which the plot is hatched. And so on until nothing remained but to film the big explosion itself.

Then someone discovered that there were no dry batteries in the studio with which to spark the gunpowder, and before they could be obtained the sun went back on us.

On the morrow, however, Charlie was up betimes and at the studio in readiness for the blow-up. Five handfuls of gunpowder had been obtained and placed in a receptacle, but Charlie was dissatisfied.

"Shove a half barrel in," he ordered. "I want a real explosion, not a puff of tobacco smoke."

Five handfuls of gunpowder exploded under compression would scarcely have the effect of a puff of tobacco smoke, be it said; but Charlie wanted to blow everything in sight to the four winds, I suppose. At any rate, he had his wish, and a half barrel of gunpowder was added to that already in the box, the clay covering freshly compressed on top of it, the fuse attached, and then—

It was some explosion, I give you my word. The lookers-on and operatives had backed away fully two hundred feet—and not too far at that. That gunpowder went off with a noise that would have gladdened the heart of our old friend, Guido Fawkes, had he been on earth to hear it. It carried with it a goodly section of the studio floor, and brought the adjacent wall down to earth with a resounding crash. The wall fell right into the picture, and can be plainly seen on the screen.

Then Charlie began to ponder upon how he could make the big blow-up even more thrilling to the public. He wanted to show Eric Campbell crawling out of the pit just as the powder was fired, and although it was, of course, impossible to endanger our comrade's life by doing this in actuality, Charlie and Sydney finally evolved a scheme whereby the effect is produced on the screen by trickery.

They photographed both methods and it is a toss-up which one will remain in the picture, but enough that both showed Eric just about to crawl from the hole into which he has been kicked when there is a blinding flash and a pillar of smoke soars into the air right behind his back, and everything the next second is a mass of debris.

It forms a thrill sufficient to satisfy the most bloodthirsty picture-goer in the world, and is a fitting climax to a comedy which is one succession of quick situations and gags.

Poor Charlie was all shot to pieces, figuratively speaking, of course, by the end of the picture, and I daresay he would have sneaked away to the hills for a rest but for the fact that he has so little time in which to complete his next production. We have all of us had a pretty hard row to hoe this time, and eagerly grabbed the opportunity to absent ourselves from the plant for a day or so.

I was sitting in my chambers, writing as usual, when the 'phone rang, and Sydney Chaplin informed me he was on his way up in the lift to solicit my aid in shaping up the continuity of the picture.

"What, am I on the cutting committee now?" I gasped.

"No," he reassured me. "But the picture's going to be slammed together and shown in its rough three-reel form at the Liberty Theatre to-night. I want you to help me by writing out the continuity of it so the joiner can get busy."

"Come ahead, then," I told him, and inside the next five minutes this old machine of mine was going nineteen to the dozen, writing the gist of the story. It was soon done, and within an hour and a half I was speeding downtown (in the best company in the world, of course) to witness the premiere of *Behind the Screen. [It is a bit puzzling that Syd would show up at Goodwins's apartment to utilize his skill as a typist to produce a continuity guide, and even more puzzling that the cutter could have put the film together in the hour-and-a-half time frame that Goodwins seems to indicate. However, what is significant is the clarification that this was a true preview, in which an un-subtitled rough cut was shown to gauge audience reaction before trimming the film to its final shape. Also significant is Syd's evident involvement in the process.]*

When we arrived Charlie was already there, in company with Harry Caulfield, the manager, Edna, and one of the officials of the Mutual Company. Sydney entered at the same time as my companion and I, and, the party being presumably complete, the attendant drew to the little curtains that had been kindly placed in readiness along the section in which the Chaplin party sat.

The picture, which was unannounced in front of the theatre, because that would have been a violation of the Mutual's agreement with the Garrick Theatre (which has sole rights to Chaplin's first runs in Los Angeles), looked very ragged and odd the way it was run that night. It was devoid of sub-titles, of course, for those are added in New York from a list dictated by Charlie before the picture is despatched, and it needed trimming closer so that the action would appear snappier, but the way that audience yelled their appreciation was a treat, and there's not a question that *Behind the Screen*, trimmed down and glorified with sub-titles, will add yet another bunch of leaves to Charlie Chaplin's mighty wreath of laurels.

How he keeps on evolving new gags and keeping the public interest at such a pitch is a mystery to me, as it is to many of his even greatest admirers, but he does it, and it seems he always will.

"There's such a sameness about Chaplin," I've heard some people say, and their argument has an element of truth. But the odd part about it is that with all Charlie's sameness he is for ever giving them something different, something new, and while they continue to get a heartier laugh out of Charlie Chaplin than they do out of anyone else in the whole wide world, why, they're going to stick!

36

A Racy Account of *The Rink*

March 31, 1917

It seems an age since I closed my weekly series of Chaplin notes, doesn't it? Of course, I may be flattering myself, but that's how it seems to me, and, since I have had quite a small shoal of letters from *Red Letter* readers inquiring the reason of the sudden cessation of them, it would seem that I was not the only one that missed the little chats you and I were wont to have together.

The fault however was no more mine than it was yours or the kindly editors. Let me explain.

Those of the "Red Letterites" who followed my series will have a pretty good idea of Charlie Chaplin's method of work and of the time it usually takes him to turn out those inimitable two-reel comedies of his. His schedule times for releasing them to the public were precisely one month apart—ample for the average director to turn out a satisfactory two-reeler. But Charlie was 'most always one or two days behind the clock, and towards the latter his tardiness grew into weeks, what time the authorities back in New York presumably danced up and down the Mutual offices tearing at their locks (if any) and wondering the whys and wherefores.

The real whys and wherefores were, however, nothing more or less than the comedies themselves. Anyone of average skill and experience can, as I say, turn out a two-reeler in a month with an ease paralleled only by the facility with which some Californians eat peas off their knives.

Not so Chaplin, however. His pictures are superlative, and each one exhausts enough comedy ideas to supply the average producer with half-a-dozen plots. When those ideas are used up, therefore, it behooves Charles to sit him down and think out a host more for his next picture—and it is not long before he finds himself getting near to his official closing day, while he has yet to finish about a third of the picture.

To come to the hosses, then, Mutual grew tired of waiting and trying to beat Father Time at his own game, consenting finally to Charlie's oft-repeated plea for his release dates to be set six weeks apart instead of four-and-a-bit.

So, you see, since this was the case it became relatively difficult for your Uncle Fred to put up real, newsy chatter week after week when those weeks were half of them almost devoid of a happening worthy of note.

I am, however, going to give you a report of each picture as that picture is completed, this week being devoted to the production that followed the making of *Behind the Screen*.

One fine bright day (they're not so plentiful here at this time of the year) we put in our usual midday appearance at the plant to find the stage in the hands of an army of strange men, some of whom were littering it with old pieces of electrical machinery while others strove to negotiate the straightening-out of what looked then like a family of oily black snakes.

Investigation proved however, that the conglomeration of oddities was, in fact, nothing worse than a surfacing machine imported for the time being from a local skating rink. This weird contrivance, which, when assembled, looked rather like a small edition of one of those tanks we hear so much about, soon began to emit angry internal rumblings; the several wheels that jutted from its sides began to spin merrily, and it travelled slowly across the floor, throwing up into the air a choking cloud of sawdust. It would have been an unnerving thing to meet in the early dawn following a "night before," but in the bright light of the noon day sun the only emotion it aroused in our bosoms was that of curiosity.

"What seems to be the idea of this odd-looking animal?" someone asked.

"Surfacing machine," answered the head carpenter, and, after the manner of the Laconian of old, closed up like a clam.

"What's its object on earth, though?" I asked. "It's kicking up an unholy mess and choking everyone."

"Making the stage into a rink," replied the laconic one.

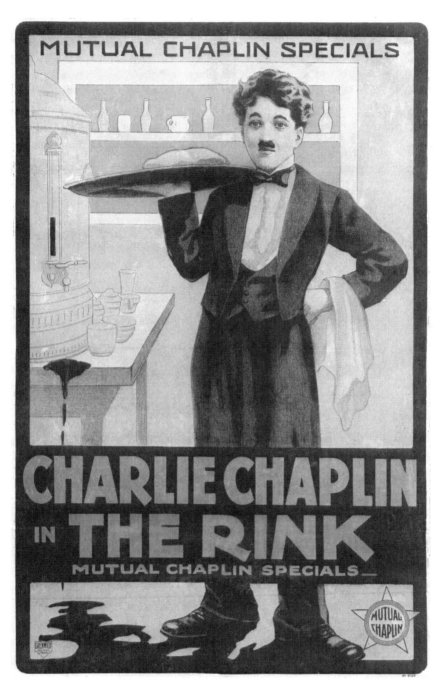
Original release poster for *The Rink*.

And then there dawned upon this mighty brain of mine the true meaning of the whole procedure.

Chaplin was going to make a skating-ring *[sic—rink]* picture!

I wandered to the office in pensive mood. The mere mention of that now superannuated sport brought back to me forcibly two things; the one, more personal, the days of the old skating clubs at Stamford Hill, Clapham, and Finsbury Park respectively (of which I was an active member in their palmy days), the other, the second time I had seen Charlie Chaplin.

It was at one of the West End music halls in London, and he was playing the part of a professor in Fred Karno's topical trifle *Skating*, which enjoyed a goodly run while the rinking boom lasted.

[While Goodwins offers no hint as to Sydney's involvement with the production, it is probably no coincidence that he co-created Skating *in 1909 and trained many Karno actors, including Charlie, to perform the skating stunts and falls in the sketch. While the plot bears no apparent resemblance to the plot of the film, it is unclear from existing scripts and reviews whether the brothers borrowed any of the physical business—aside from Charlie's spectacular skating skills, of course, which he honed touring the sketch for the better part of a year.]*

It also brought back to me a lot of other things, but they have nothing to do with Charlie Chaplin so I must desist.

When I arrived in the office I found His Majesty reading the mighty pile of mail that invariably awaits him there.

"Hello, Charles," I greeted him.

"Hello, Tiddley-winks," he responded—I don't know when he'll get through inventing new nicknames for me! "You're up early."

I looked hurriedly at my watch, which registered 1 p.m., realised he was kidding me, and ignored the reference.

"Going to make a skating picture, I hear."

"You're hearing is in good trim, then," he replied, still reading. "I am. Why?"

"That'll be nice, won't it? I'm an ex-professional roller-skater, you know."

He opened another letter.

"That so? Too bad; we'll have to keep you in the background then. I don't want anyone skating better than me!"

But after a few moments he ceased his heartless kidding, and we wandered out to the stage, where, during my absence, the company had foregathered and was putting roller-skates of doubtful age and mechanical condition onto its unaccustomed feet.

There was hardly a man-jack among them who had ever had a set of rollers on before, so you can imagine the varying expressions their faces bore as they tried to master the task of perambulating the floor and at the same time keeping their balance.

With all the vanity and case-hardened amusement of the old hand, Charlie and I watched their struggles and applauded their tumbles on that day. But to give them their due I never in my life saw the art of epatination [*a faux-posh word derived from* patinage, *the French word for skating*] mastered so quickly as it was by Campbell, Austin, and Rand. Eric Campbell, with his three-hundred-pounds of weight, had never even set foot in a skating-rink, yet on the second morning I turned up at the studio to find him careering gaily around the floor with all the aplomb of an expert.

A mishap in *The Rink*. Edna and Fred try to help Charlie, Eric, and Albert.

However, to business. The picture is called *The Rink*, and starts off with Charlie as a waiter in a restaurant, where he succeeds in making a mess of things in general, but, by means of repeated strategies gets the blame shifted on to the shoulders of the other waiter (played by John Rand). This restaurant faction, which takes up practically the whole of the first reel, is replete with absurdly funny gags, most of them having to do with the various viands that are served up to the long suffering customers, or should be served up, to be precise, for the majority of them contrive by some means to turn into very inedible objects before they reach the diner for whom they were intended.

For example, a brush with the kitchen swamper (sculleryman), is responsible for his brush, plus soap and floor-swab, getting on to a plate which Rand had placed in readiness for a juicy leg of chicken. Imagine the diner's expression when he finds on raising the cover what he has been served with!

[Members of Chaplin's stock company often appear in several roles in a single film, and this is the case with Goodwins in The Rink. *In the first restaurant scene he is easy to spot as a diner a couple of tables behind Eric Campbell; dapper-looking, he wears a light suit and sports a neatly trimmed blond mustache and an expanse of balding pate. As the action between Charlie and Eric proceeds, Fred converses enthusiastically with his table companion, at one point lighting a cigarette and getting a bit of something—possibly cigarette ash—in his eye. After Charlie infuriates Eric by pocketing his change for a tip, he rushes past Fred with Eric in hot pursuit. We cut to the lobby to find Fred already there; having apparently just arrived from the outside, he has his back to an attendant who is about to remove his overcoat. Instead, in a neatly staged bit of business, Charlie dashes in, grabs Fred by the back of the coat and twirls him around as a human shield. Eric grabs Charlie and forcibly retrieves his money as Fred looks on, very annoyed at having been drawn into their fracas. When Charlie returns to the dining room Fred is still seated where we left him. Such continuity gaps were common in the Mutuals, given the breakneck pace at which they were produced. But Chaplin was justifiably confident that no one would notice—indeed, your annotator failed to notice Fred's omnipresence in the scene until he carefully scrutinized the film for these notes.]*

In another scene Charlie got a notion to have the studio cat served up to one of the gentlemen—a Sybaritic *[luxury-loving]* soul of epicurean tastes (played by Lloyd Bacon). Lloyd, my own particular crony, has since

Charlie "helps" Fred Goodwins with his coat.

gone from our ranks, and the epicure was the last part he played under the Chaplin banner. But of this more later. *[Goodwins does not explain Bacon's departure.]*

A search was promptly instituted for one of the army of cats that makes the Chaplin studio its headquarters, but grimalkin evidently had no desire to become an actress, for there was not a cat to be found within a radius of half a mile.

The whole Chaplin forces turned out, headed by Charlie himself, and an exhaustive search resulted in the discovery by the night watchman of Sam, father of the flock, who registered his disapproval by emitting sundry howls of discomfiture. He played his part well, however, at the start, leaping on to the kitchen table at the crucial moment and devouring the dainty morsel that lay upon the platter, while Charlie and Rand indulged in fisticuffs around the coffee-urn. A yell from the dining-room terminates the fight prematurely, however, and Charlie hastily slamming a cover on the platter—wotting not that Samuel the cat is beneath it—hurries off to fill the diner's order.

Here it was that Sam begins to misbehave. Natural historians tell us that darkness is the natural element of the feline species, but if this be so Sammy is a most unnatural member of his kind. He rent the studio welkin while the cameras were being shifted hurriedly to the dining-room scene for the purpose of registering his escape, and continued to rend it until the cover was removed by Charlie. There sat Sam, in place of the eggs in aspic, or whatever it was the diner is supposed to have ordered, but he didn't sit there long. He just waited long enough for the cameras to show what he was, and then, with one final howl of disgust, leapt through the air like a comet, and disappeared beneath the studio stage, whence he did not emerge until the day's work was done.

It was the most ludicrous sight you ever saw in your life. The expression on Bacon's face, the startled look of the cat were too much for Charlie. Instead of registering surprise, as he had intended to, he just threw back his head and yelled with laughter. The picture in its finished form shows him thus.

Events follow close upon each other, culminating in Charlie's exit—to lunch, if you please! His meal over, he stops before a skating-rink (in reality one of the local picture shows in Los Angeles) and enters. From the ensuing trouble the plot of the picture emanates, for he meets Eric Campbell, who, in the part of a dashing old libertine is vainly trying to overtake Edna. The latter, when Charlie arrives, has just about given up the ghost, for she has been dodging her pursuer all the afternoon, but the redoubtable Charles starts right from his whirlwind entrance to literally make rings around the villain of the piece, until the latter has so far lost his sense of safety that he throws up his feet and goes to grass (or rather to maple) with a thud that would have awakened the Seven Sleepers of Ephesus.

Hence, the fun is fast and furious. Campbell has no more chance than the man in the moon with his elusive tormentor, and the latter downs him time after time while Edna, surrounded by a bevy of fellow-rinkers, stands by and applauds gleefully the undoing of the pest. In one melee Charlie upsets at one sweep three of the skaters and calls me—as the rink instructor—to eject one of them for disturbing the peace!

[For his role as "rink instructor" Goodwins loses the mustache and dons a dark uniform. In the film as released Charlie knocks down two skaters (John Rand and Albert Austin, doubling from their earlier roles as waiter and cook), and Fred enters and firmly escorts Rand out, as though Rand were the trouble-maker and not Charlie, who looks on innocently. Then Fred demonstrates the

*skating prowess he bragged about to Charlie by gliding gracefully backwards as
he keeps watch over the other skaters.*

*For the second rink sequence, described below, Goodwins becomes a tux-
edoed attendant who takes Charlie's hat and cane, then participates in the fast
and furious chase-on-skates that ends the film.]*

Before the picture is over Charlie has brought about a beautiful family
tangle, which shows that several trusting but faithless spouses have been
gently putting it over on each other, and, as the song says, trotting round the
town with other fellows' wives. He makes himself such a general nuisance,
however, that the whole male element finally decides to give chase and eject
him from the assembly, whence they pursue him down the open street. He
finally escapes, however, by hanging on to the back of a speeding motorcar,
and the picture ends in his pursuers falling in a heap over each other.

Considering the nature of the production, it is a wonder that some of us
weren't injured, but nothing happened worse than a few minor bruises sustained by Eric Campbell in the fall on the street, which, considering about ten
men were piled on top of him, is not surprising. But the picture passed without mishap worthy of note, and is a very good example of Charlie's peculiar
sense of humour.

"Another off the fire," said Charlie on the day of its completion. "Now for
the next."

"What's it to be?" I asked him in my best reporter style.

"*Easy Street*" he replied. "The one I began a few months ago, and afterwards switched into *The Pawnshop*. If it runs as smoothly as this one has I
shan't grumble."

[Goodwins actually gets more screen time in The Rink *than in any other
Mutual film, which is fitting, since it would be his last appearance for Chaplin.
He is credited in modern filmographies for his roles in the Essanay films, but
not for his appearances in the Mutuals. Though less prominent, these performances are well done and certainly deserving of mention, so we hereby set the
record straight: Goodwins appears in* The Floorwalker, The Fireman, The
Vagabond, The Count, Behind the Screen, *and* The Rink.]*

37

A Million Dollar Contract and *Easy Street*

April 28, 1917

Theatrical people are perhaps the most superstitious souls—next to sailors—in the whole wide universe. They have their odd little hunches concerning the effects of various things on their work and careers that fairly stagger their less romantic brothers of the commercial world.

Thus, for example, there is no greater inducement you can offer a fellow-player to commit murder than to whistle in his dressing-room, the penalty wherefore, 'twould seem, is the ultimate sacking of the one nearer the door, whether or not he be the whistler. Again, making quotations from *Macbeth*, the singing of Tosti's "Good-Bye" and "The Light Cavalry March" are things that are utterly taboo in theatrical circles, all of them supposedly marking a premature failure of the production.

And one of the worst things you can do, if you happen to be a playwright, is to give your play a name that signifies success or the like. Plays with titles like "The Money-Makers" are invariably predestined to utter failure and loss of money, and because of this it was something of a surprise to me that Charlie Chaplin decided to make his ninth Mutual picture under the working title of *Easy Street*. It seemed to me to be simply asking for trouble, and thus it proved. With the exception of *Shanghaied* there has never been a picture made by Chaplin that has marked upon the map a greater series of misfortunes than that hopelessly misnamed comedy.

I came across Charlie a few days before *Easy Street* was born or thought of; he was walking across the bare stage humming to himself a tune that seemed familiar to me.

"What seems to be the idea of all the music?" I enquired.

But he ignored me and continued to sing softly about the stage in the pensive way that is his wont when a new picture is shaping itself up in his mind.

Then I caught the drift of what he was murmuring, and it carried my mind away back into dim recesses, to my surreptitious vaudeville visits when I was an Eton-collared, callow youth. Thus it was—

> "'old yer row, 'old yer row,
> we ain't said a word abaht 'alf wot occurred:
> 'old yer row. Wot'd yer say?
> We always kills coppers wot comes dahn our way!"

Yessir, Charles' mind was as far away from California and motion pictures as the two continents themselves.

It was not, however, until he finally condescended to come down from the clouds that I discovered that there was some definite connections between his reminiscent humming of Tom Woottwell's classic melody and the forthcoming picture.

"Did you hear what I was singing?" he questioned, with the air of one who doesn't care particularly whether he's answered or not.

I assured him that I had, and he proceeded to ruffle the hair on the back of Billy the goat, who had hoofed his way onto the stage for his morning caress.

"What made you think of that old thing?" I asked him.

"Oh, I wasn't particularly thinking of what I was humming," he said, with a faint smile, though I darcsay there was more than a shade of unconscious cerebration (this is a new one of his) about it. I'm going to finish off that set we had built just before we made *The Pawnshop*."

"Then you're going to make *Easy Street* after all," I said, as one upon whom a great light has suddenly broken in. "Is that it?"

"After all," he repeated, grinning abstractedly. "Did you think I was going to leave a big set unused?"

I shrugged my shoulders non-committally.

"Of course I'm going to make it," he continued. "What I've been trying to do is get a natural theme to build the story around. The old crook story I had in mind is too gruesome."

"Then you were thinking—"

"That old song has put an idea in my head," he confessed. "'We always kill coppers wot comes dahn our way.' What a classic sentiment to build a comedy on!" [*In his* Autobiography *Chaplin names several songs that inspired specific films, but not "Old Yer Row." The notion of slum dwellers killing cops proved to be a potent inspiration; policemen had always been Charlie's natural enemies, and the irony of Charlie becoming one himself stimulated some of Chaplin's most inventive comedy. In addition, Charlie's new role and the grimly realistic slum setting elicited a surprisingly incisive vein of social commentary, and both the Tramp character and Chaplin's filmmaking took on added depth as a result.*]

The classic sentiment in question sounded more to me like a good excuse for an underworld melodrama than the basis for a comedy, but when I began to see the minor sets springing up and to learn bits of the plot ahead of their execution I saw where the comedy was to come in.

Then, like a cruel bolt from the blue, down came the Californian evening climate and caught me unawares immediately after a strenuous game of golf, with the result that for six days I reclined in the throes of that wretched malady which has once before deprived me of my pictorial activity—I mean, of course, the "flu." So the starting of *Easy Street* was taken while I was absent from the plant—not that I am hinting that it suffered as a consequence; I merely record it as a fact.

News came to hand from time to time that the production was proceeding merrily, and that the opening scenes, which are laid in a slum mission, were "as funny as the dickens," and by the time I was up and doing again around the studio Charlie had completed them, and had gone out to the big street set.

This scene, as I think I told you several months ago, resembles nothing so much as a by-street in the heart of Whitechapel, and was built, every stick and pane, by those wonderful knights of scenic art that have their field in the Lone Star Studio. Indeed, so realistic is this mimic slum that few of those who saw the picture when it was released ever dreamed that it was anything but a real street somewhere in the under-world of Los Angeles.

Edgar Brewer, for two years Charlie's master carpenter, has achieved a triumph second to none in this particular piece of work, and I feel I ought, out of sheer justice to him and his henchmen, to ask my readers to remember, when they have the chance to see *Easy Street*, that they are looking on a piece of stage craftsmanship. It will add to their enjoyment of the picture, which, for all the little trials and tribulations of its making is no end of a good story. Many, indeed, regard it as Charlie at his best.

The plot, in brief, shows Charlie a poor human derelict, who goes to sleep outside a mission house and is awakened by the singing within. Craving warmth, he enters, and after a lot of interludes becomes so converted by the lady missionary (Miss Edna) that he even hands back the collection box which he had (unknown to anyone, and least of all to the audience!) hidden in the folds of his voluminous breeks *[Scottish term for trousers]*.

Thence he proceeds towards his slum rendezvous, the big boss of which (Eric Campbell) rules his domain by sheer intimidation. But en route Charlie,

Charlie's got his hands full in *Easy Street*.

his lesson still in mind, accepts a job as a policeman, and is told to make "Easy Street" his beat. Right away he encounters Eric, whom he tries to brain half-a-dozen times with his truncheon, but without getting as much as a blink from that hardy soul; and then begins the fun.

Then also began the list of casualties. Just as Charlie arrived at the studio on the first morning of the big scene news came to him that his old property-man, one George Gramer, of whom Charlie had thought very highly, had died the previous night after a lingering illness of a tubercular nature, and that his last few words had been for the boys at the Chaplin studio.

I need hardly record that work was out of the question for that day, Charlie takes hardly the thought of another's demise or misfortune, and it was impossible for him to think comedy that day as if he himself had been the sufferer. But he couldn't afford to delay over-long, and after making lavish contributions to poor old George's burial, and to the fund that was forthwith raised for his widow, he set to on the fight with Campbell.

All other means proving unavailing, Charlie tries to seek safety in flight, but is caught bodily by the gigantic bully and pinned to the wall with one hand, while the latter removes his own coat with the other.

Then, to demonstrate his strength—and Eric's is some strength in very truth!—the bully seizes the lamppost and bends it double. "See that?" he growls. "That's how I'll bend you in a few moments." Delighted at the expression of terror on the little policeman's face, the bully tortures him still more by bending the post lower yet, and Charlie, seized with a sudden inspiration, leaps on his back and jams his head through the glass side of the lamp with the purpose of turning on the gas and suffocating him into unconsciousness, the idea being that by the time the burly brute regains consciousness sufficiently to sing "We always kills coppers wot comes dahn our way" again, he will safely be in the cells.

So far so good; but in making the leap Charlie had reckoned without his host in the shape of the bent lamppost. He landed on Eric's back securely enough, but as he did so he struck his nose violently against the sharp edge of the ornamental iron that surrounded the lamphouse, inflicting a bone-deep gash that must have nearly blinded him for the time being. But he stuck gamely on until he had Eric's head inside the lamp, none of the company having noticed the accident, and only gave in when his face became so covered with blood that he could hardly breathe. Then he slid off feebly and walked towards the cameras, which, before they ceased to turn, registered the whole gruesome sight on the film.

Of course he was rushed to the nearest medical man, who fixed him up with an antiseptic dressing, but it was two days before he was able to get about, and nearly ten before he could resume the interrupted scene. When the rough-run was made in the projecting-room it was quite a little tragedy to see the black streaks on his pale make-up as he slid off Eric's back and turned to the lens for the first time.

He will bear a trifling scar to his grave, but otherwise there is nothing amiss with him now. Considering the rough stuff he had to go through in his early stage and picture career, it is a marvel he hasn't sustained an injury before. Isn't it the perversity of things that a simple little piece of business like that should choose itself as a means of injury, while bigger stunts have left him unscathed?

The accident caused the production to fall a way behind time, and things weren't particularly enhanced by the fact of Charlie's lay-off. When you've been away from active work for over a week it's awfully hard to get back into your swing, and to gather up the loose ends of the work where you discontinued it, and consequently it was a long time before Charlie could get going with the same vim as he had when the accident put him hors de combat. Eventually, however, the picture was well on its way once more, and proceeded thus:—

Eric, temporarily stifled by the gas fumes, falls to earth, and Charlie, coolly brushing a few specks of dust from his uniform, telephones to headquarters that he has captured the terror. Twenty policemen hurry to the spot full of trepidation, but forthwith become bold men and true when they find the giant in a state of coma with Charlie sitting reflectively on his face! They transport the bully to the station, where he comes to, smashes his "darbies," [British slang for handcuffs] and proceeds to "clean" the entire police department, escaping afterwards in search of the diminutive Charles.

Then comes the inevitable Chaplin chase, interspersed at intervals with free fights. Charlie is ultimately slugged with a life-preserver [British slang for a billy club] and hurled down a coal-chute into an underground "hell." Here he finds Miss Edna, who has also been captured by the bully's mates, engaged in a hand-to-hand fight with a dope fiend. He immediately proceeds to clean up the latter, but is again "outed," and falls into a corner. Here, however, he

Charlie demonstrating crowd control on Easy Street.

sits on the drug maniac's cocaine needle, which infuses him with new vigour to such an extent that he fights fourteen men single handed, knocks out the "dope," and makes his getaway with Edna. Thence he enters one of the buildings, gets into another fight with Eric, and finishes by dropping a huge iron stove out of the first floor window onto the latter's head. *[In the finished film Charlie dispatches Eric with the stove before being knocked out and dropped into the dope fiend's lair, where the action proceeds as described above.]*

This puts the final crimp in the courage of the local toughs, and Charlie is hailed as their hero. The picture then fades out and in again on the new "Easy Street." Gone are the dope-dens and red-light houses. *[Easy Street remains remarkable even today for its unflinching look at how poverty goes hand-in-hand with urban violence, spousal abuse, and drug addiction.]* The saloon becomes an employment agency, the old lodging-house becomes a huge mission-house, pot-plants and canaries take the place of old milk bottles, &c. on the window-sills and the entire populace of the district is seen wending its way, all brushed up and reformed, toward the mission, at the door of which two ministers wait to greet the newly formed congregation.

But the greatest reformation of all is that of Eric the bully. He has taken unto himself a clean collar and a silk hat which, if they contrast oddly with his old tweed coat and corduroy breeks, nevertheless indicate a literal acceptance of the old saw that "cleanliness is next to godliness"! He is a striking instance of Charlie's triumph, for not only has he turned over a new leaf in regard to his character and person, but he has also blossomed out into a modern edition of Chesterfield. His manners towards his spouse, with whom he was wont to fight so strenuously in the days gone by, are beyond reproach, and he carries his defeat so graciously that he even raises his new and shining "lid" to constable Charles as he passes the latter on the way to church.

The thing is a pure travesty, and, touching though it does lightly on religion, it is treated in so delicate a way that not the most prejudiced Puritan could take exception to it. After all, it points to the advantages of a better viewpoint on life, and may strike home on a tender spot in certain of the rougher communities where such characters as Big Eric are far from being myths.

[Some critics did object to Chaplin's use of a mission in the film, and particularly to the scene within it in which Charlie believes a baby he is holding is urinating on his lap (Charlie is simply holding the baby's bottle upside down). Others objected to a later shot of the addict shooting up, which was removed for the 1932 sound reissue. Contemporary reviews were mostly ecstatic, however, stressing how funny the film was.

A few prescient commentators also recognized that it was more than funny. It was, in fact, a glorious fulfilment of Chaplin's goal, discussed throughout Goodwins's articles, of infusing serious content into his slapstick comedies. Without stinting on the laughs Easy Street *expresses a profound and optimistic vision of a broken world made whole. Far from being gratuitous, the film's use of a religious mission and its theme of conversion set the stage for a modern retelling of the David and Goliath story. Disguised as another of Charlie's slapstick comic adventures, this unpretentious little film aspires to—and achieves— biblical grandeur.]*

The picture was nearing its end, and everyone was more than a trifle glad, for it had, as I say, been fraught with unpleasant touches. But the gods of mischief were not through with us yet, for the next thing that happened was a collision between a heavy trolley-car and an automobile which was carrying one of the property boys to Los Angeles. Nothing fatal resulted, but the shock and concussion succeeded in depriving the boy of his hearing, which, although it is not essential to his work, is quite an important faculty. Small wonder that Charles and we all breathed a sigh of relief when the last scene was filmed at 10.30 a.m. that Sunday.

It is odd how smoothly some productions will run throughout, while others are fraught with mishap after mishap, for all the world as if a Jinx were at work behind the scenes.

Do you wonder that actors are superstitious?

• • •

Saint Patrick's Day, March 17, 1917, marked the official termination of the Chaplin contract whereby he beat the world's previous record by earning £134,000 for making twelve two-part comedies. Following *Easy Street*, Chaplin started on a sort of Baden-Baden picture, having its locale in a health resort, and this was finished upon the very day the contract ended. *[This film was released as* The Cure, *and once again Chaplin borrowed a setting—in this case a health spa—from a Karno sketch that Sydney had helped to create,* The Hydro *(1912). Little is known about the sketch, but Chaplin probably wasn't able to recycle much of it, judging from his outtakes, which reveal him pursuing an agonizing number of false starts. The film took him two months to complete, a record for him at the time, but one that he would soon surpass.]* He still has two more pictures to make under the contract and must, of course, work these out of his own time (his contract having expired). Rumour says that Adolph Zukor, head of the World Film Corporation, has offered him 1,000,000 dollars (nearly 200,000 guineas) for next year, during which he is to make four four-reel pictures. But rumour often lies. In any case it is certain that Charlie Chaplin's 1916–17 contract will be far overtopped by his 1917–18 one, whoever countersigns the latter, and although I may not recount these happenings hereafter I propose to communicate the news of his re-engagement to you through the *Red Letter* immediately something definite comes to hand.

[Zukor did offer Chaplin a million, as did Mutual, but he chose to go with the newly formed First National Exhibitors' Circuit, which paid him a million plus a $75,000 signing bonus to write, direct, and star in eight pictures over the

next year. While the financial offers were comparable, First National offered Chaplin more autonomy. He would produce his own films, and, critically, after five years the ownership would revert to him. This shrewd business move—the contract was once again negotiated by Sydney—ended up earning Chaplin and his heirs many millions of dollars, as the First National films remain commercially viable to this day. The contract received as much publicity as the one for Mutual, and the films were advertised as Chaplin's "million-dollar comedies."]

For your kind attention and appreciation of these little chats, for the opportunity they have given me of meeting, if only by mail, one of the most courteous and professional of editors, and for the many, many personal letters that have come across these 7,000 miles of sea and land from my homeland and my fellow country men and women because of these little chats I am very grateful. If by my efforts to give you an insight into the personality and methods of my friend Charlie Chaplin I have succeeded in interesting you, and in establishing him deeper into your hearts, then these articles have not been written in vain.

It is probable that at a not far-distant date I shall be wending my way hence towards the metropolis in which I was born to meet you all in closer intimacy through the medium of the screen. The need of "better British pictures" for the British has become more and more an obsession with me, and it is my intention to do what I can, backed by my three years of intimate experience in the U.S.A., to lend a hand in the furtherance of that requirement.

In the meantime, au revoir.

And Then . . .

While Goodwins doesn't tell us why his employment with Chaplin ended in his gracious but very brief farewell, we can deduce a few things from the content and timing of his last three articles. First of all, his claim that the four-month gap between the installment of November 25, 1916, and that of March 31, 1917, on *Behind the Screen* and *The Rink*, respectively, was due to the extension of Chaplin's release schedule from four to six weeks is unconvincing. His reason—that there wasn't as much to report, given the additional downtime—doesn't jibe with the fact that he never had the slightest problem filling his pages with gossipy news about the extracurricular activities of the company during previous periods of downtime.

The timing is also suggestive. *The Rink* was released in the United States on December 4 and *Easy Street* on January 22. In his final article Goodwins reports that Chaplin had begun working on *The Cure*, but offers not much more information about the film other than telling us that it was to be set in a health spa. So it seems most likely that he left the studio sometime in late January or early February, before the production got under way. But again, why the four-month gap?

Another wrinkle is that in his *Rink* installment Goodwins promised to report on each film as it was completed; in other words, when he wrote his penultimate article he had no idea that he was nearing the end of his time with Chaplin. And indeed, why would he, given his prominence as an actor in *The Rink*? In addition, he relates several pleasant conversational exchanges with Chaplin in those last couple of articles, making his abrupt departure all the more puzzling. There may, of course, have been a falling out that he was unable to report, given his mandate to extol the virtues of his boss.

Nor can we discount the possibility that Goodwins left because of his own cinematic ambitions. After leaving Chaplin's employ he worked as a film actor for two more years in Hollywood. In 1919 he fulfilled the promise he made in his last installment and returned to his homeland, immediately writing, directing, and starring in three comedy shorts. He went on to direct seven feature films, two of which he also wrote, before his untimely death from bronchitis in 1923, at the age of thirty-two.

But whatever the reason for his departure, it is unfortunate that Goodwins didn't report on the making of *The Cure*, considered by many to be the funniest of the Mutuals, or the two superb films that brought the series to a close, *The Immigrant* and *The Adventurer*. A new studio manager, John Jasper, succeeded Henry Caulfield in June 1917 and hired a new press agent, Carlyle T. Robinson, who did not write the sort of personalized articles Goodwins had been turning out for *Red Letter*. Robinson was to remain with Chaplin for fifteen years, a turbulent period in Chaplin's life during which Robinson's skill at damage control would be severely tested; he would later joke, in the tell-all book he wrote after he was fired in 1931, that he had gone from being press agent to "sup-press agent."[1]

Unlike Robinson, Goodwins wrote no tell-all following his time with Chaplin. There is little doubt that he could have revealed much more than he did in his *Red Letter* series. However, we can be grateful that, despite the constraints of his role as staff writer, he managed to provide us with so many unguarded glimpses of the great comedian at work and play during what Chaplin later described as his happiest years. It was a time when a war-torn world—and British fans in particular—were finding precious moments of solace and joy in the irrepressible onscreen antics of the man Goodwins dubbed, without a trace of press agent hyperbole, "the world's jester-in-chief."

Charlie Chaplin's New Contract: Record Salary and One Film a Month

April 1, 1916

[This anonymous syndicated article was probably written by Terry Ramsaye, Mutual's new publicist.[1]]

All doubts have now been set to rest as to Charlie Chaplin's future.

He has formed a Chaplin Comedy Producing Company, and his pictures are to be released through the Mutual Corporation, a big American concern controlling Flying A, Thanhouser Beauty, and other well-known films.

Charlie will receive a salary of 670,000 dollars (£134,000) for his first year's work under the contract. The total operation in forming the Chaplin Producing Company involved the sum of 1,550,000 dollars (£310,000). This stands as the biggest operation centred about a single star in the history of the motion-picture industry, it is said.

The closing of the contract ends a war of negotiations involving unending conferences and diplomatic exchanges for weeks. In this time five or six motion-picture concerns and promoters have claimed Chaplin and audibly whispered figures—with every guess too low.

The president of the Mutual put Chaplin under an option, pending the completion of arrangements for the organization of a special producing company. At that time the negotiations were entirely personal between the president and Chaplin.

The final conference was held, and the ceremony of singing [sic] up with the Mutual proceeded, with all due array of attorneys, notaries, &c., including, of course, a battery of arc lamps and a motion picture camera.

Charles Chaplin was accompanied by his brother, Sidney Chaplin, who conducts the younger comedian's business affairs and salary negotiations.

The directors handed Chaplin a bonus cheque for 150,000 dollars (£30,000). In addition to the bonus paid Chaplin, he will receive a salary of 10,000 dollars (£2,000) a week.

The new Mutual Chaplins will be produced in studios now being equipped in Los Angeles, California, where the comedian started work on March 20. One two-part comedy will be produced each month. *[During the silent era film length was given in number of reels rather than running time. A 35 mm reel was approximately one thousand feet, which would run about eleven minutes if projected at twenty-four frames per second. However, neither shooting speed nor projection speed was standardized until the sound era; cameras were hand-cranked and projectors had rheostats. Films were run at anywhere from sixteen to twenty-two frames per second. Some films came with instructions as to how fast to run them, but others did not, so film speed varied from theatre to theatre according to the whim of the projectionist and theatre manager. Comedies were expected to run at a more accelerated pace than dramas, and we know that Chaplin carefully controlled the shooting speed; however, he exercised little control over the projection speed. The correct projection speed for silent films therefore, is a matter of some debate.[2]]*

The Chaplin contract contains more than 20,000 words and provides conditions and clauses to cover numerous contingencies. An element of "war risk" enters into the contract. Chaplin is a British subject. It is stipulated that he shall not leave the United States within the life of the contract without the permission of the corporation. Incidentally, the company has insured the comedian's life for 250,000 dollars (£50,000). *[The war clause was to cause Chaplin considerable grief in England. Soon after the contract was signed on February 26, 1916, Lord Northcliffe's* Daily Mail *began a smear campaign against him. Northcliffe was not only a media mogul but also the director of propaganda in the British War Office, and he vigorously pursued an anti-Chaplin campaign through his nationalistic tabloid. Chaplin soon began receiving white feathers, a symbol of cowardice, in the mail, and he continued to receive them for years after the war ended. However, Northcliffe's campaign did little to affect his popularity. To most people, particularly the soldiers, it was patently obvious that Chaplin was doing more for the war effort by boosting morale than the diminutive comedian could possibly do as an indifferent*

Tommy in the trenches. Chaplin also contributed thousands of dollars to the British cause, and helped to sell millions of dollars' worth of American war bonds through a 1918 personal appearance tour with Mary Pickford and Douglas Fairbanks.

And in the end he did make it to the trenches, at least on film; his 1918 war comedy Shoulder Arms *featured him as an American doughboy who captures the Kaiser and ends the war. Chaplin released the film with considerable trepidation three weeks before the Armistice. He needn't have worried; it became a worldwide sensation that was especially popular with the Allied soldiers. The film also served as proof to many, such as the pioneering film critic Louis Delluc,[3] that cinema had come of age as a major art form, with not only the means but the responsibility to comment upon the times.]*

Charlie himself is not much inclined to talk about business. "A great many people are inclined to make wide eyes at what is called my salary," he remarked. "Honestly, it is a matter I do not spend much time thinking about.

"Money and business are very serious matters, and I have here to keep my mind off them. In fact, I do not worry about money at all," he admitted convincingly.

"It would get in the way of my work. I do not want people to think that life is all a joke to me," he added with an air of seriousness, "but I do enjoy working on the sunny side of it.

"What this contract means is simply that I am in business with the worry left out, and with the dividends guaranteed.

"It means that I am left free to be just as funny as I dare, to do the best work that is in me, and to spend my energies on the thing that the people want. I have felt for a long time that this would be my big year, and this contract gives me my opportunity. There is inspiration in it. I am like an author with a big publisher to give him circulation." *[Whether Ramsaye is quoting Chaplin verbatim or crafting his eloquent comments, the modest response is brilliant public relations. Ramsaye would later report him saying, "Well, I've got this much if they never give me another cent. Guess I'll go and buy a whole dozen neckties."[4] Goodwins's articles, of course, reinforce this regular-guy image. But Chaplin's Mutual salary sent a shockwave around the world, eliciting resentment as well as awe. Pundits and cartoonists were quick to pick up on the gulf between the millionaire creator and his shabby creation, a divide that would only widen as the years passed.]*

I'VE JOINED.

Cartoonists loved imagining Charlie as a soldier. This 1916 British postcard is from a series featuring Charlie at war by William Ellam.

Appendix B

Charlie Conducts Sousa's Band

April 8, 1916

[Upon the completion of his Essanay contract the company made Chaplin an offer of $350,000 for twelve new films, which Sydney advised Charlie to reject while he sought better terms for his brother in New York City. Chaplin's performance at the Hippodrome, described in this anonymous article, is usually presented as a small sidelight to his New York visit. However, R. J. Minney, one of Chaplin's biographers, claimed that the other studios were dismayed by the astronomical amount Charlie was demanding and gave Sydney the cold shoulder. According to Minney, Syd arranged the Sousa concert to demonstrate Chaplin's drawing power. If so, it had the desired effect; Chaplin's concert was February 20, and two days later he confirmed a record-breaking deal with Mutual which made him the highest-salaried employee in the world. There is no corroboration for Minney's account, but as his source was Syd himself it can't entirely be discounted.[1]]

At the New York Hippodrome Charlie Chaplin made his first public appearance in New York, and what an audience there was to welcome the little comedian! The capacity of the Hippodrome is 4,000, but even this vast space would not hold all Charlie's New York admirers, so a further 1,000 seats were arranged at the rear of the stage, and the orchestra pit was also crammed to overflowing.

Charlie made this one and only appearance on behalf of charity; in fact, that was the only condition on which he would make an appearance at all.

When one knows that Chaplin's share of the evenings receipts total 7,700 dollars (£1,500), one can imagine the total box office receipts. Charlie has decided to divide his share equally between the British and American Actors' Funds. *[Chaplin actually received $2,600, which he divided between the funds.]*

After a brief speech, Charlie proceeded to conduct Sousa's band, first through the mazes of "The Poet and Peasant" and then through one of his own compositions, "The Peace Patrol." Learning that her little favourite was to conduct the band, a lady admirer of Chaplin's sent him a solid silver-headed baton with which to perform his arduous task.

In the wings before his appearance Charlie appeared intensely nervous. "If only it was over!" he kept saying.

So changed was the appearance of the world-renowned little man when he made his bow in evening dress that many would have failed to recognise him had it not been for his introduction by Mr. Tom Wise, and, indeed, there was some slight feeling of disappointment, as everyone hoped against hope that they might see the original tabloid moustache, shabby derby and baggy trousers.

After his musical efforts, and by the way this is the only time that anyone but Sousa or his trained assistant has had the privilege of conducting the band, and thanking the shrieking gallery boys for their welcome, Charlie made his final bow, and with about three steps of the famous Chaplin walk, quitted the stage. *[Chaplin doesn't mention this performance in his* Autobiography, *but it was covered extensively in the press. He made no secret of the fact that he was rattled by the audience's apparent indifference to his musical abilities: "I have positively and absolutely made my last public appearance in person. No one realizes my shortcomings on the speaking stage more than I. It is not my sphere. I am timid, awkward, ill at ease and disappointing to the audience, who are led to expect so much from me after having seen me on the screen."[2] He was as good as his word, seldom appearing onstage after this time. Ironically, he became a consummate party entertainer, able to hold groups spellbound with his mimicry.]*

The sight of that little trot which is known throughout the civilised world woke re-echoing cheers and until Chaplin had again returned and informed the audience in pantomime that his tricks were only for the camera, the performance could not proceed. *[This interesting little detail is usually omitted from accounts of the event.]*

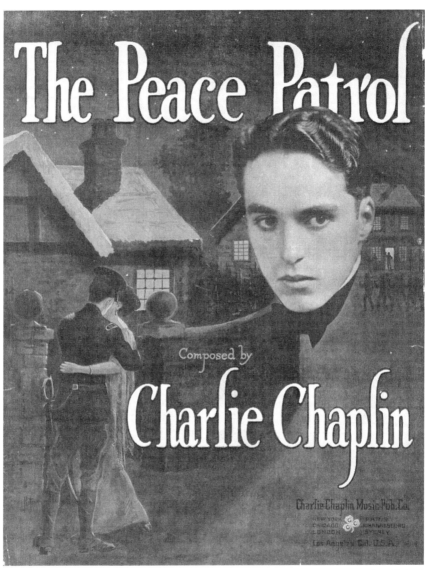

Chaplin played "The Peace Patrol" with Sousa's band, and also had it self-published and recorded. His musical abilities would be put to better use as the composer of his film sound tracks, which included haunting melodies that were spun off into hits like "Smile."

Chaplin is a very slight little fellow about 5 feet 3 inches tall. He weighs less than 130 lbs., and is 26 years old. "Are you married?" Charlie was asked. "Well," he laughed, "I'm kind of semi-detached." *[At this point Chaplin's relationship with Edna was a marriage in all but name, but he never spoke about her publicly until much later. Here he compares his marital status humorously to a semi-detached home, or duplex, as such buildings were called in America.]*

We sincerely wish that all Chaplin "doubters" could have been at the Hippodrome, when they could not have failed to realise that his personality is so strong and so unique that it does not require the prop of pails, brushes, and his usual screen impediments to make him felt across the footlights.

Such an ovation as Charlie received would make every Londoner feel proud that dear old London is the birthplace of the little comedian who has drawn more honest laughter than any man living, and, indeed, what better record can one wish to break than that of making laughter? *[Chaplin had musical ambitions too, which would not be fully realized until he began scoring his own movies in the sound era. In late 1915, as mentioned in chapter 30, he established a short-lived music publishing company that published three of his compositions, including* The Peace Patrol.*]*

Appendix C

His Doings in New York
April 15, 1916

[Chaplin was aware by mid-1914 that his films were steadily growing in popu-larity, but he hadn't viscerally experienced the full extent of his fame until the cross-country train journey he made in February 1916 to negotiate and sign his Mutual contract. At every stop the stations were jammed with eager fans hop-ing for a glimpse of their idol, and even when the train didn't stop fans lined the platform and waved from the fields. At Grand Central in New York the crowd was building to such alarming proportions that the chief of police sent a telegram instructing him to disembark a stop earlier. "I had always thought I would like the public's attention," he lamented in his Autobiography, *"and here it was—paradoxically isolating me with a depressing sense of loneliness."[1] In fact, he was riding a roller coaster of emotions that ranged from exhilaration at this indisputable proof of his success to blind panic as the crowds seemed about to engulf him.*

This article, consisting mostly of a breakfast interview with Chaplin, is for some reason heavily filtered through the editorial voice of someone at the maga-zine. Nevertheless, it is both fascinating and revealing. We get a ringside seat to watch Sydney's endearingly protective attitude toward his brother, and the smooth way the two work together to charm the unnamed reporter, who proves sensitive to the comedian's rapidly fluctuating moods. The reporter (whose sex is never made clear, but whom I suspect was female based on her questions and observations) begins by asking Chaplin about his childhood, unwittingly

putting the comedian on the defensive; it would be many years before Chaplin
admitted publicly that he was the son of a man who drank himself to death and
a mother who went insane. One can sense Chaplin's relief when the reporter
changes the topic to some of the technical aspects of his craft—the origins of
his now-famous costume, makeup, and some of his characteristic movements.
Chaplin's answers to these questions are, for the most part, disarmingly candid
and accurate, particularly in his precise analysis of the rationale behind his
mustache and his reaction to seeing himself on the screen.]

You will all be wanting to know of Charlie Chaplin's doings in New York,
where he went to arrange the terms of his great contract with the Mutual
Corporation, a big American concern controlling many well-known films.

Our representative visited Charlie in a magnificent New York hotel, where,
as Charles Spencer, he was having the time of his life of twenty-six years.

Charlie could be found nightly at any of the gay resorts—as Charles Spencer—and although the night throng literally rubbed shoulders with him, little
did it dream that it was the real Charlie.

"I'm out for a good time," said the little man. "My brother Syd is a good
business man." Thus Charlie enjoyed while Syd deployed. At the fashionable
Claridge, with its soothing ochre candelabra lights, the folks were "getting
wise," for Charlie was there nightly.

However, the moment he was discovered he ducked to the Winter Gardens,
where he mixed with a new jabbering throng. Then on to the Knickerbocker
Grill, where ladies danced amid tables in the calcium light. Then on to the palm
room of the Astor—the place that foreign ammunition buyers call "home" these
days. *[This bold reminder that amid the gaiety, opulence, and celebrity-sighting*
in America some people were profiting handsomely from the war would have
struck a responsive chord with Red Letter *readers.]* On and about he went as
Charles Spencer, notwithstanding the fact that there were twelve Charles Spen-
cers in the New York directory, who ranged from managers down to porters.

Our representative had an appointment with Mr Chaplin at The Astor.
Charlie was on time, which was going some for a chap who didn't have to be,
and who had been dodging publicity for weeks.

"Grape fruit, bacon and eggs, and some coffee," he said to the waiter in the
grill-room a few minutes later. Honest, he seemed like a rosy-cheeked boy as
he fingered the big menu rather nervously.

He is little, small-waisted. His hair is brushed back on his forehead, with a
little more than painstaking care. It is liberally sprinkled with grey at the temples.

"Yes, I'm twenty-six," he laughed, showing a magnificent set of teeth.

His eyes were big and grey—almost blue—bashful at first, but enthusiastic and alive as the conversation became more animated. A splendid face—always smiling. It is surprising what an eyebrow or a moustache can do.

Perhaps he is five foot four *[Chaplin was five feet six and a half, but people often thought he was shorter]*, and his suit of brown and grey homespun fitted him like a glove. Beneath the neat wing collar and bat-wing tie of green and black, the only conspicuous part of his dress was noted, a blue and white striped shirt, with many, many tiny stripes that seemed to somehow go with little Charlie.

It was his hands, though that attracted the reporter the most. They were remarkable hands, tiny, graceful hands, with delicate, almost lady-like fingers, which were forever drumming on the white cloth or else twisting and wiggling in gesture. The nails were perfectly manicured.

"Above all else, he detests an interview," said Brother Syd, who sat just across the table.

"Oh, but that doesn't mean I'm not mighty glad to see you," said the little comedian with a most engaging smile.

He has a decided touch of "Cockney" in his speech. He began slowly at first to answer the various questions asked him, self-conscious and embarrassed. Then all of a sudden he seemed to change, and shortly he was talking with enthusiasm.

"I was born in London," he was saying. "There was father, mother, and Syd and myself—why do you have to have all that?"

"Because any detail about your life is most interesting to people," said the interviewer.

Chaplin laughed, literally all over.

"Well, he said, recovering. "Yes, I used to hold shows out in the back yard when I was a kid. I would see some drama, and then try to reproduce it out on the back lawn, with a carpet hung from the apple tree to the corner of the house. I always gave out the parts to the children in the neighbourhood, and we used to have great times."

"And at the early age of twelve did you aspire to be an actor when you grew up?"

He chuckled and dug at the last remaining bit of grapefruit.

"No," he answered with a droll expression in his eyes. "I aspired to be a member of parliament."

He paused. The bacon and eggs had arrived—eggs whose yolks were a brilliant yellow, and bacon that looked clean and curly, like pigs tails.

"However," he resumed, helping himself generously, "the time came when I had to go to work, and I got a job with a stage company, and travelled about playing a minor part. Later I got into comedian work, and did the music halls for a while. When Gilette [*sic*] came to London I got a job in his company, and played the part of Billy in *Sherlock Holmes*. [*The American actor-playwright William Gillette wrote and starred in the first stage play featuring Sherlock Holmes. Following a successful Broadway run and American tour he did a long run in London in 1901, then toured the British Isles. By the time he reprised the role in London in October 1905, Chaplin had been playing Billy the page boy for over two years in various road companies, and was considered so good in the role that he was transferred to Gillette's company for its prestigious West End run.*] Then I got on in a sketch called *A Night in a London Music-Hall*."

The reporter interrupted.

"You used to play in that over here, didn't you? You were the drunk that used to fall out of the box?"

"Yes," laughed Chaplin. "I afterwards sold it out to Billy Reeve. I brought it over here when I came to this country about three years ago." [*There are so many errors in this short sentence that it's likely the reporter's careless notetaking rather than Chaplin that is to blame. Billie Reeves (not Reeve) originated the role of the drunk in* A Night in an English Music Hall *in 1904, four years before Chaplin joined the Karno Company; Chaplin had been in the States for six years, not three, when this interview took place; and, of course, he could not have sold Reeves or anyone else the rights to* A Night in an English Music Hall, *which was the exclusive property of Fred Karno.*]

"Now, let me in on the magic secret of the moustache, the cane, and the big feet—you have little feet," switched the reporter.

"Surely," answered Charlie, obligingly, "I'll begin with the feet first. I got my so-called walk from an old character I used to see in London. He was a poor old fellow, who used to stand outside a saloon, and when the drivers of the hansom cabs used to drive up for their drink, the poor old fellow, who had sore feet, would shuffle out to the side walk with a 'Hey yar, sir!' to hold their horses for a tuppence or anything they might give him. I used to imitate him after I got home, and the imitation stuck with me."

"Then you mean," went on the reporter, "that while you are posing before the camera with that funny walk you always have the idea that you always have sore feet?"

"That is just it. I simply play the character of the old fellow, and always have in my mind the idea that my feet are sore." *[Chaplin repeated this story to many early interviewers, calling the character "Rummy" Binks, and it is certainly true that he often affects a footsore amble. However, others have claimed credit for originating the famous walk, including, most credibly, Karno comedian Fred Kitchen. But, as we've already seen, Chaplin was loath to credit his important theatrical mentors, preferring instead to nurture his image as a solitary creator who drew his inspiration from life. True or not, the Binks story was certainly more colorful—and less likely to lead to a lawsuit—than admitting that he stole the walk of another comedian.]*

"In other words," laughed the reporter, "you get about a thousand every time you play your feet are sore?"

Charlie was drinking coffee and it bubbled as he laughed into it.

"Did the old chap do that funny side motion with one foot when he went around a corner?"

"No," answered Chaplin, serious now. "It seemed to me a natural thing for him to do when he went round the corner with his feet hurting him so, I just carried the character right through, that is all, and that is where the side motion comes in, I suppose." *[Comedian Will Murray, who directed Chaplin in* Casey's Circus, *claimed credit for Chaplin's much-praised corner-turning move, which involved hopping on one foot and extending the other straight out as he changed direction.]*

"Now, the moustache?"

It does one good to see Charlie Chaplin laugh. It is contagious, and for the life of him he couldn't see why people wanted to know all about those little things. However, he was always willing to explain, and while explaining the laugh left him completely.

"I haven't a natural comedian's face," he was saying. "I had to have some kind of a make-up. I started in by wearing a red false nose and a big moustache, but I found that when I looked at the pictures the nose took black and the big moustache covered up all expression of the mouth. I had to have something, so one day I stuck on the eyebrow. It was surprising how it changed me. It really is a convenience, that's all. It changes my face into that of a comedian and at the same time, as it is small, allows full play for the expression of the mouth.

"The baggy trousers, the big feet, the tight-fitting coat, and the cane are all old British music-hall stuff."

"Just think of it Char—Mr Chaplin, you're getting more salary than the President of the United States," put in the reporter, as the thought of Charlie's earnings hit him between the eyes.

"I was talking with a New Yorker last night, and he said the same thing. When I answer, 'Yes, but he is only the President,' the fellow didn't get it at all. They say a Britisher hasn't a sense of humour. There are one or two over here that don't possess that quality. But he was a good fellow, just the same," he added quickly.

Sydney, the manipulator, had been silent up to this time, listening to his illustrious brother talk. Now he suddenly broke in to explain that Charlie, when he was with the Essanay people, got a bonus of £2,000 for every picture taken last year. *[Syd exaggerates here, though not by much. Chaplin's Essanay films were making so much money that when, midway through the series, he asked the company for two weeks off to do a lucrative engagement ($25,000 for two weeks of fifteen-minute appearances at the New York Hippodrome), Essanay paid him the same amount NOT to go. In July 1915, as an additional incentive and to guarantee his services, they began paying him a $10,000 bonus for each film completed. This netted Chaplin an additional $60,000 by the time he parted ways with the company at the end of 1915. However, the bonus payments came back to haunt him, because Essanay claimed that they were contingent on Chaplin making an additional ten films beginning in July; since he completed only six the other four factored into the suits and countersuits that followed. For more on Chaplin's conflicts with Essanay, see chapter 20.]*

"You must have salted away close to £125,000," gasped the reporter.

Chaplin laughed, and looked wisely at his brother, he said, "We picked up quite a bunch last year, didn't we, Syd?"

"Did you ever dream of such wealth as you are now rolling up at twenty-six years of age?" went on the reporter.

"I had a presentiment once," answered Charlie soberly.

Moods—he is full of moods—and romantic, he is so full of it that it is hard to conceive that he has not up to date been married.

"Let's have the presentiment story?" urged the reporter.

Charlie's eyes lighted up. He pushed his empty plate back along the cloth, and leaning his elbows on the table, started off.

"You know the People's Theatre in Philadelphia? Well, I was playing *A Night in a London Music Hall* there just two and a half years ago. I was working five shows a day, and was getting a small salary for it. I knew a fellow in New York who had loads of money, and one Sunday night I made an appointment to meet him in New York. We never played on Sunday nights in Philly—I was never envious of this chap's worldly goods, but every time I saw him I would get clean discouraged when I thought how hard I worked and how little I was getting for it. I loved to go to New York, even if it was to go alone. I just loved to walk up Broadway or Fifth Avenue and look around and to feel that I was in the midst of life and all that sort of thing. Well, to get back, I had about £80 saved up, and the night before I went to New York to meet my friend I said to myself—'Now, why not live for just once, anyway?'

"I yearned to live like a rich man, even if only for one night. It was rather a kid trick, but nevertheless a natural one. The more I thought it over the more determined I was to do it. So, when the time came, I took my £80, and started for the big town. I wasn't to meet my friend until late, and so I marched up to this very hotel and hired a room. I had never stopped at such a hotel before, and it gave me a thrill."

He paused, and a reminiscent smile came into his eyes.

"Go on, that's a great story," hurried the reporter, fearing he was changing his mind about telling it.

"I went down to the street," resumes Chaplin slowly, "and I summoned a cab with great gusto. Then I rode all over town all alone, I was spending money. The thought took possession of me and it felt good.

"After a while I drove to one of the finest cafes in town, and ordered a big dinner all by myself. I didn't like champagne, but I ordered a bottle because it meant money—and I wined and dined and tipped, the latter when any opportunity offered itself. Sometimes I tipped twice. Then I called another cab, and was driven to the Metropolitan Opera House, where I heard that wonderful opera, *Tannhauser*, all by myself.

"Back I went to the café afterwards and went through a second dinner, wine and all, and then I met my friends, and we did the late places. I never was a so-called sport. It was just a momentary impulse to live the rich man's life. The minute I struck my good friend I began to get discouraged again. I felt, modestly, too, that I was really cleverer than he was—yet I was a slave, and he was living like a king always. Then I went back the next morning to Philly to the five performances with £50 less in my pocket, and I felt blue. Now here is where the presentiment comes in.

"Just before the afternoon first performance I received a message to come to some lawyer's office in the Longacre Building. The first thought that flashed into my mind was that a relative of mine had died and left me a lot of money. I was sure of it. After the show I went over the Longacre Building, and I was terribly disappointed when I found it was the Keystone Film Company that wanted to talk with me about moving picture work.

"They offered me £40 a week, and it seemed like a lot of money to me. I grabbed the job of acting for the camera. A Mr Castle [sic—*Adam Kessel, one of the partners in Keystone Comedy Company*] had seen me at the theatre, and he was convinced I would make good on the screen. Do you know, I began to lose weight worrying about my job. I kept wondering whether I would make good. It was the start of my good fortune."

[The story Chaplin told in his Autobiography *a half-century later remained substantially the same, except that he gives Mack Sennett credit for discovering him, not Adam Kessel. He also omits several telling details in this account. The "rich man" he met in New York was Arthur "Sonny" Kelly, whom he first met in England as the stage manager of a company of dancers that included his sister, Hetty, who became Charlie's first serious love interest. Charlie impulsively proposed to her a few days after they met, and was crushed when she refused.*

Arthur was not rich, but he was the employee of a rich man, as another of his sisters had married the American millionaire Frank J. Gould, who offered him a job. In the later account Charlie bumps into Arthur quite by accident, at the end of a solitary evening on the town. They go to Arthur's Madison Avenue flat, but their conversation and Charlie's memories of Hetty only increase his melancholy mood.

After Charlie became one of the founders of United Artists he arranged for Arthur to be hired by the company in 1925, after which Arthur would work in various capacities for UA or Chaplin until his death in 1954. Hetty died during the influenza epidemic of 1918, but Charlie didn't find out about it until he returned in triumph to England in 1921 and Arthur informed him. The news cast a pall over his homecoming, and the memory of Hetty would haunt him for the rest of his life.]

"It's like a romance, isn't it?" supplemented Syd, as the story ended.

"It is," answered the reporter. "And, speaking of romances, why isn't there a lady, Mr Chaplin?"

"I am afraid I would turn into a tragedian," laughed the movie star. "I somehow never gave the matter any serious thought. Perhaps some time—but they do not interest me enough now." *[Chaplin is being evasive here, since he was in the midst of a torrid romance with Edna. Presumably the two had an understanding that their offscreen relationship should remain private, and, remark-*

M—m—m—m! A Peach ! !

This image of Charlie and Edna from *A Jitney Elopement* was painted for the cover of the March 1916 issue of *Film Fun*.

ably, it did, until he told the story of their romance in his Autobiography, *where he also recounts with great poignancy the story of his unrequited love for Hetty.]*

"You get a lot of letters from women, don't you?"

"You can't help that," he answered. "Nowadays the women are proposing in letters, and it makes you weary. I love the letters from children," he went on. "I get hundreds of them. There is something about children that is so true and square. I always fall for them very hard."

"Then you don't think the woman the equal of the man?"

"No. I don't wish to be ungallant, but I believe man is cut out to do the bigger things."

The boy philosopher was at work.

"You never saw a woman Shakespeare, or, a Balzac, or a Burns, did you. Men excel in all lines."

The conversation switched back to the movie world. Chaplin was arguing how the movie situation was in a critical state at present owing to the trash that is being unloaded on the market.

"But it will right itself shortly, I believe," he said. "Then you will see only the beginning of the great moving-picture industry."

"Tell me, what was your first impression when you first saw yourself on screen?"

Syd was the finest listener you ever saw, and all the while there was a light of pride in the grey eyes above his black moustache. He thinks Charlie is "some fellow." And I guess he's right.

"It was uncanny at first," Chaplin was answering. "You know, when you see yourself on the screen you simply can't take your eyes off yourself. I never know what else is going on in the picture. I simply see myself all the time, and I always feel that I have never seen that chap before me. But you can't keep your eyes off yourself.

"Sometimes when I look at myself I feel that the mannerisms and expressions of the Charlie Chaplin on the screen are forced, and immediately make plans to correct the fault in the next picture."

"Do you ever laugh at yourself? Do you ever seem funny to yourself as you see yourself on the screen?"

"Oh, I never laugh at myself," answered Chaplin seriously. I can't see anything funny about it, and I wonder why people think it so funny." *[Despite his self-effacing comment Chaplin often laughed at his onscreen antics, as reported by Goodwins in chapter 13, and by many other observers as well.[2]]*

Notes

CHAPTER 1

1. By 1915 Chaplin was already famous in Japan under the name "Professor Alcohol," presumably a reference to his many drunken portrayals in the Keystones.

2. A. G. Gardiner, *Portraits and Portents* (New York: Harper and Bros., 1926), 225.

3. He was far more discreet in bragging about his popularity than John Lennon, whose similar comment in a 1966 British newspaper interview that the Beatles were "more popular than Jesus" became infamous; later that year the group was hounded by Bible-belt protesters and the KKK during what became their last American tour. Chaplin, at least, had the good sense to say such things only privately, in this case over lunch with co-star Virginia Cherrill during the making of *City Lights*. Cherrill, Kamin interview, 1978.

4. G. P. Huntley was a popular British stage and music hall comedian.

5. White claimed to be from Manchester, but David Kiehn found evidence that he was born in Graudenz, Germany, a fact that he may well have wanted to hide, given the war. See David Kiehn, *Broncho Billy and the Essanay Film Company* (Berkeley, CA: Farwell Books, 2003), 191.

6. An area north of London.

7. Jamieson (the name is usually spelled Jamison in modern filmographies, but Goodwins varies the spelling considerably in his articles) plays a flirtatious gay man

in the film. While Chaplin rarely featured overtly gay characters, feminine grace notes became an important part of his own character, such as the hairdresser's flair he exhibits when grooming Edna in *The Vagabond*. Such behavior humorously counterbalances the Tramp's scruffiness and aggressive masculinity. In *Behind the Screen* burly Eric Campbell thinks Charlie is gay at one point, and does a mincing dance to mock him. In 1936, when such humor was banned from the screen, Chaplin slipped a gay character past the censors and into the prison scene in *Modern Times* as a subtle acknowledgment of the reality of homosexuality in prisons.

8. Charlie Chaplin, *My Autobiography* (New York: Simon and Schuster, 1964), 195–99.

CHAPTER 2

1. The apostrophe before "cute" isn't a typo; the word was originally derived from "acute," meaning "clever" or "sharp"; as the twentieth century dawned it took on the additional associations of "small," "adorable," and "attractive."

2. See David Kiehn, *Broncho Billy and the Essanay Film Company* (Berkeley, CA: Farwell Books, 2003), 205–7. For a later account of the dual aspects of Chaplin's personality, see May Reeves's fascinating *The Intimate Charlie Chaplin* (tr. Constance Brown Kuriyama, Jefferson, NC: McFarland & Company, Inc., 2001).

3. Chaplin gives a vivid account of his encounter with Barrie in his travel memoir *My Trip Abroad* (New York: Harper and Brothers, 1922), 85–88.

4. Herbert Rawlinson was a prominent leading man during the silent era who made a successful transition to character roles after sound came in.

5. In his *Autobiography* Chaplin specifically recalls buying the first three volumes of the work in Philadelphia in 1913, and reading them "off and on, never thoroughly, for over forty years." Charlie Chaplin, *My Autobiography* (New York: Simon and Schuster, 1964), 497.

CHAPTER 3

1. Gerith von Ulm, *Charlie Chaplin, King of Tragedy* (Caldwell, ID: The Caxton Printers, Ltd., 1940).

2. Peter Bogdanovich filmed an interview with Chaplin for the 1976 documentary *The Gentleman Tramp*. Chaplin, always a reluctant interview subject, shut down and deflected most of Bogdanovich's questions; his comment

about not liking to improvise may well have reflected his resistance to being forced to "improvise" responses to Bogdanovich's rather heavy-handed interview style—or possibly his resentment at not being asked to help direct the interview himself. In any event, none of the Bogdanovich footage made it into the documentary.

3. Charlie Chaplin, *My Autobiography* (New York: Simon and Schuster, 1964), 326. For a detailed study of Chaplin's physical approach to acting and directing, see Dan Kamin, *The Comedy of Charlie Chaplin: Artistry in Motion* (Lanham, MD: Scarecrow, 2010).

4. This is also a Gus Elen song. Chaplin calls it "Jack Jones," the name of the song's protagonist, in his *Autobiography*.

5. Chaplin's understudy in his American Karno tours was Stanley Jefferson, later to achieve fame as Stan Laurel, who spoke eloquently about what they both learned from Karno in several books by John McCabe, notably in *Charlie Chaplin* (New York: Doubleday, 1978). In the book Laurel offers fascinating descriptions of Chaplin both on stage and off.

6. Charles Chaplin Jr. with N. and M. Rau, *My Father, Charlie Chaplin* (New York: Random House, 1960), 9.

7. For more on this subject, see "Chaplin's Collaborators," in Jack Spears, *Hollywood: The Golden Era* (Cranbury, NJ: A. S. Barnes and Co., 1977), 226–54. See also Hooman Mehran, "Chaplin's Writing and Directing Collaborators," BFI, http://chaplin.bfi.org.uk/programme/essays/collaborators.html.

CHAPTER 4

1. This variant spelling of "wagon" persisted slightly longer in England than America.

2. Site of an annual Guy Fawkes fireworks celebration in England.

CHAPTER 5

1. Mack Sennett, with Cameron Shipp, *King of Comedy* (Garden City, NY: Doubleday, 1954), 189.

2. Charlie Chaplin, *My Autobiography* (New York: Simon and Schuster, 1964), 169.

3. Max Eastman, *Heroes I Have Known* (New York: Simon and Schuster, 1942), 186.

4. Fred Goodwins, "The Little Lady of Laughter," *Pictures and the Picturegoer*, May 6, 1916.

5. Chaplin, *My Autobiography*, 170.

6. David Kiehn, *Broncho Billy and the Essanay Film Company* (Berkeley, CA: Farwell Books, 2003), 194–95.

7. See Joyce Milton, *Tramp: The Life of Charlie Chaplin* (New York: HarperCollins, 1994), 114. Considering her prominence in Chaplin's films Edna maintained a remarkably low profile both during and after their time together. What we know for certain is that she was born on October 21, 1895, in Paradise Valley, Nevada, and moved at age three to the even more evocatively named town of Lovelock, Nevada. She left for San Francisco in 1913, where she attended a business school for two years before Chaplin hired her. Chaplin and Edna fell in love shortly after they began working together, and their offscreen romantic relationship lasted until sometime in 1917. In 1923 Chaplin tried to establish her as a star in her own right with *A Woman of Paris*, a serious drama he wrote and directed as a vehicle for her. While the film made a star of Adolphe Menjou, it marked the end of Edna's film career. She married happily in the 1930s, and remained on Chaplin's studio payroll until her death in 1958.

8. Chaplin, *My Autobiography*, 159.

9. Charlie Chaplin, *My Trip Abroad* (New York: Harper and Brothers, 1922), 60.

10. Kiehn, *Broncho Billy and the Essanay Film Company*, 203.

CHAPTER 6

1. David Robinson, *Chaplin: His Life and Art* (London: Penguin Books, 2001), 248.

2. King of England from 1016 to 1035, who purportedly tried to command the sea to stop rising in order to demonstrate to his courtiers that even the power of the king could not influence the inexorable power of nature.

CHAPTER 7

1. Sime Silverman, the founder of *Variety*, was particularly appalled by what he saw as the indecencies in Chaplin's films, and was one of a number of self-appointed advisors who called upon the comedian to hire a scenario writer to create better, more acceptable stories.

2. For a thorough examination of how Chaplin's artistic evolution was intimately connected with his public image, see Charles Maland's brilliant *Chaplin and American Culture* (Princeton, NJ: Princeton University Press, 1989).

3. Goodwins, quoted from *Pearson's* (no date given) by David Robinson, *Chaplin: His Life and Art* (London: Penguin Books, 2001), 151.

4. Charlie Chaplin, *My Autobiography* (New York: Simon and Schuster, 1964), 189.

5. Charles A. McGuirk, "Chaplinitis," *Motion Picture Magazine*, July and August, 1915.

CHAPTER 9

1. Gaspard was a miserly character in the enormously popular 1877 French operetta *The Chimes of Normandy* (*Les cloches de Corneville*).

CHAPTER 10

1. In America the artificial hair used for fake beards and mustaches is spelled *crepe* hair.

CHAPTER 11

1. Since the 1960s steady efforts have been made, spearheaded by film historian David Shepard, to locate and preserve the best existing elements of the Mutuals and restore the films to their original glory. Chaplin took no part in these efforts; he had no ownership stake in the Mutuals, and never sought to purchase the rights as they changed hands through the years. However, in 1925 he purchased the outtakes, largely to prevent them from being used to create spurious new Chaplin films, as had already happened with both his Essanay and Keystone releases. Eventually he ordered them destroyed, but most survived, and a judicious selection became the basis for the documentary *Unknown Chaplin*, which presents a tantalizing glimpse into his working methods. The cloak-and-dagger story of how this precious footage was rescued is recounted in Kevin Brownlow's *The Search for Charlie Chaplin* (Bologna, Italy: Cineteca di Bologna, Le Mani, 2005). For more on the history of the Mutuals, see Michael J. Hayde, *Chaplin's Vintage Year: The History of the Mutual-Chaplin Specials* (Albany, GA: BearManor Media, 2013).

2. For this reason the current official release prints of the First National films, particularly *A Dog's Life*, do not represent Chaplin's best performances, which

are tighter and funnier in the originals. Original First National prints, however incomplete or poor in picture quality, have therefore become the grail for Chaplin enthusiasts. For more on this subject, see Dan Kamin, *The Comedy of Charlie Chaplin* (Lanham, MD: Scarecrow, 2010), 172–79.

3. In his February 26 installment Goodwins refers to Vincent Bryan as a writer of the Chaplin films, and here he refers to him as co-director. Chaplin, always reluctant to credit the creative contributions of others, had Goodwins issue a retraction in the June 17 installment (chapter 15).

4. Charlie Chaplin, *My Autobiography* (New York: Simon and Schuster), 174–75.

5. Chaplin is paraphrasing the line "Like some tanned reaper in his hour of ease" from the poem "The Closing Scene" by Thomas Buchanan Read.

CHAPTER 12

1. Readers would have been familiar with Turpin because he had co-starred in Chaplin's first two Essanay films, *His New Job* and *A Night Out*, and was on his way to becoming a major star in his own right. David Robinson neatly described his screen character as "a wizened little man who resembled a prematurely hatched bird, with permanently crossed eyes and a prominent Adam's apple dancing up and down his scrawny neck." David Robinson, *Chaplin: His Life and Art* (London: Penguin, 2001), 140–41. Readers would also have been familiar with Leo White, who appeared in most of the Essanays, often in the role of a French dandy. White would go on to play in five of the Mutuals and appear in hundreds of other films in the course of his career. He reunited with Chaplin in 1940 for a small role in *The Great Dictator*.

2. Charlie Chaplin, *My Autobiography* (New York: Simon and Schuster, 1964), 139.

3. Laurel's story was quoted in John McCabe, *Charlie Chaplin* (New York: Doubleday, 1978), 47–48.

CHAPTER 13

1. Charlie Chaplin, *My Autobiography* (New York: Simon and Schuster, 1964), 219.

CHAPTER 14

1. Lester was a popular British comedy star whose repertoire included a sketch called *The Village Fire Brigade*.

CHAPTER 15

1. The teacher's comments were quoted in the *Daily Mail* on September 2, 1921, during the run-up to Chaplin's triumphal return trip to London, when dozens of stories about his youthful years were appearing in the papers. A tip of the bowler to Barry Anthony, who found this intriguing item and cited it in his excellent *Chaplin's Music Hall: The Chaplins and Their Circle in the Limelight* (London: I. B. Tauris, 2012), 185–86. In his *Autobiography* Chaplin also wrote about his time with the Field family, confessing to his erotic interest in the landlady's youngest daughter but not mentioning his evening stroll with the schoolteacher. Charlie Chaplin, *My Autobiography* (New York: Simon and Schuster, 1964), 95–97.

2. A popular 1909 song by Carrie Jacobs-Bond. In 1920 Buster Keaton ended one of the disastrous days in his breakthrough film *One Week* by placing a copy on a piano which has just crashed through the floor of the prefabricated home he is building.

CHAPTER 16

1. *Faction*, for some reason, was a term used in both the Chaplin and Harold Lloyd studios to refer to scenes, rather than simply calling them "scenes," "sections," or "sequences." As Lloyd explained, "Faction . . . is our term for a sequence within a picture—any set of incidents turning on a common theme or locale." Harold Lloyd, with Wesley Stout, *An American Comedy* (New York: Longmans, Green and Co., 1928), 168.

CHAPTER 17

1. We cannot, of course, discount the possibility that Goodwins is correct—he repeats the running time a bit further along in his article. Some theatres may have projected Chaplin's films at a slower pace to allow the audience to better savor them, or simply to extend their running time, since the Chaplin films were both the most expensive and the most popular films on the bill. A second possibility is that this was a preview performance—all the major silent comedians previewed their films, often changing them after gauging the audience reaction. But *The Floorwalker* went into general release on May 15, the day after the showing discussed above, so this wasn't a preview. A third possibility is that Goodwins simply got the time wrong.

CHAPTER 18

1. Phrenology was an early nineteenth-century system for diagnosing people's character and mental capacities from the bumps and fissures in their skulls. By Goodwins's time it was considered a laughable pseudoscience.

2. In 1915 Henry Ford financed a "Peace Ship," sailing to Sweden with prominent peace activists in hopes of mediating the conflict and bringing the war to an end. He soon abandoned the mission in the face of discord and illness among the activists and widespread mockery by the press.

CHAPTER 19

1. This is the third time that Goodwins has pegged the running time for a single reel of film at twenty minutes. At that rate *The Birth of a Nation* would have run four-and-a-half hours, not the three-hour running time that is widely reported; and Chaplin's 1921 feature *The Kid* would have run two hours. See discussion in chapter 17.

2. In *The Immigrant.* See Theodore Huff, *Charlie Chaplin* (New York: Henry Schuman, 1951), 59. Also see David Robinson, *Chaplin: His Life and Art* (London: Penguin Books, 2001), 827, for a list of shooting ratios for Chaplin's 1918–1952 films.

3. As electrical lighting replaced gas over the next couple of decades this transitional term reverted back to "chandelier," a word originally borrowed from the French word for candlestick, and which became the generic name for elaborate oil, gas, or electrical fixtures featuring multiple sources of light.

4. Known as the Panama-California Exposition, the 1915–1917 celebration commemorated the opening of the Panama Canal and the role of San Diego as the Canal's first northern port of call.

5. Chaplin visited San Francisco's rival Panama-Pacific Exposition during the making of *A Jitney Elopement* in March 1915, but there was never to be a "Chaplin Day" in San Diego. The Expo succeeded despite his absence, drawing 3.8 million visitors.

CHAPTER 20

1. *Reel Life*, June 24, 1916, 1. It is unclear whether Chaplin actually shot this alternate ending, but given its inclusion in the magazine he must at least have considered it. The magazine is almost certainly the source of the persistent rumors that he did shoot it, although there is no trace in the surviving outtakes.

2. Charlie Chaplin, *My Autobiography* (New York: Simon and Schuster, 1964), 174.

CHAPTER 21

1. David Robinson, *Chaplin: His Life and Art* (London: Penguin Books, 2001), 217–18.

CHAPTER 22

1. He was 6 feet 4 inches, according to David Robinson, *Chaplin: His Life and Art* (London: Penguin Books, 2001), 173.

2. *Moving Picture World*, January 5, 1918, 53, and January 12, 1918, 220.

3. *What a Woman Can Do*, released April 29, 1911. See David Kiehn, *Broncho Billy and the Essanay Film Company* (Berkeley, CA: Farwell Books, 2003), 50.

4. Alistair Cooke was one of them; a 1933 interview turned into two summers of work on a script for Chaplin's long-contemplated but never made Napoleon film. See Cooke, "The One and Only," in *Six Men* (New York: Alfred A. Knopf, 1977).

5. A. J. Marriot, *Chaplin: Stage by Stage* (N.p.: Marriott, 2005), 181–82.

6. *Variety*, August 11, 1916, 21.

7. Alf Reeves had selected Chaplin to lead the Karno company tours of America between 1910 and 1913, and he traveled with the company as tour manager. In 1918 Chaplin returned the favor by hiring Alf as his studio manager, a post he held until his death in 1946.

8. Among Ayer's many hit songs were "Oh, You Beautiful Doll," "If You Were the Only Girl in the World," and, in 1915, "That Charlie Chaplin Walk," which he wrote for the British revue *Watch Your Step* and also recorded.

CHAPTER 23

1. Goodwins is once again indulging his taste for fancy words and comic irony. A *conversazione* is a social gathering with the purpose of fostering lofty conversation about literature and the arts and sciences—hardly the kind of chatter one would expect on the set of a "comedy manufactory."

CHAPTER 24

1. There are tantalizing rumors that Chaplin played the Artful Dodger to Tree's Fagin in a one-night-only performance of *Oliver Twist*. Tree's daughter Iris reminded Chaplin of this occasion much later, as related by journalist Alastair Forbes: "(A)t Charlie Chaplin's Swiss table I recall her halting the host's pro-Soviet rot with memories of her father's First World War American production of *Oliver Twist* in which Charlie had played the Artful Dodger, earning a

prophesy by Tree that he would have a great career on the stage when he was through with the movies" ("Mummer and Daddy," *The Spectator*, May 12, 1979, 20). Unfortunately, I have been unable to find confirmation that any such performance occurred. If it had, it surely would have received significant media coverage, including in Goodwins's articles. It may have been something the two did at a private party—Tree was much feted during his two visits to Hollywood in 1916, and Chaplin delighted party guests all his life with impromptu performances.

2. In 1906 La Rue became a musical theatre star on Broadway, and in August 1913 she made a big hit in England, introducing the song "You Made Me Love You (I Didn't Want to Do It)" at the Palace Theatre and recording it. I have been unable to find confirmation that she toured the UK earlier, although she and Chaplin are almost certainly reminiscing about their encounters during his 1908–1910 British Karno tours.

CHAPTER 25

1. The term "typewriter" originally referred to the person—usually female—who operated the machine, rather than the machine itself.

2. Wormwood Scrubs is a men's prison in London.

3. A common nineteenth-century expression derived from the popular Colley Cibber adaptation of *Richard III*; the line does not occur in the original play.

4. Charlie Chaplin, *My Autobiography* (New York: Simon and Schuster, 1964), 187–88.

5. Frank Richardson (1870–1917) was a prolific humorous writer and self-proclaimed expert on facial hair.

6. The phrase "I Should Worry," became a national craze in the 1910s, appearing in everyday speech, cartoons, and a popular 1913 song called "*Isch Ga-Bibble (I Should Worry)*," with words by Sam M. Lewis and music by George W. Meyer. Chaplin must have been fond of the expression, because it became the working title of his 1918 film *A Dog's Life*. Roughly equivalent to today's shrug-of-the-shoulder comments "Whatever" and "It is what it is," "I should worry" had quite a long shelf life; in 1956 it morphed into "What, Me Worry?" the slogan of *Mad* magazine's happily dimwitted cover boy, Alfred E. Neuman. The craze, the phrase, Alfred's visage, and even his name can all be traced to a comic play from 1894 called *The New Boy*.

CHAPTER 26

1. Chaplin's paean to his technical crew may also have been inspired by the truly extraordinary work they had done on *One A.M.*, in which the set and props— particularly the miraculously mobile Murphy bed—became his antagonists in the film.

CHAPTER 27

1. British term for a festive celebration, derived from "beanfeast."

2. Goodwins puts the word "some" in quotation marks because at this time the ironic use of "some" to mean "a great deal" was still new enough to merit emphasis. Max Eastman, who in 1919 became a close friend of Chaplin, wrote two books on humor following periods spent discussing the subject with the comedian. See "The Humor of Quantity," in Eastman's *The Sense of Humor* (New York: Charles Scribner's Sons, 1922), 46–57.

3. Alexia Durant, "Charlie Chaplin in 'One A.M.,'" *The Photoplayers Weekly*, July 15, 1916, 1.

4. Chester Courtney, "The Mystery of the Chaplin Women," *Film Weekly*, February 28, 1931, 9. When Chaplin discovered his old music hall crony working as a bellboy at the Los Angeles Athletic Club he hired him on the spot. Courtney played small roles in several of the Mutuals, but isn't credited in any filmography. He can be seen as the rather cadaverous-looking shoplifter in *The Floorwalker* and a bar patron in *The Vagabond*. In 1931 he wrote a series of three articles on Chaplin for the British magazine *Film Weekly*, and his account of the Mutual days is in every way consistent with that of Goodwins. An excerpt from the series was reprinted in Peter Haining, *Charlie Chaplin: A Centenary Celebration* (London: W. Foulsham & Co., 1989), 79–84. Evidently Courtney didn't socialize with the other cast members, for Goodwins never mentions him.

5. For a detailed account of *One A.M.*'s reception see Michael J. Hayde, *Chaplin's Vintage Year: The History of the Mutual Chaplin Specials* (Albany, GA: BearManor Media, 2013), 94–99.

6. Roland "Rollie" Totheroh, who began working with Chaplin as second cameraman with *The Floorwalker*, became cinematographer and chief cameraman following William C. Foster's departure, shooting all the films through 1952 and helping to edit them. His contribution to Chaplin's work is incalculable. For more on Rollie, see Timothy J. Lyons's fascinating "Roland H. Totheroh Interviewed: Chaplin Films," *Film Culture*, Spring, 1972, 229–85.

CHAPTER 28

1. Charlie Chaplin, *My Autobiography* (New York: Simon and Schuster, 1964), 96–97.

CHAPTER 29

1. British slang for a stealthy departure to avoid paying the landlord or other creditors.

2. These telegrams are in the digital collection of the Chaplin Research Centre, Cineteca del Comune di Bologna.

3. Goodwins is referring to his military service in one of the British possessions.

4. Sir Thomas Lipton was a wealthy merchant and yachtsman whose persistent efforts to win the America's Cup were unsuccessful, but made his self-named tea a household word in America.

CHAPTER 30

1. Charlie Chaplin, *My Autobiography* (New York: Simon and Schuster, 1964), 226.

CHAPTER 31

1. Chaplin used reversed action shots discreetly and effectively throughout his film career, including in *Work, The Fireman, The Bond*, and *Limelight*. Generally, he uses the device to enhance his apparent physical skill rather than for funny but obvious "impossible" gags. The most inspired instance features him as an astonishingly agile bricklayer in *Pay Day*, catching and stacking bricks so convincingly that most viewers simply accept it as another of his incredible skills. Even those who are aware that the film is reversed are dazzled by the brilliance of the choreographic design and Chaplin's flawless execution. His use of special effects such as reversed or speeded-up action to subtly enhance his performances was central to his cinematic achievement.

CHAPTER 32

1. Goodwins is using this term in its archaic meaning of *prudent*.

2. The variety stage figure was almost certainly "Dr." Walford Bodie, discussed in an annotation in the September 23 installment (chapter 28). Chaplin reprints both

pictures in his Charlie Chaplin, *My Autobiography* (New York: Simon and Schuster, 1964), 91, and Charlie Chaplin, *My Life in Pictures* (New York: Grosset and Dunlap, 1975), 52–53. In his *Autobiography* he mentions performing as Bodie and Dick Turpin in *Casey's Circus* (95), but it is unclear whether he ever imitated Fagin in the show or played the Master of Ceremonies or other roles. He was the star of the company, but contemporary reviews mention only his performances as Bodie and Dick Turpin. For detailed accounts of Chaplin's time with *Casey's Circus*, see A. J. Marriot, *Chaplin: Stage by Stage* (N.p.: Marriott, 2005), 64–80, and David Robinson, *Chaplin: His Life and Art* (London: Penguin Books, 2001), 68–71.

CHAPTER 35

1. The Lee-Enfield was a bolt-action military rifle introduced in 1895. Bisley is a shooting range area in Surrey, just outside of London.

CHAPTER 36

1. He is referring to the ancient Spartans, who were known for their terse speech, from which is derived the term *laconic*.

AND THEN . . .

1. *La vérité sur Charlie Chaplin: Sa vie, ses amours, ses déboires (The Truth about Charlie Chaplin: His Life, His Loves, His Disappointments).* Traduit et adapte par Rene Lelu (Paris: Editions de Mon Cine, Societe Parisienne d'Edition, 1933), 245.

Regrettably, Robinson's book has never been published in full in English. An abridged and sanitized version was serialized in *Liberty* magazine in 1933 and reprinted in the same magazine in 1973, as well as in Frank C. Platt, *Great Stars of Hollywood's Golden Age* (New York: Signet New American Library, 1966).

Additional portions were translated by Constance Brown Kuriyama as an appendix to her translation of another French work on Chaplin, May Reeves and Claire Goll, *The Intimate Charlie Chaplin* (Jefferson, NC: McFarland & Company, 2001). Robinson's comment about being a "sup-press agent," quoted above, was from her translation of excerpts from Robinson's book.

Readers of the present volume will be interested in both Robinson's and Reeves's later unauthorized accounts, and particularly that of Reeves, who was Chaplin's lover during his 1931 world tour. Reeves's book fully lives up to its title, with passages that are sometimes squirmingly uncomfortable to read. Yet, as Kuriyama makes clear in her superb introduction, it is arguably the best-written and most insightful of all the memoirs written about Chaplin by those close to him, and an indispensable resource for anyone interested in how Chaplin's complex personality intertwined with his art.

APPENDIX A

1. Ramsaye would go on to write *A Million and One Nights: A History of the Motion Picture* (New York: Simon and Schuster, 1926), the first definitive history of the industry, now considered a classic.

2. For an examination of this issue, see Kevin Brownlow, "Silent Films: What Was the Right Speed?" *Sight and Sound*, Summer, 1980, 164–67. See also pianist/film scholar Ben Model's intriguing series of motion studies on YouTube at https://www.youtube.com/user/silentfilmspeed/videos?view=0, in which he convincingly demonstrates that the silent comedies of Chaplin and Keaton lose much of their humor when slowed down to real-life speed.

3. Louis Delluc, *Charlot* (Paris: Maurice de Brunhoff, 1921). This was the first book-length study of a film artist. English edition, *Charlie*, translated by Hamish Miles (London: John Lane The Bodley Head, 1922).

4. Ramsaye, *A Million and One Nights*, 735.

APPENDIX B

1. R. J. Minney, *Chaplin, the Immortal Tramp* (London: George Newnes Limited, 1954), 49–51.

2. *New York Dramatic Mirror*, March 4, 1916, cited in Michael J. Hayde, *Chaplin's Vintage Year: The History of the Mutual Chaplin Specials* (Albany, GA: BearManor Media, 2013), 69.

APPENDIX C

1. Charlie Chaplin, *My Autobiography* (New York: Simon and Schuster, 1964), 181.

2. See, for example, Charles Chaplin Jr., *My Father, Charlie Chaplin* (New York: Random House, 1960), 93; and Jerry Epstein, *Remembering Charlie* (New York: Doubleday, 1989), 21.

Index

Bryan, Vincent, 12–13, 74, 86, 176, 180, 192, 220, 229, 242, 312n11:3
Bunny, John, 40
A Busy Day, 130
By the Sea, 51–52, 54, 79, 172, 177

Campbell, Eric, viii, 62, 81, 86, 89, 93, 98, 119, 128, 139, 146, 150, 167, 168, *169*, 170, 176–77, 181, 182, 193, 199, 202, 206, 213, 214, 219, 251, 257–58, 263–64, 266, *272*, 273, 275, 276, 280–*83*, 284, 308n1:7
Carmen (Cecil B. DeMille and Raoul Walsh film versions), 64
Carr, Sadie, 45
Caruso, Enrico, 122
Casey's Circus (aka *Casey's Court*), 7, 66, 219, 248, 301, 318–19n32:2
Cassey, Jim, 172–73
Caulfield, Harry, 73, 74, 91–92, 135, 144, 154, 198–99, 267, 288
The Champion, 5, 6, 47–48, *49*, 53
Chaplin, Charles, Jr. (Charlie's son), 29
Chaplin, Charles, Sr. (Charlie's father), 216, 298, 299
Chaplin, Charlie: ability to speak in foreign language gibberish, 11; and the war, 9–11, 116–18, 151–153, 290–91, *292*, 298; artistic training and discipline, 83, 95; attitude toward anti-Semitism, 223–24; celebrates 27th birthday, 102–7; coming up with new gags, 99, 191; concern for welfare of animals and crew, 62, 186–88, 221–22; conducts Sousa's band, 293–96; contract negotiations with Mack Sennett, 39–41; directs company

in "The Peril of Primrose" charity sketch, 167–70; dismisses influence of Fred Karno, 28, 95; encounters intellectually disabled boy, 120; entertains the company with clog dancing, 83, 205–6; ethnic characters in films of, 164, 223; fame of, vii–viii, 1; feminine characteristics of, 307–8n1:7; gay characters in films of, 307–8n1:7; love of boxing, 28–29; memories of early poverty, 216–17; nostalgia for stage touring days vs. film, 87–88; on actors as foils to his character, 245; on American cafeterias, 16–17; on comic technique, 24, 109–10; on directing technique, 207; on happiness, 20–21; on his costume and makeup, 79–80, 300–301; on how speaking affects performance in silent film, 183–85; on parks and loneliness, 45; on privacy, 18–19; on self-confidence, 28–29; on watching himself on the screen, 306; on women's inferiority to men, 306; plays Billy Armstrong's role in *A Night in the Show*, 62–63; praises technical crew, 204–5, 317n26:1; pressure of work, 4:7, 76–77, 128, 163–64, 166, 170–73, 188–89; reaction to Mutual salary, 291; rehearses gags, 202–3; responds to charges of vulgarity in his films, 58–60; responds to a negative article, 234; sympathy for the plight of underemployed actors, 240–41; undercranking to make falls look more violent, 189; use of closed sets, 155, 176, 178, 183, 248; use of

271, 285, 300, 301; Chaplin leaves
    Karno Company, 97
Keaton, Buster, 47, 75, 180, 313n15:2,
    320nAA:2
Kelly, Arthur "Sonny," 304
Kelly, Hetty, 304
Kelly, James T. (aka Kelley), 5, 13, 168
Kessel, Adam, 304
The Kid, 18, 163
Kid Auto Races at Venice, 52
"King Chanticleer" (song), 181
Kiehn, David, 44, 45–46
Kitchen, Fred, 301
Kitchener, Lord Herbert, 152
Kono, Toraichi (aka Harry O'Brien),
    23, 78

La Rue, Grace, 195, 316n24:2
Laurel, Stan, 97, 264–65, 309n3:9
Lennon, John, 307n1:3
Leno, Dan, 235
Lester, Alfred, 108
Levy, Albert, 213
Life, 4, 5, 22, 54–56, 57
Lloyd, Harold, 180
Lloyd, Marie, 139
Lloyd, Rosie, 139

May, Phil, 248
The Masquerader, 56, 130
McPherson, Quentin, 95
Merson, Billy, 44
Mineau, Charlotte, 62, 119, 259
Minney, R. J., 70, 293
Modern Times, 11, 27
Monsieur Verdoux, 29
Mumming Birds, 63, 87. *See also A Night
    in an English Music Hall*; *A Night in
    the Show*

Murray, Will, 301
Mutual Film Corporation: Chaplin's
    outtakes, 24, 85, 311n11:1; contract
    and salary, viii, 71–75, 85–86, 107,
    285–86, 289–91, 293, 297; Lone Star
    Studio, 75; sale of British rights to the
    Chaplin Mutuals, 244; two cameras
    shooting each scene, 85

The New Janitor, 60
*A Night in an English (or London) Music
    Hall*, 63, 95, 300, 302
A Night in the Show, 62–64, 63, 172
A Night Out, 37, 43
Normand, Mabel, 71
Northcliffe, Lord, 291

Oakman, Wheeler, 24
"'Old Yer Row," (song), 278, 281
One A.M., 33, 62, 64, 175–76, 183,
    286–87, 189, 212; Chaplin's problems
    with, 190–92, 194, 198, 317n26:1;
    first public showings of, 196, 209–11;
    sources of inspiration for, 177–78,
    180–81
One Week (Keaton), 313n15:2

The Patchwork Girl of Oz, 75
The Pawnshop, 228–29, 232, 276, 278–
    79; difficulty casting wedding ring
    scene, 235–36
"The Peace Patrol" (song), 294, 295,
    296
The Perils of Pauline, 210
Persons, Tom, 24
Peter Pan (Barrie), 17–18, 105
Pickford, Jack, 24, 134, 148
Pickford, Mary, 24, 56, 291
"Poet and Peasant Overture," 294

About the Contributors

AUTHOR

Fred Goodwins was a twenty-four-year-old British actor on tour in America when Charlie Chaplin hired him to be part of his newly formed stock company. Goodwins remained with Chaplin from 1915 through early 1917, appearing in many of the Essanay and Mutual comedies that confirmed Chaplin's reputation as the funniest man alive. Before long, Goodwins, who had been a London correspondent for the *New York Times*, was also writing publicity releases describing life at the studio, including the thirty-seven articles for the British magazine *Red Letter* that make up this book. Following his time with Chaplin Goodwins had a successful film career in the United States and England as an actor, writer, and director, until his untimely death from bronchitis at the age of thirty-two.

EDITOR

David James is a senior lecturer in film and media at Manchester Metropolitan University in the UK. His diverse research interests include the portrayal of class in British wartime films, British war films of the 1950s, and sitcoms of the 1960s, 1970s, and 1980s. He is also interested in (particularly British) comedy and light entertainment. His current research is based around music hall performers and audiences, and the transition from live performance to film.

ANNOTATOR

Dan Kamin is the author of *The Comedy of Charlie Chaplin: Artistry in Motion* (2008). A performer and mime expert, he created the physical comedy sequences for the films *Chaplin* and *Benny and Joon* and trained Robert Downey Jr. and Johnny Depp for their acclaimed starring performances. He also played the wooden Indian that came to life in the cult classic *Creepshow 2*, and created the Martian girl's weird movement for Tim Burton's horror spoof *Mars Attacks!* Dan performs his one-man shows internationally, and is a frequent guest artist with symphony orchestras, combining comedy, movement, and classical music in his popular series of "Comedy Concertos." You can find out more about Dan and see him in action by visiting www.dankamin.com.